The Retail Development Process

The last forty years have seen an enormous growth in retail trade and the increasing involvement of corporate finance in shopping centre development. Familiar patterns have emerged of hypermarkets, retail parks, sub-regional and regional centres, which have radically transformed the environments of most Western economies and led to major growth and change in already established town centres.

In this volume Clifford Guy describes and explains the characteristics of modern shops and shopping centres and their institutional context. We see that while many older areas of shopping developed gradually, in an uncoordinated way, most shops built in the last forty years have been the outcome of planned and specialised retail development. Clifford Guy relates retail growth and change to the world of property development and finance. He shows how the land use planning system has been able to apply strategic control over retail development in the public interest. Highly up-to-date, the volume raises some interesting questions about possible future directions for retail development.

Establishing general principles capable of transcending national boundaries, this text will be invaluable to students of geography, planning, land and estate management, and to practising planners, surveyors and retail and property consultants.

Clifford Guy is Senior Lecturer in the Department of City and Regional Planning at the University of Wales, Cardiff. He has widespread research experience in the fields of retail development and retail planning and policy.

The Retail Development Process

Location, property and planning

Clifford Guy

London and New York

First published 1994
by Routledge
11 New Fetter Lane, London EC4P 4EE

Simultaneously published in the USA and Canada
by Routledge
29 West 35th Street, New York, NY 10001

Reprinted 1995

© 1994 Clifford Guy

Typeset in Times by LaserScript Limited, Mitcham, Surrey

Printed and bound in Great Britain by
Biddles Ltd, Guildford and King's Lynn

British Library Cataloguing in Publication Data
A catalogue record for this book is available from the British Library

Library of Congress Cataloguing in Publication Data
A catalogue record for this book is available from the Library of Congress

ISBN 0-415-07504-1 (hbk)
ISBN 0-415-07505-X (pbk)

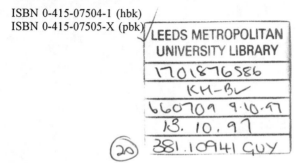

Contents

Figures

Tables

Acknowledgements

This book arose out of a degree of frustration with the academic literature on retail development. Several years of experience in teaching an option course in Retail Planning and supervising student dissertations suggested a lack of appropriate texts. Keeping one's own teaching material up to date was feasible for an academic with access to technical journals and ephemeral reports, but difficult for students who tend to rely more on published text books. As explained at greater length in Chapter 1, existing books offer either a detailed and critical account of retail location with a cursory treatment of development processes, or a detailed account of the processes but without the critical social science perspective which an academic accustomed to the geographical and planning literature would expect. Writing a book on this topic became a way of solving this problem, and it appeared that a 'gap' in the literature might be plugged.

A considerable debt is due to Neil Wrigley, who recognised the potential in this topic, helped me to choose a title, and presented the idea successfully to Routledge. Credit should also be given to two anonymous referees who at this early stage suggested a focus set firmly in the world of property development rather than retail location, perhaps knowing my background as a former geographer. Researching and writing this book, however, meant investigating some strange new topics such as investment appraisal, portfolio management and shopping centre design. Here, I am particularly grateful to Mark Teale, Jonathan Reynolds, and Peter M. Jones, who set aside some of their valuable time to explain patiently these mysteries, answer my naïve questions and suggest further reading and contacts. I am also grateful for permission to use the research libraries at Hillier Parker and Templeton College, Oxford. Tim Westlake and Mark Tewdur-Jones provided further material and helped me understand the niceties of central and local government planning procedures. Dennis Lord introduced me to the very different shopping patterns and retail development attitudes in North America.

Thanks are also due to the University of Wales, College of Cardiff, for granting me a term's study leave to research and write the first draft of this book. In my Department, many colleagues including Jeremy Alden, Huw Williams, Ian Bracken and Philip Cooke offered encouragement. My tutees and option course students showed remarkable tolerance of my frequent temporary absences from the office and increasingly distracted behaviour as deadlines loomed.

The final stages of writing were graced by the help of Susan Hodgkinson in typing the tables and Geraldine Davies and Janice Cole in producing most of the figures. Francesca Weaver and Laura Large at Routledge were tolerance and helpfulness personified.

I would like also to thank Healey & Baker, the Unit for Retail Planning Information, and the editors of *Town Planning Review* and the *European Journal of Marketing* for permission to reproduce diagrams originally published in their reports or articles.

During the latter stages of writing, my friend and former colleague Larry O'Brien died after several years of physical disability and intermittent illness. His bravery under stress and success in maintaining a praiseworthy research output should serve as examples to all of us.

Finally, my greatest debt is due to my family, for their dedication to consumerism and enthusiasm for visiting shopping centres, old and new.

Glossary

Note: Terms appearing in italics within the Glossary are also discussed as separate entries.

Anchor store (anchor tenant): The largest, or any very large store within a *shopping mall* or *focused centre*: usually a supermarket, variety store or department store, owned by a major *multiple retailer*.

Catchment area: The area from which any given store or shopping centre derives a large part of its trade, and within which shoppers tend to use the store or centre in preference to other stores or centres.

City centre: An area, central to the city as a whole, in which the main land uses are commercial. In Western Europe, it forms the most important retail area in the city, and may include both unplanned and planned retailing. It also serves a wider purpose as a business, cultural and entertainment focus for the community.

District centre: Either a relatively important unplanned suburban retail area, or a *focused centre* anchored by a *superstore* or *hypermarket*.

Edge of town: A site at or beyond the residential limits of an urban area, probably with good road access.

Festival marketplace (festival shopping): A *speciality centre*, which combines retailing with eating out and entertainment. Often converted from old warehouse or other non-retail buildings.

Financial institution: Any large company that provides loans or invests capital in development projects. In the context of retail development, the term is often restricted to insurance companies, pension funds, property investment companies and property unit trusts.

Focused centre: A shopping centre consisting of one or more large, free-standing stores, plus a few smaller stores.

Gilts: Government-issued, 'gilt-edged' securities, seen in Britain as a completely risk-free investment medium.

Gross lettable area (gross leasable area) (GLA): The total enclosed floor area of a store, or of all shop units within a shopping centre.

Hierarchy of shopping centres: A classification of shopping centres (and/or retail areas) in which the importance of the centre is related to the size of its *catchment area*.

Hypermarket: In Britain, a *superstore* of at least 50,000 sq. ft. or 5,000 sq. m. sales area. In other Western European countries, the term is often used to describe *superstores*.

Institutional lease: The rental arrangement favoured by *financial institutions*. Retail space is usually let on 21- or 25-year leases, with the tenant taking responsibility for insurance and repairs. Rents are usually reviewable every five years, on upward-only terms.

Local plans: These plans are prepared by district councils. They present the council's view of the most desirable pattern of land use within its area, usually over a ten-year period.

Long-term finance: This is required to repay the capital costs of a development project.

Major space user: A relatively large store within a *shopping mall*. May include *anchor stores* and other large stores.

Multiple retailer: (As conventionally defined in the UK) Any company that operates at least two retail outlets ('small multiple') or at least ten retail outlets ('large multiple').

Net present value (NPV): The sum of all discounted net annual returns, minus the capital cost of a development project.

Off-centre (out of centre): Any site outside the limits of a town centre or other established *retail area*.

Out of town: In the retail context, can be used to mean either *edge of town* or *off-centre*.

Peppercorn rent: An annual rent payment of a very small amount, usually associated with long leases.

Planned retailing: A building or group of buildings deliberately developed in a co-ordinated manner for retail use.

Property company: A company whose rationale is commercial property development and which is large enough to be quoted on the Stock Exchange.

Property developer: An individual or company that carries out property development. The 'developer' may be a *property company*, a *financial institution*, a local authority or other public agency, or any combination of the three.

Property development: In a market economy, the process of transforming a plot of land from one state to another: the main motive is usually financial profit.

Rate of return: The amount of capital or rental increase over a period of time, expressed as a percentage of the present value of a site or building.

Regional centre (regional shopping centre): A large free-standing *shopping mall*, usually defined as exceeding 400,000 sq. ft., or 500,000 sq. ft., or 50,000 sq m. GLA.

Repositioning: An attempt to alter the nature of one or several shops, so as to serve a different type of consumer from that previously served.

Retail area: Any urban area in which the predominant land use is retailing; can also describe that part of a building that is devoted to retail use.

Retail developer: A person or company that assembles land, researches demand, negotiates finance, designs and organises construction of one or more buildings intended mainly for occupation by retail firms.

Retail park: An organised development of at least three *retail warehouses*, defined as single-storey retail units of at least 10,000 sq. ft., totalling at least 50,000 sq. ft. GLA.

Retail warehouse: A store of at least 10,000 sq. ft. GLA that sells a narrow range of non-food goods direct to the public from a warehouse-type building, in an *off-centre* location with stock stored on the premises.

Sales area: The part of the internal floor area of a store that is used for selling and displaying goods and services.

Securitisation: The financing of a property development through the spreading of loan guarantees over a wider basis than the conventional single lender.

Shopping centre: A planned retail development comprising at least three shops, which is under one freehold ownership and managed and marketed as a unit. The term has also been used in the retail literature to describe almost any type of *retail area*.

Shopping mall: A *shopping centre*, usually comprising one or more *anchor stores* and several smaller units, in one building or an architecturally unified group of buildings, and usually with a single ground landlord. The minimum size is often defined as 100,000 sq. ft. GLA.

Short-term finance: This is required to cover the developer's costs during preparation and implementation of a project. It may be used to purchase land, and pay the building contractor and professional consultants.

Speciality centre: A shopping centre that serves a particular segment of the market. Speciality centres comprise mainly small shop units and do not usually contain *anchor stores*.

Speculative development: A property development carried out without prior knowledge of the identity of the tenants.

Structure plans: These plans are prepared by county councils (in England and Wales) and regional councils (Scotland). They set out the authority's view of the most desirable pattern of land use within its area over the next fifteen years.

Supermarket: A single-level, self-service food store of less than 25,000 sq. ft. (or 2,500 sq. m.) sales area. The lower size limit has been variously defined as 5,000 sq. ft., 500 sq. m. or 10,000 sq. ft.

Super-regional centre (super-regional shopping centre): A free-standing *shopping mall* of at least 800,000 sq. ft. GLA.

Superstore: A single-level, self-service store offering a wide range of food and non-food merchandise, with at least 25,000 sq. ft. (or 2,500 sq. m.) sales area and supported by car parking. The term can also be used to describe non-food stores of the *retail warehouse* type.

Town centre: An area, central to the town as a whole, in which the main land uses are commercial. In Western Europe, it forms the most important retail area in the town, and may include both unplanned and planned retailing. It also serves a wider purpose as a business, cultural and entertainment focus for the community.

Town centre management: The process of planning and taking action to improve the vitality and viability of a town or city centre as a whole, involving inputs from both public and private sectors.

Turnover rent: A rental charge based on the tenant's retail turnover.

Unitisation: Multiple ownership of a single property, through a Single Property Ownership Trust or some other means.

Unplanned retailing: A *retail area* that has evolved in a gradual and/or piecemeal manner, often through conversion of buildings originally designed for some other purpose.

Year's purchase: The value of a property, divided by a year's rent: the inverse of the *yield*.

Yield: The current annual income from a property, expressed as a percentage of the property's freehold price.

Zone A: The space extending 20 ft. back from a shop frontage, for which rents per unit area are higher than 'Zone B' and 'Zone C'.

Chapter 1

Introduction

Retailing is one of the most important sectors in all developed economies. In Britain, the retail sector employs over two million workers. It can be estimated that retail sales constitute around one-quarter of Britain's entire gross domestic product.

Retail companies form some of the largest enterprises in developed economies. In Britain, ten of the largest 100 companies are involved wholly or mainly in retail trade (Table 1.1). These ten companies were valued at some £39 billion on the Stock Exchange in November 1992.

Retail property – shops and shopping centres – constitute an important part of the country's built environment. There are almost 350,000 retail outlets in Britain, plus some 200,000 outlets devoted to 'service' uses of the type normally found within shopping centres (Schiller and Boucke, 1989). The amount of floorspace devoted to retail and service activities in Britain is over 70 million sq. m. or about 800 million sq. ft. (ibid.).

Table 1.1 Retailers among Britain's top 100 companies

Company	Market capitalisation (£m)	Position in top 100
Marks & Spencer	8,939	12
J. Sainsbury	8,635	14
Boots	5,097	27
Tesco	4,344	30
Argyll Group	4,032	32
Kingfisher	2,744	41
Ladbroke Group	1,757	64
Sears	1,385	76
W. H. Smith	1,260	89
Kwik Save	1,115	96

Source: *Sunday Times*, 8 November 1992

Development of new retail floorspace has been one of the most important areas of capital expenditure in Britain in the last two decades. To take an extreme example, Tesco plc spent around £1 billion in the financial year 1991/1992 on the development of new superstores. Commentators speak of the 'Tescoisation' of the urban and suburban landscape, meaning the replacement of open space by retail superstores with their access roads, car parking and signposting. Part of the popular reaction to this phenomenon concerns the uncompromising appearance of many of the buildings concerned, and their similarity from one region of Britain to another. Thus, the development of new retail space is of great significance both as source of economic growth and change, and as a social event that can arouse both positive and negative reaction.

At the same time, town and city centres have radically changed in their appearance and function during the last thirty years. The patchwork pattern of small shops, mixed with office, residential and other uses, has in many cases been replaced by giant buildings containing perhaps over one hundred shops. A small number of property companies and financial institutions have been prominent in these development or redevelopment schemes.

The student of retail development faces some difficulty in obtaining an understanding of this topic from existing academic and professional literature. Standard texts tend to be of two kinds. First, books written for a geography/town planning readership can give an excellent account of the broad factors affecting retail growth and change, and also present clearly the more important relationships between consumer purchasing behaviour and the location of retail activity. Examples of specialist texts include Davies (1977a; 1984), Beaujeu-Garnier and Delobez (1979), Dawson (1979; 1982), Berry and Parr (1988), Jones and Simmons (1990), O'Brien and Harris (1991) and S. Brown (1992). In addition, some of the more general human geography texts such as Carter (1981) and Herbert and Thomas (1990) include well-informed and detailed discussions of the geography of retail activity. However, these texts tend to provide little information on the processes through which retail space as such comes into existence. The reader may gain the impression that new or redeveloped retail space is provided by some 'hidden hand' in response to pressure of demand from shoppers, or the wishes of town planners. The exception to this rule is the book by Dawson (1983), which provides detailed material on the financing and organisation of retail development in several settings and countries, as part of a wide-ranging treatment of shopping centre development.

Another type of text is that written from a professional perspective, such as the architect (for example, Gosling and Maitland, 1976; Scott, 1989; Beddington, 1991); or the estate manager and surveyor (for example, Morgan and Walker, 1988; Thomas, 1990). These texts can provide excellent detailed descriptions of various types of retail development, and of ways in which these types are funded and organised. However, the wider perspective relating development to the 'outside world' of shoppers, retail firms, financial institutions and town planners is not always well explained. To a reader more used to critical social science approaches, this literature appears overly descriptive and uncritical. And because its focus is so much on recent and current professional practice, this literature is unable to provide useful advice about retail development patterns should some major changes occur in the wider political, economic and social background.

This book attempts to remedy the deficiencies of these various approaches by taking the production of new retail space as its central focus. It attempts to describe and explain this phenomenon in its many contemporary forms. The core concept used is the 'development process'. It is held that there are common features of retail development, which should be explained before particular cases such as grocery superstores or town centre redevelopment are discussed. A greater understanding of these and other cases can be gained by exploring their variations around the common elements of the development process.

A major emphasis is given to the roles of institutional factors in influencing rates, types and locations of retail development. Particularly important are sources of finance for development, and land use planning by public sector organisations. The view is taken that the development of various types of retailing can be better understood through knowledge of these institutional factors. Furthermore, tensions exist between the requirements of retailers, property developers, financiers and planners, and these tensions are often resolved in the form of uneasy compromises which are not fully satisfactory to any of these 'actors' involved in retail development.

These arguments determine the structure of this book. The first two chapters are introductory in nature, making definitions and establishing general contexts for the more detailed and specific discussions of later chapters. Thus, Chapter 2 presents a straightforward classification and description of the typical products of retail development – shops and shopping centres. Chapter 3 discusses models of retail development from an economic perspective based upon rent theory. The retail development process is presented as a variant on a generalised property development process.

The next two chapters examine the role of institutional finance (Chapter 4) and land use planning (Chapter 5). The focus in these chapters is mainly on the British situation, so that detailed case studies can be examined.

The following three chapters discuss three types of retail development: 'unplanned' development (Chapter 6), the result of unco-ordinated decisions at various times in the past by various landowners and retailers; more organised development by retailers themselves (Chapter 7); and modern shopping centres (Chapter 8), the largest, most expensive and most complex examples of retail development. In these chapters the roles of retailer, developer, financier and planner are examined and their influences on the built outcomes discussed.

From this discussion it will be clear that an 'actor' perspective is used frequently in this book. Criticisms have been expressed that 'actor' models of the development process are simplistic, and that they ignore the frequent tendency for the various roles to be combined in *ad hoc* coalitions. However, the models can be altered easily to take account of complexity or simplicity in real life.

Finally in this introduction, three problems should be mentioned that have affected the way in which this book has been written. The first of these is the unsatisfactory coverage and quality of published information about the property and spatial aspects of the retail sector. Many writers have complained about the lack of any recent government census of retail distribution, which would allow analysis of retail trends for specific geographical areas. This reflects a lack of concern by government interests (Guy, 1992). However, much information about retail development is concealed by retail and development companies for reasons of confidentiality. Other important information is available only in publications with restricted circulation, such as stockbrokers' analyses or the series of brief reports issued by property consultancies such as Hillier Parker, Healey & Baker, and the Investment Property Databank. This book has made extensive use of those sources available to the author, but it is likely that some important 'semi-publications', which would have added to the reader's understanding of retail development, have been omitted.

The second problem is a paucity of critical theory in many of the topics discussed in this book. Theories of the spatial characteristics of retailing are well developed (Jones and Simmons, 1990; Brown, 1992). However, the academic study of property development and its relationships with institutional factors, particularly development finance and land use planning, seems still to be in its infancy. Many of the cause-and-effect relationships suggested in this book rely on simple comparisons of time series, or the anecdotal evidence much used in the gossip-prone estate management and financial investment industries. It is to be hoped that some of these ideas will be taken up elsewhere and subjected to more rigorous analysis. One way in which this might be done would be through international comparisons of retail development and its institutional influences. Some such comparisons are suggested briefly at points in the book, but a thorough treatment must await further research.

The third problem in writing any book on property development is in keeping up with events. At the time of concluding the preparation of this book (March 1993), the property sector is still in 'slump' condition after the collapse of demand for new space in the years following 1989. The retail sector appears to be emerging from a prolonged standstill in consumer expenditure and a period of contraction in the numbers of certain types of retail outlet. This may then be a good time to write such a book, at the end (it is hoped) of a particularly marked boom–slump cycle. However, development activity has still been substantial over the last two years in some areas of the industry; and the land use planning background appears to be in a state of change. The critical reader will need to beware of all short-term analyses and predictions made in this book, and supplement its contents with careful reading of up-to-date material in the property and planning journals and consultants' reports.

Chapter 2

Retail development – a descriptive outline

INTRODUCTION

This chapter presents an overview of the main types of retail development that characterise advanced Western economies. Particular use is made of British examples. The emphasis is on description – of size, physical characteristics and location – of the various types of development. The intention is to provide the background for the more detailed explanations of development processes and trends that occur in later chapters.

Retail development takes place broadly as the result of demand from two sectors of the service economy. One source of demand – the property investment industry – is discussed in detail in Chapters 3 and 4. The second and most obvious source of demand is the retail firms themselves. These are discussed in the first main section of this chapter. Responding themselves to changes in consumer needs and preferences, retailers' plans for expansion, contraction or changes in retailing methods have implications for retail property development. The next section describes typical forms of modern retail development. This involves a sevenfold classification based mainly upon the physical characteristics of the development itself. A typology of retail locations is also introduced, and its relationship with shopping centre types is discussed.

RETAIL GROWTH AND CHANGE

This section reviews briefly the structure of retailing and the characteristics of retail growth and change, referring mainly to Britain. More comprehensive explanations of retail growth and change are available in several texts (e.g. Dawson, 1982; Davies, 1984; Jones and Simmons, 1990; O'Brien and Harris, 1991).

Two broad trends underlie changes in retail demand and retail provision. These are, first, changes in the population and its expenditure on consumer goods; and, second, changes in the structure of the retail sector, often arising from competition between retail firms.

Changes in population and expenditure characteristics

Population changes in total have been relatively unimportant in Britain for many years because total population growth has been slow. However, changes in age structure, and in consumer tastes and preferences, have been important in encouraging the development of new consumer goods and new forms of retail marketing. A whole new science of 'geodemographics' has grown up in recent years, studying the relationships between consumer demand, demographic structure of the population, and characteristics of residential areas. This helps retailers to target particular geographical areas for particular ranges of retail products and/or marketing methods; and it helps retailers to adjust the product mix within their stores to the tastes and preferences of the local catchment population (Beaumont and Inglis, 1989; Johnson, 1989).

Two trends that occurred during the 1980s were of particular importance in explaining the growth of retailing in Britain. These were an increase in the volume of consumer expenditure, and the growth of narrowly defined specialist retail markets. The former was associated with growth in real incomes, and increasing availability of means of credit, so that extra income was spent rather than saved. Much, though not all, of this extra expenditure was translated into retail sales, which rose substantially during the 1980s after several years of stagnation (Figure 2.1).

This growth in consumer expenditure was concentrated largely into comparison and specialist goods rather than the more staple convenience goods, for which demand per head has remained remarkably steady over the years

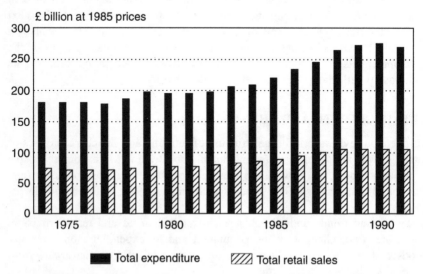

£ billion at 1985 prices

■ Total expenditure   ▨ Total retail sales

Figure 2.1 Consumers' expenditure in the UK and retail sales, 1974–1991

Source: Central Statistical Office (1992)

(Figure 2.2). Growth in demand for home improvement materials, furnishings and domestic electrical goods was also considerable. This partly comprised a new level of demand from householders who had bought their property from local authorities, following pressure from the Conservative government upon local authorities to sell their rented properties to tenants.

The end of the 1980s, however, saw the beginnings of an economic recession in Britain, as in many other Western countries. Consumer expenditure and retail sales grew only slightly in 1990 and fell, in real terms, in 1991 (Figure 2.1). The main reasons for this appear to have been, first, a lack of consumer confidence during a period of falling house values and increasing unemployment and, second, a preference amongst consumers to repay old debts to retail and finance companies rather than take on new ones.

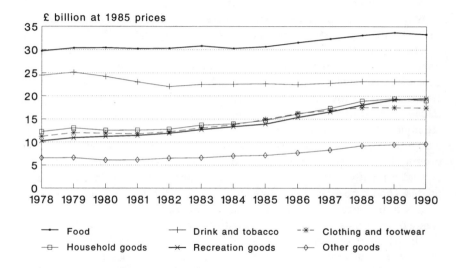

Figure 2.2 UK consumer retail spending, 1978–1990

Source: Central Statistical Office
Notes:
The categories relate to those listed in CSO data (Annual Abstract of Statistics 1991, Table 14.9) as follows:

Food:	Food (household expenditure)
Drink and tobacco:	Alcoholic drink; tobacco
Clothing and footwear:	Clothing and footwear
Household goods:	Do-it-yourself goods; furniture; pictures; etc.; carpets and other floor coverings; major appliances; textiles and soft furnishings; hardware; cleaning materials and matches
Recreation goods:	Radio; television and other durable goods; TV and video hire charges; licence fees and repairs; sports goods; toys; games and camping equipment; other recreational goods; books, newspapers and magazines
Other goods:	Pharmaceutical products and medical equipment; toilet articles and perfumery; jewellery; silverware; watches and clocks; other goods

The retailing and development outcomes

The growth in specialist retail markets was manifested in two principal ways: 'lifestyle retailing' and 'niche retailing'. Lifestyle retailing was developed from the notion that in many areas such as clothing, the mass market was breaking up. Subgroups of the population, defined by variables such as age and social class, were each seen to require their own versions of consumer goods. These could be sold in special shops that were designed to appeal to that particular group of the population. Hence, the Burton's retail empire diversified into thirteen differently named retail outlets, each aimed at a particular target market (Table 2.1). The idea also grew that lifestyle retailing could be narrowly focused on a target market but extend to a broad range of goods. The Habitat furniture and household equipment shops were an early manifestation of this idea, while in the 1980s the Next group of stores diversified into a wide range of clothing and eventually furnishings, from its original base in men's clothing.

Niche retailing concentrated on very narrowly defined areas of merchandise. In Britain the classic 1980s examples were Sock Shop and Tie Rack.

These trends resulted in an increase in demand by retailers for premises in the larger central shopping areas. The general growth in comparison shopping expenditure also encouraged the major 'high street' variety and department store companies to improve and, where possible, expand their outlets. Companies that traded from smaller, more specialist units (such as fashion and shoe retailers) attempted to move into shopping areas where they had been previously unrepresented. The lifestyle retailers were eager to operate several stores, each catering to a different market, within close proximity. The niche retailers also expanded rapidly. Thus, the 'space bandit' retailers competed for scarce retail premises and were prepared to pay ever higher rents for their new stores. This led rapidly to the situation, described in more detail in Chapter 8, where shopping centre developers sought to enlarge existing centres or build new ones. Finally, the increase in demand for household goods such as furniture and home improvement materials led to rapid expansion programmes by the retailers concerned. The resulting development boom in 'retail parks' in the late 1980s is also discussed in Chapter 8.

The cessation in growth of consumer expenditure at the end of the 1980s had major effects upon the retail industry. Some retail goods continued to sell well whereas others, particularly household goods and the more luxurious types of clothing and leisure goods, entered sharp decline in real terms. The 'space bandits' continued to pay high rents while faced with declines in trade, leading several of them to run into financial losses, followed by contraction, restructuring and even liquidation. Even a small reduction in annual profits could confound the Stock Market's expectations and lead a firm into considerable difficulties.

This all suggests another characteristic of the retail development market. Success, failure, growth and decline among retailers depend largely upon vagaries of consumer expenditure and preferences, and are highly visible to the

Table 2.1 Burton Group outlets, 1988

Outlet	Market	Profile	Target market age	Total no. outlets
Burtons	Men Youths	Mainstream formal and casual clothing and accessories	20–40	467
Alias	Men	Fashionable colour co-ordinated leisure and casual clothing	25–40	33
Top Man	Men Youths	Fashion-aware formal and casual clothing and accessories	11–30	252
Radius	Men	Individualistic formal and casual clothing and accessories	20–35	32
Principles for Men	Men	Modern classic clothing and accessories for business and pleasure	25–45	105
Champion Sports	Men Women Children	Fashionable sportswear and equipment	15–35	100
Dorothy Perkins	Women	Mainstream formal and casual clothing and accessories	18–40	467
Secrets	Women	Fashionable lingerie and nightwear	15–45	27
Top Shop	Women	Fashion-aware casual and occasion clothing and accessories	11–30	302
Principles	Women	Sophisticated fashionable classic clothing and accessories	25–45	192
Evans	Women	Mainstream fashion size 14+	25–60	196
Debenhams	Men Women Children Home	Mainstream mass-market fashion for the individual and home	All ages	71
Harvey Nichols	Men Women Children Home	Exclusive and designer fashion for the individual and home	All ages	1

Source: Burton (1988)

general public. This means that development prospects can change rapidly with the fortunes of the retail industry, and the likelihood of uninformed 'bandwagon' behaviour is high. Examples of this process will be discussed later in this book.

Retail competition

The second broad area of change – in retail ownership patterns and the nature of competition between retail firms – has been equally important. It has affected not so much the overall level of demand for new floorspace, but the nature of the floorspace itself, and to some extent, its location.

The years since the 1950s in Britain have been marked by a steady transformation of retail firm ownership, from domination by small independent firms to domination by large multiple organisations (Figure 2.3). These large firms also dominate most sectors of retailing (Table 2.2). In 1989, the five largest retail firms accounted for 19 per cent of all retail sales, and the 800 or so 'large multiple retailers' (owning ten or more shops) accounted for 61 per cent (Healey & Baker, 1992: 8). In the grocery sector, the five largest companies account for between 37 and 60 per cent of all sales, depending upon the base used for calculation.

This concentration of retail distribution has given certain retail companies enormous influence over the development process. Some companies can dictate terms to shopping centre developers who wish to entice them into new developments (see Chapters 3 and 8). In addition, much retail development has been carried out by a few of the major retailers, particularly in the grocery industry (see Chapter 7).

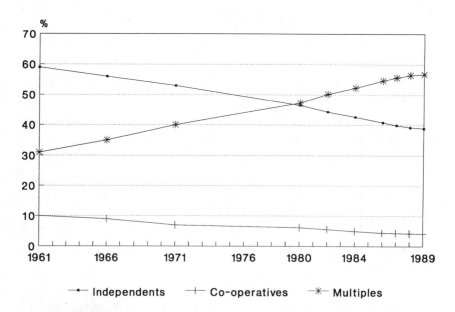

Figure 2.3 Shares of retail turnover in Britain, 1961–1989

Source: Business Statistics Office (1992)

Table 2.2 Retail concentration ratios, 1989

Commodity group	Total turnover (£m)	Percentage of turnover:	
		Largest 5 retail groups	Largest 10 retail groups
Food	35,809	41.3	54.1
Drink, confectionery and tobacco	17,189	22.0	33.4
Clothing, footwear and leather goods	19,901	36.5	49.5
Household goods	27,606	18.5	28.7
Other non-food goods	20,738	23.3	31.9
Hire and repair	1,653	64.6	68.6
All Retail	123,313*	19.3	30.0

Source: Business Statistics Office (1992: Table 13)
Note: *Numbers in source do not add up to exact total

TYPES OF RETAIL DEVELOPMENT

The pressures outlined above have led to development of a number of typical retail forms, which can now be summarised. The following classification bears some similarity with those of other authors (e.g. Davies, 1984; Dawson, 1983; Morgan and Walker, 1988), and is based largely upon physical characteristics. The intention in this section is to present brief descriptive summaries; the historical background and economic circumstances of these types of development will be discussed in later chapters. The types of centre described are typical of Western Europe: centres found mainly outside Western Europe, such as the strip centre (Dawson, 1983: Chapter 2; Carlson, 1991) are not discussed here.

Planned and unplanned retailing

An initial distinction should be made between 'unplanned' and 'planned' retailing, following the tradition established in early American studies of urban retailing (e.g. Berry, 1963). An *unplanned retail area* is one that has evolved in a gradual and/or piecemeal manner, often through conversion of buildings originally designed for some other purpose. Its ownership is likely to be fragmented between several companies, including some of the retail occupiers. Planned retail development can take place within unplanned areas; but if this development is small in relation to the retail area as a whole, the area can be said to have remained 'unplanned' as a whole. Most central shopping areas of towns and cities in Western Europe comprise mainly unplanned retailing, and the neutral term 'town centre' or 'city centre' can include both unplanned and planned retail areas. Smaller suburban clusters of shopping in European towns and cities are typically unplanned.

Some confusion can arise through the British habit of referring to unplanned retail areas as 'shopping centres', whereas in American usage (and in this book) the latter term is normally reserved for planned centres. Unplanned retailing is discussed in more detail in Chapter 6.

Planned retailing, on the other hand, is deliberately developed in a co-ordinated manner for retail use. Planned development creates either (a) a single building, with one or more retail stores contained within it, or (b) an organised group of physically separated retail stores with common arrangements for vehicle access and car parking. Planned centres are usually under one ownership and managed and marketed as a unit. The following classification extends from simple to complex forms of retail development, and is based upon physical characteristics (see Figure 2.4).

The free-standing store

In this, the simplest type of retail development, a single store is built together with access and car parking facilities. 'Free-standing' implies that the store is physically separate from other shopping areas. Often it is the case that a retail firm will take responsibility for acquiring land and building the store, to its own specifications. Development by retailers is discussed in Chapter 7.

Conventional classifications of free-standing stores are into food (or grocery) and non-food; and by size. Figure 2.5 relates store types to store size and typical

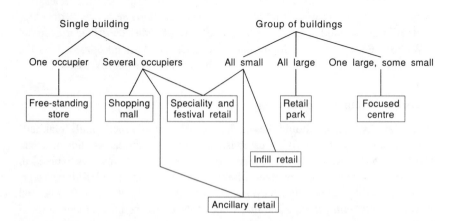

Figure 2.4 Retail development: a typology

Size (sales area)	Food stores	Non-food stores
Under 25,000 sq. ft.	Supermarket	Electrical goods Video hire Fast food
25,000–50,000 sq. ft.	Superstore	Retail warehouse: DIY carpets furniture toys
Over 50,000 sq. ft.	Hypermarket	Retail warehouse: furniture

Figure 2.5 Free-standing stores: a typology

goods sold within. The most prominent forms of free-standing store in Britain are the superstore and the retail warehouse.

The *superstore* was defined by the Unit for Retail Planning Information as follows:

> single level, self service stores offering a wide range of food and non food merchandise, with at least 25,000 square feet sales area (2,500 square metres) and supported by car parking. Stores with 50,000 square feet or more are commonly referred to as hypermarkets.
>
> (Unit for Retail Planning Information, 1976)

It should be noted that 25,000 sq. ft. and 2,500 sq. m. are not identical. The Unit subsequently altered its lower limit to 2,500 sq m. However, other sources of information such as the Institute of Grocery Distribution have retained the 25,000 sq. ft. lower limit.

A further qualification normally adopted in practice is that car parking should be free of charge and on one level.

Hypermarkets are normally defined in Britain as described above. Stores of hypermarket size are, however, often included in lists of 'superstores'. In contrast, in continental Europe the term 'hypermarket' is often used to denote food stores of over 2,500 sq. m. sales area.

Retail warehouses have been defined by Gibbs (1987: 19) as: 'characterised by the sale of a specialist range of non-food goods direct to the public from a warehouse type building in an off-centre location with stock stored on the premises'. No lower size limit is specified in this definition, although 25,000 sq. ft. is probably appropriate for all such stores apart from electrical goods outlets (Figure 2.5). Retail warehouses are usually single-storey, and possess free car parking for customers. The mention of 'off-centre location' signifies that purpose-built retail warehouses are unlikely to be found within established retail areas: this topic is discussed below and in Chapters 5 and 7.

Generally, modern free-standing stores are purpose-built, notwithstanding their similarity to warehouses. Access for shoppers and for delivery of goods are at opposite sides of the building. Car parking is provided for shoppers, typically at a rate of around ten spaces per 1,000 sq. ft. of gross retail area, for grocery stores, and around five per 1,000 sq. ft. for retail warehouses in Britain (Burt and Sparks, 1991; Thomas, 1990: 56). The store's design – both external and internal – is typically utilitarian, the main objectives being externally to provide obvious signals of the store's location and identity to the passing customer; and internally, to allow free movement of both shoppers and fork-lift vehicles around the store.

The focused centre (neighbourhood centre, district centre)

This type of centre consists of one or more stores similar to those described above in the 'free-standing' category, plus some smaller stores. These may be built in line facing a car park, or on either side of a short pedestrian walkway. Internal divisions between the small stores are often of lightweight construction and can be moved to allow variations in size between one store and another. The small stores will probably operate under covenants that forbid the sale of goods already sold in the main store. In this way the centre developer ensures that the small stores are complementary to the main store and add to the variety of goods sold in the centre as a whole.

In Britain many of these centres, usually known as 'district' centres, have been developed by grocery retailers, who also operate the largest store in these centres. Reasons for this situation are discussed in Chapter 7. In France and other Western European countries, these centres tend to include a food hypermarket and are known as 'Centres Intercommunaux' (Reynolds, 1992). In North America, such centres would normally be known as 'neighbourhood' centres. Larger 'community centres' are of similar physical layout but are anchored by a small department store or discount (non-food) store, as well as one or more super- markets (Dawson, 1983: 22).

Two examples of focused centres are shown in Figure 2.6.

The retail park

The retail park is a term adapted from the 'retail warehouse park' first discerned in the early 1980s. It consists basically of a cluster of stores of the type described above as 'free-standing'. It can include any of the free-standing types discussed above, although retail warehouses are most typical.

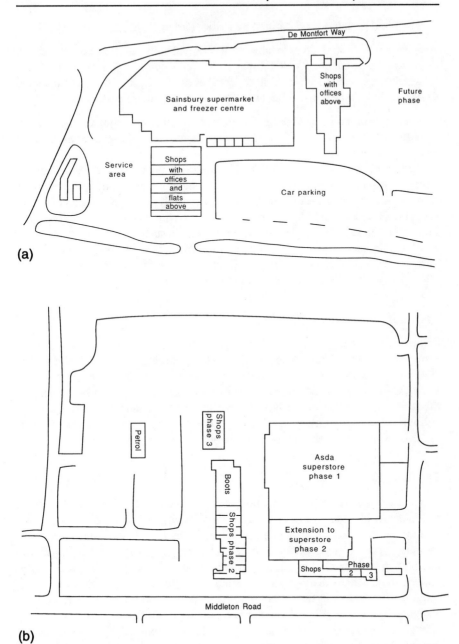

Figure 2.6 Focused centres: (a) Coventry: Cannon Park Centre; (b) Manchester: Chadderton Centre

Source: Unit for Retail Planning Information (1977: 58–9, 62–3)

The retail park has been defined by Hillier Parker (1989) as:

at least 50,000 sq. ft. gross lettable retail area, and built and let as a retail entity. It should be sited outside the town centre and contain at least three retail warehouses, defined as single-storey retail units of at least 10,000 sq ft. It should also include some purpose-built pedestrian area or joint car parking facilities.

The stores within a retail park may be physically separate, or joined together, or a mixture of the two styles. Some retail parks include leisure uses such as cinemas or indoor bowling arenas.

The retail park appears to be mainly a British phenomenon. Free-standing stores in off-centre locations are common throughout North American cities and in most Western European countries, but are rarely developed deliberately in clusters. Two examples of retail park layouts are shown in Figure 2.7. The first, Fforestfach Retail Park, represents an early stage in such developments, with the retail warehouses separated by a major road. The second, Telford Bridge Retail Park, is a more integrated development and typical of retail parks built in the late 1980s and early 1990s. Further information is provided in Chapter 8.

The infill development

Opportunities often arise within older unplanned shopping areas either to develop retail units on unused land, or to redevelop a large existing store or group of stores. Where the scale of such development is small relative to the retail area as a whole, this type of development can be termed 'infill' (Morgan and Walker, 1988: 2). Physical characteristics of this type of development are hard to summarise, as they will reflect local circumstances. Most typical is probably a group of small stores, sited along one side of an existing street, or both sides of a pedestrian route.

The shopping mall

The most complex form of shopping development, and yet one of the most common world-wide, comprises one or more large 'anchor stores' and several smaller units. Such centres attempt to replicate the amount and variety of shopping space in long-established central shopping areas. Small comparison goods shops selling clothing, footwear, leisure and luxury items are particularly important, and help distinguish the centre from retail parks or from focused centres. The American term 'shopping mall' is becoming used in Britain (e.g. Morgan and Walker, 1988: 2) and appears appropriate. This type of centre is in effect contained in one very large building, although some of the internal spaces may not be roofed over. Its lower size limit may be taken as 100,000 sq. ft. of gross retail area, to distinguish it from the focused centre or retail infill. Shopping malls typically have a strong marketing profile, with a well-known name and logo, and are managed and marketed as a unified shopping destination. They can be built either within existing shopping areas, or free-standing.

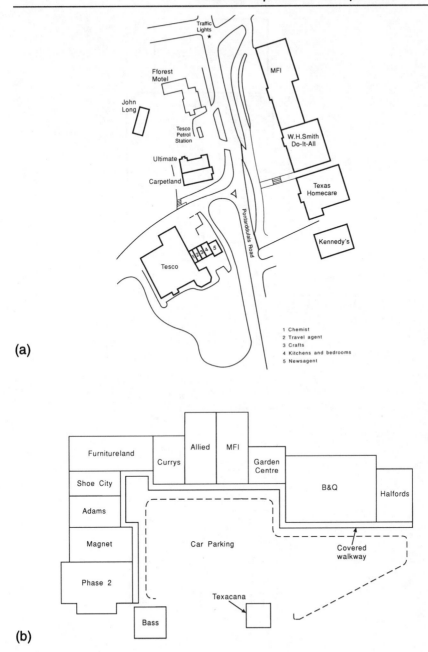

(a)

(b)

Figure 2.7 Retail parks: (a) Fforestfach Retail Park, Swansea;
(b) Telford Bridge Retail Park

Sources: Bromley and Thomas (1989a: 48, 50); Brown (*European Journal of Marketing*, 1990, 24, 9)

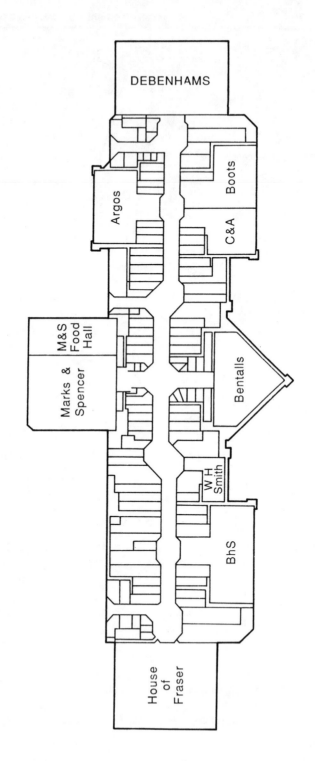

(a)

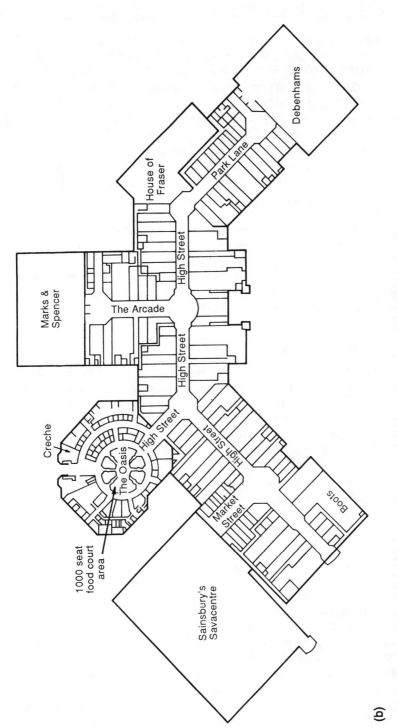

Figure 2.8 Shopping malls: (a) Lakeside Centre, Thurrock; (b) Meadowhall Centre, Sheffield
Sources: Your Personal Guide to Lakeside (nd); *Shopping Centre Horizons*, Winter (1991)

(b)

Larger malls, when built in free-standing positions, are generally known as 'regional centres'. The lower size limit to this type of centre has been variously stated as 300,000, 400,000 or 500,000 sq. ft. or 30,000 or 50,000 sq m. Such centres are marketed as a 'one-stop' shopping destination: the intention is that the centre should sell a very wide variety of goods, at a range of prices and styles.

Since the mid-1960s in Britain, shopping malls have usually been partly or wholly covered from the elements. Pedestrian ways, lined by shops, generally link the anchor stores with one another and with car parks. In the larger centres, junctions between pedestrian ways are often used for restaurants, food courts or even ice skating rinks. Centres built or refurbished in the 1980s tend to display better quality landscaping and building materials than those of earlier generations, and are often climatically controlled. Very large centres of over about 800,000 sq. ft. are usually built on two levels, in order to reduce the total land take of the centre and to shorten the amount of walking that shoppers have to carry out within the centre itself. In such a centre, the major space users will probably trade from both floors. Figure 2.8 shows the layouts of two recently built regional shopping malls, the Lakeside and Meadowhall centres. The location and design of shopping malls is discussed in depth in Chapter 8.

Speciality and 'festival' centres

These types of centre have recently become important in Britain, following trends in North America. The speciality centre is targeted on a particular segment of the market, whereas the festival centre combines retailing with eating out and entertainment (Morgan and Walker, 1988: 8–9). In both cases the attraction to the shopper should be the centre as a whole, rather than individual shops within it. Such centres do not usually contain anchor stores, and comprise mainly small shop units, of a size smaller than that typically used in shopping malls. Both types of centre frequently arise through the conversion of older multi-storey buildings, for example, department stores or warehouses.

Ancillary retailing

'Ancillary' retailing is a term used to describe groups of shops that exist simply to serve the incidental retail needs of people who are in the area for some other purpose. These shops may form part of a mixed development of various land uses. The most common instance is probably where retail uses occupy part of the ground floor of a multi-storey office or hotel building in a city centre. The retail use is designed partly to provide a service to the building's other occupants, and partly to take advantage of the flows of pedestrians at street level which are normally found within city centres. Other common instances are transport interchanges and tourist complexes (Dawson, 1983: 34–35).

A variation on this theme is the underground shopping mall, found in some major cities such as Montreal, Toronto and Sydney, where climatic conditions can be adverse. Here, shops line the pedestrian subways which link major pedestrian attractors. These cannot really be considered as integrated centres, since they follow rather than create the pedestrian routes; and are unlikely to include anchor stores, for reasons of lack of space.

RETAIL LOCATION

The question of location has been important to developers and retailers for many years. Brown (1992: 16) summarises conventional thinking about retail location as three-stage: first, decisions about whether to operate in a particular geographical region; second, decisions concerning whether to operate in a particular shopping centre or retail area; third, 'site' decisions relating to particular premises. Each of these decisions is (or should be) informed by methods of analysis specific to that geographical scale. These methods are beyond the scope of this book, but are explained elsewhere (e.g. Davies and Rogers, 1984; Ghosh and McLafferty, 1987; Wrigley, 1988; Jones and Simmons, 1990).

The location of retail development is, however, a key issue to which this book devotes considerable attention. One of the most important locational issues is whether development is carried out within or outside existing retail areas. Simple classifications, such as 'in-town'/'out of town', 'in-centre'/'off-centre', 'centralised'/'decentralised', have been in common use since the early 1960s. Concern arose in Western Europe when it was noticed that major new retailing was beginning to occur in locations well outside the existing town centres and other retail areas. The first examples of this were probably the hypermarkets built in suburban or edge-of-town locations in France and Germany. Attempts to build such stores followed in Britain. Up to this time, new retail development in suburban locations had consisted simply of small-scale, neighbourhood centres serving the local residential population. The new hypermarkets, in contrast, were in some cases nearly as large as neighbouring town centres, and clearly posed a threat to existing retail interests.

The history of free-standing suburban retailing is discussed in more detail in Chapter 7, while the planning issues and attitudes are examined in Chapter 5. This section simply serves to introduce the locational dimension into the discussion of retail development, and to define a typology of retail locations within urban areas.

Locational classifications

Surprisingly, there seems to be no generally agreed typology or classification of retail locations. The commonly used classifications of shopping centres discussed by Dawson (1983), Davies (1984), Guy (1984) and other writers relate to centre size and catchment area rather than location. These classifications are derived from central place theory (Christaller, 1966; Berry and Parr, 1988), and are still used in retail planning practice despite the outdated and restrictive assumptions of that theory (S. Brown, 1991).

A point at issue is whether locational typologies should simply describe potential locations for retail development, without reference to existing retailing, or include reference to existing retailing or proposed retail development. The first type – a classification of potential locations within urban areas – should bear some relationship to the main features of urban development generally. In the European context a simple typology would be:

- town or city centre
- inner suburban
- outer suburban
- edge of town.

Conventionally, 'inner suburban' refers to areas developed mainly before 1914, typically high-density residential which includes scattered industrial and commercial uses. 'Outer suburban' areas built after 1918 are of lower residential density, with more clearly separated industrial and commercial areas. 'Edge of town' refers to undeveloped sites beyond the residential limits of the urban area but within easy reach, and probably with good road access.

Most locational classifications also refer in some way to characteristics of retail areas themselves. An example is that used in Britain by the Institute of Grocery Distribution:

- purpose-built shopping centre
- traditional 'high street'
- local or neighbourhood centre
- edge of town (free-standing).

Thorpe (1991) criticises this classification for not distinguishing between 'in-town' and 'out-of-town' purpose-built shopping centres. Guy (1988), writing specifically on grocery superstore development, used another classification:

- town or city centre
- inner urban
- new 'district centre'
- edge of town.

For more general use it would appropriate to break 'inner urban' into at least two further categories: for example: existing unplanned retail area; industrial area; other. The 'other' category can include, for example, waterfront locations which are popular for specialist retailing. The 'new district centre' type mentioned above is itself a form of development rather than a location, and 'new residential area' seems more appropriate for the present purpose. This leads to a more comprehensive typology:

- town or city centre
- suburban unplanned retail area
- industrial area

- other urban
- new residential area
- edge of town.

Location and type of retail development

This locational classification may now be related to the various forms of retail development outlined earlier in this chapter. Figure 2.9 shows the most common combinations.

Free-standing stores and retail parks are usually located outside existing centres, for reasons of space and easy access for vehicles. Focused centres can be provided either in new residential areas, in existing centres as part of an urban renewal programme, or at the edge of town. They are usually inappropriate to central shopping areas, because of their car parking requirements. Infill and ancillary development usually takes place in existing central areas of towns. Speciality and festival centres may be developed either around the fringes of

Type of centre	Location					
	TC	SUA	IA	OU	NRA	ET
Free-standing store			✓	✓	✓	✓
Focused centre		✓		✓	✓	✓
Retail park			✓	✓		✓
Infill	✓	✓				
Shopping mall	✓			✓		✓
Speciality/festival	✓			✓		✓
Ancillary	✓					

Key:

TC   town centre
SUA   suburban unplanned area
IA   industrial area
OU   outer urban
NRA   new residential area
ET   edge of town

Figure 2.9 Typical locations of planned centres

central shopping areas or in other urban locations related to tourist or waterfront attractions.

Shopping malls, despite their requirement for sites of substantial size, are found in a variety of urban locations. An important distinction should be made between shopping malls that are themselves free-standing (often loosely termed 'regional' or 'out-of-town' centres), and those that are themselves part of a central shopping area. Free-standing shopping malls are the norm in North America, where the response to the growth of suburban population has been to build new centres in the newly developed suburban areas (Lord, 1988). Regional or even 'super-regional' centres (of over 800,000 sq. ft.) here form the highest level in the hierarchy of planned centres. In Western Europe, however, it has been much more common to build shopping malls within the fabric of existing central areas. Dawson (1983) terms such developments 'renewal centres'. This pheno-menon reflects both the preference of financial investors for town centres, as discussed in Chapter 4, and the strength of land use planning control in European countries, as discussed in Chapter 5.

Finally in this section, we can return to the discussion of potential locations for retail development. In Figure 2.10, the simple typology of urban locations is mapped against a threefold categorisation based upon retail use or 'status': non-retail, unplanned retail and planned retail. The entry in each cell of this diagram expresses the characteristics of the location as it might be seen by a developer. Some cells contain retailing, some offer potential for new develop-ment. Figure 2.11 shows the types of retail development opportunity which these sites could present, using the classification of planned centres introduced earlier in this chapter. The issues and choices which are implied in these diagrams are discussed in later chapters.

CONCLUSIONS

This chapter has provided an introduction to the study of retail development. Some common physical forms of development have been described, and the underlying dynamics of retail expansion and change briefly discussed. The important issue of retail location, and its relationships with shopping centre deve-lopment, has been addressed. The discussion of these issues has been brief and the reader is referred to the other texts mentioned for a more detailed approach.

What has been missing from this chapter is any discussion of the typical economic appraisal and other processes of decision-making and negotiation which occur before and during the development of shopping centres. Centres do not arise simply through pressure of demand from consumers or retailers, although these pressures are a prerequisite. The remainder of this book attempts to provide a full discussion of these issues. The development process involves several stages which are described in Chapter 3. It also requires financial backing, and approval from land use planners. These requirements are discussed in Chapters 4 and 5. More specific and detailed discussion of various types of retail development is provided in Chapters 7 and 8.

Location	Non-retail	Retail status	
		Unplanned retail	Planned retail
Town or city centre	Ancillary uses	Traditional 'high street'	Infill or shopping mall
Inner suburban	'Brownfield' site	Retail ribbon	Infill or district centre
Outer suburban	Industrial estate	–	Free-standing or district centre
Edge of town	'Greenfield' site	–	Free-standing or district centre or shopping mall

Figure 2.10 Retail status and retail location

Location	Non-retail	Retail status	
		Unplanned retail area	Planned centre
Town or city centre	Ancillary specialist	Infill or Shopping mall	Refurbishment
Inner suburban	Free-standing Retail park	Focused centre	Refurbishment
Outer suburban	Free-standing Retail park Focused centre	–	Refurbishment
Edge of town	Free-standing Retail park Shopping mall	–	Refurbishment Enlargement

Figure 2.11 Retail development opportunities

Chapter 3

The development process – an introduction

THE SCOPE OF THIS CHAPTER

This chapter provides an introduction to property development processes in developed economies. The principles of property development apply widely across many different types of development, scales of activity and locations. However, the emphasis in this chapter is on commercial development rather than residential or industrial. The final section discusses particular features of retail development.

The literature on property development falls broadly into two types. There is a descriptive or explanatory literature, written largely for students of surveying and land management, which explains the economic principles of land value, land use and development (e.g. J. Harvey, 1992), or describes typical property development decisions and processes from the point of view of the developer and/or valuer (e.g. Cadman and Austin-Crowe, 1991). Then there is a critical literature in which property development is placed within wider economic and political contexts. This literature tends to derive from geographers and sociologists (e.g. Ambrose and Colenutt, 1975; D. Harvey, 1985; Massey and Catalano, 1978). Recently the two viewpoints have begun to merge in critical reviews of development practice (e.g. Healey and Nabarro, 1990; Healey *et al.*, 1992).

The main purpose of this chapter is to provide a background from which to discuss retail development and change in later chapters. The approach taken is founded in a pragmatic view of current practice although perhaps more critical than that found in the average surveying or valuation textbook. The analysis is based mainly in neo-classical rather than Marxist economics, although some insights are drawn from the latter. This eclectic approach is a matter partly of personal preferences. It also seems important to be able to provide an account of property development principles that is reasonably sympathetic towards the perceptions of leading practitioners.

The key to understanding property development lies in relationships between land use, land value and rent. These relationships are dealt with first in this chapter. There follows a brief description and economic justification for private sector property development in a market or mixed economy. The next section describes some models of the development process. Thereafter the discussion turns to more technical matters, although still adopting a very broad and general approach: these are development appraisal, and sources of finance for development. The final main section explains briefly how retail development in particular relates to the more general principles established in this chapter.

LAND USE, LAND VALUES AND RENT

This section establishes some general relationships between land use, land values and rent, drawing widely from the economic literature. A brief and non-technical explanation is provided: readers seeking a deeper understanding or more rigorous presentation should refer to the texts cited.

Land value

The value of a piece of land or a building, expressed as its freehold price, may be determined in various ways. A simple explanation is that its value is the maximum that anyone is prepared to pay for it, should it be available for sale. Prices may be determined, using these notions, by something akin to an auction sale. Offers or 'bids' are made by prospective purchasers, and the highest bid obtains the property. Hence the concept of the 'bid-price': the maximum amount that any prospective purchaser is prepared to pay. Similarly, the 'bid-rent': the maximum rent that any prospective tenant is prepared to pay.

A second basic principle is that of comparison. Prices are set with reference to recent sales of similar areas of land or buildings. This is essentially how house prices are determined in the short term. Experienced valuers can estimate a price by referring to prices that have been paid very recently for similar houses in similar locations. Similarly, rents may be set, by landlords, from information about rents actually being paid in comparable buildings or for comparable land elsewhere. In this way the bid-price or bid-rent offered in one instance becomes (for a short time) the standard for sellers' and buyers' price (or rent) expectations.

It will be shown later in this chapter that property prices and rents are themselves linked in conventional valuation practice. Where the building(s) concerned is to be let to tenants, and the market rent can be estimated in advance, then the value of the building is estimated as the rent multiplied by some ratio normally adopted for that type of property. Hence, land values and rents are intimately linked.

Determination of land prices and rents

These arguments do not explain why prices or rents vary from one building or one place to another. One explanation for this might be that the purchaser will pay more for a building that is in good condition than for one in bad condition; or more for a large house than a small house. Also, location is an important factor in affecting prices, for several reasons which are discussed later in this chapter.

More formally, two theoretical approaches exist to the determination of land prices and rents, and the whole topic of land and property development. The *neo-classical economic* approach focuses on the price mechanism. Prices are related to factors of demand and supply, and the *land market* acts as a forum for buyers and sellers, attempting to establish an equilibrium in which demand matches supply (Healey, 1992: 34). Implicit in this model is the notion that 'an unrestricted land market will allocate land in the most efficient manner by ensuring that it goes to the highest bidder' (Sheppard and Barnes, 1990: 101).

This introduces to the study of the land market the familiar notions of supply and demand. A property of a type which is in short supply, and/or in heavy demand, will (other things being equal) be worth more than one in plentiful supply and/or low demand. An increase in demand for that type will, in the short term, lead to a price rise. In the longer term, the market should respond to this situation by increasing the supply of properties. A decrease in demand will lead to reduced prices and/or a 'glut' of unoccupied and unsold properties.

The second broad approach is associated with *Marxist* economists, or more generally the *political economy* approach. This bases the study of the land market within an analysis of the struggle between groups for the control of the surplus generated in production (Healey, 1992: 34). Landlords are defined as a 'class' and use their monopoly power to limit access to land. However, the extent of this power varies according to the type of 'rent' that is being paid. The simplest distinction is between *monopoly rent* (which pertains to particular individual landlords and exists even for land at the lowest margin of productivity) and *differential rent* (which arises when land is used for productive activity). The latter is of more concern here, and was divided by Marx into two categories. *Differential rent I* has been defined by Sheppard and Barnes (1990: 304) as: 'The difference in rents paid on two plots of land when the same production method is used on both, as a result of differences in fertility or location.' This type of rent is determined essentially by the amount of profit that producers derive from using land, hence rent levels are derived through a bidding process amongst potential users (see above).

Differential rent II is defined as: 'The difference paid on two plots of land of the same fertility and locational advantage, as a result of differences in the production methods used' (Sheppard and Barnes, 1990: 304).

Differential rent II introduces the notion that capital can be invested in a plot of land to increase its rent-bearing capacity, and this is the key to the whole notion of property development. It allows landowners to make profits from development, and gives landlords greater control over rent levels, thus increasing their monopoly power (Sheppard and Barnes, 1990: 237).

Land uses and land markets

The above discussion, as well as everyday experience, suggests that property markets are organised into many categories and that each category interests certain purchasers (or tenants) only. One important, probably the basic, categorisation is by land use. Thus, markets are routinely differentiated into residential, commercial and industrial property; or residential and agricultural land, for example. Each category has its own supply of land or properties, and its own group of prospective landowners, purchasers, renters and land agents. These basic markets are further subdivided into more specialised submarkets, categorised by size of building, quality, location, etc. Thus, the 'office market' can range from two-room premises above shops, suitable for insurance brokers and the like, to complete modern office blocks in the City of London, suitable for corporate headquarters of financial companies.

This, in turn, suggests that land use and land value may be related, because each land use derives its own markets, with unique demand/supply relationships and price/rent structures. It follows also that a single building or piece of land may possess several land values: retail, office, residential and so on. Each of these land values reflects the demand/supply relationships and price/rent structures pertaining to the land use concerned.

Land valuation

In land markets in capitalist economies, the main approach to the determination of land value is related to the future income that can be derived from land. This view essentially regards land, or buildings, as an investment, and is usually adopted in the valuation of commercial and industrial property. The price offered is one that allows a satisfactory return to be made, over a period of years, sufficient to repay the costs of purchase and to provide an element of profit. The return derives from anticipated rents paid by future occupiers (tenants) of the land or of buildings constructed upon it. This model applies particularly well to agricultural land, because a clearly quantifiable income can be derived from growing crops or grazing animals on agricultural land. The principle can, however, be applied to any property in which an income is derived from tenants. For non-agricultural land, the income is related to prospective tenants' rent payments (see above), rather than direct income from the produce of the land itself. When dealing with land users who do not directly derive income from land or buildings, such as owner occupiers of housing, the model then becomes more tenuous. The notion of utility or 'psychic income' derived from occupying the property has to be used instead. It is held that prospective purchasers try to maximise utility, subject presumably to some overall limit on expenditure. Similarly, persons or companies renting property seek to maximise the utility derived from the space rented, subject to a limit on what they can pay.

When comparing alternative schemes for land or property development on a particular site, those concerned will compare the predicted flows of net incomes from the various schemes. Several methods are used, which are explained in detail in valuation and property portfolio management texts (e.g. Millington, 1988; Dubben and Sayce, 1991). Basically, these methods all attempt to predict flows of costs and revenues, year by year, from the development. Annual flow elements are usually 'discounted' so that elements in the near future are given more weight than distant elements. The scheme that maximises the stream of net incomes (discounted revenues less costs) over a period of, say, fifteen years will be selected for development. Neo-classical economists claim that the profit-maximising scheme involves the 'highest and best' use for the site concerned.

Von Thunen and Alonso

These two elements – the bid-price, and the anticipation of a stream of future incomes – were united in a theory of land pricing, by the agricultural economist von Thunen in 1826. For any piece of land, bid-prices were related to the amount of income that could be obtained from the land. Such income could be related to the physical requirements for various types of agricultural land use. The farmer who could produce the greatest income from the site would bid the highest price, and thus obtain the land. This recalls the concept of Differential Rent I, discussed above. Thus, land use would become related to land value; and land value would be different for different land uses, on the same piece of land. Von Thunen also added a locational dimension to the process. Different types of agricultural produce cost different amounts to carry to market. Thus, farmers producing output that was expensive to transport would try to obtain land close to the market, and would bid the highest prices. Hence, land uses formed concentric rings around the market; and land prices were highest close to the market. This well-known theory of land use and land value is explained in many textbooks (e.g. Haggett et al., 1977: 199–222; J. Harvey, 1992: 209–212).

Equally well known is Alonso's (1960) application of von Thunen's agricultural land model to a hypothetical city. Alonso showed that if demand for products and supply of externally derived materials were concentrated at the centre of the city, a concentric ring pattern of land uses, and a peak of land prices or rents at the centre of the town, would result from arguments similar to those used by von Thunen. Alonso (1964) also explained how variations in both costs and revenues, according to distance from the city centre, could be used to predict the location that would offer the greatest profit for any particular firm. A consistent prediction was that commercial uses (retail and office) would 'capture' the central part of the city. This was mainly because these uses needed to be at the most accessible part of the city (i.e. the centre). Only in this location would revenues be sufficiently high for operation to be profitable. But because other uses (industrial, residential) also wanted a central location, mainly to save on costs, the commercial users had to bid higher prices to obtain these essential city centre sites. On the other hand, commercial users had low valuations of sites

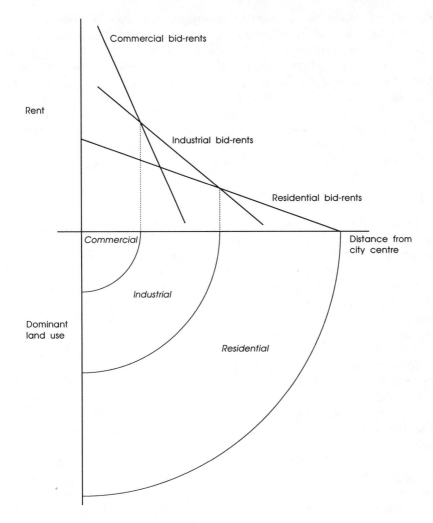

Figure 3.1 Urban bid-rent theory
Source: Adapted from Brown (1992: 54)

located away from the centre; thus other users, who valued them more highly, would obtain them. This situation is described diagrammatically in Figure 3.1.

Recent experience shows that many commercial space users do not in fact seek central sites, and the topic of retail decentralisation is studied in later chapters. Some commentators have claimed that this, along with other objections, devalues Alonso's model. However, it is still the case that central areas of cities are dominated by commercial uses, and rents are much higher in central areas than elsewhere in the city (Whitehand, 1987: 33). Decentralisation of commercial uses implies a willingness to forgo the advantages of a central location, in order to pay lower prices or rents. The trade-off between 'location' and 'rent' is an important concept in the study of urban commercial structures.

To sum up, different types of land user will bid different prices for the same piece of land, according to the anticipated future stream of incomes to be derived from the land or property built on it. Hence, for the same area of land, it is possible to estimate 'agricultural land value', 'residential land value' or 'commercial land value', for example. In other words, the von Thunen/Alonso model leads to the conclusion that land use determines land value; and the location of land can determine its land use.

PROPERTY DEVELOPMENT

Property development in a market economy is the process of transforming a plot of land from one state to another: the main motive is usually financial profit. Again, two broad explanations exist, depending upon theoretical perspectives. To the neo-classical economist, the purpose of property development is to improve the functioning of the land market, by increasing the supply of property of particular types in particular locations, to meet perceived demand by prospective occupiers. From the political economy perspective, property development increases the monopoly power of the landowning class, through the application of capital investment to a plot of land.

These two perspectives are not necessarily in conflict. They both allow the commonsense definition that the purpose of development is to increase the value of the land such that profit from the operation is maximised. The developer attempts to provide accommodation for the type of user who will provide the maximum stream of net incomes over a foreseeable period. This will involve realising the 'highest and best' use for the land concerned.

As shown above, the broad type of future land use (residential, industrial, etc.) that maximises development profits is determined mainly by location. However, site characteristics, the local demand and supply of property of various types, and the developer's own experience and preferences will all affect the result. While the use which from general principles appears to be 'highest and best' for that site should always in theory provide the maximum income from the land, excessive costs of development or problems in obtaining finance may lead to some other development solution being the most profitable.

Maximising the value of a plot of land can be done in three broad ways. First, land use can be changed from one category to another, for example agricultural to residential at the urban fringe. Residential land values in Britain are usually at least one hundred times as great as agricultural. Second, land use can be intensified: a four-storey office building can be replaced by a ten-storey one, thus increasing the income to be gained from the site. Third, a site can be modernised, with or without replacement of the existing building. Modern offices with telecommunications networks and air conditioning are more valuable than a 1950s building that possesses neither facility. Combinations of these three purposes for development are of course common.

Property developers are often criticised for making what appear to be very large profits from their activities: examples are discussed in Marriott (1967) and Ambrose and Colenutt (1975). This raises an issue about the efficient functioning of the land market. Property development, as practised in market or mixed economies, is justified by practitioners as an efficient means of providing the market with modern accommodation for its many and varied economic activities. The astute developer should be aware of supply and demand relationships, and should provide accommodation that is actually needed by potential users. The land market will, if it functions correctly, adjust land values before and after development, so that developers do not make 'excess' profits. However, commentators have also noted that the land market is not fully efficient. This is for five reasons:

1 Land and property is essentially 'lumpy': land is sold in parcels, and buildings are developed and sold as complete entities. This means, for example, that minor changes in demand may not be matched by the minimum scale of change in supply which can economically take place.
2 Property sales and purchases are subject to 'transaction costs', which may be substantial and may inhibit property market activity.
3 There are time lags between perceiving a demand for properties of a particular type, and supplying those properties. As noted above, this can lead to short-term scarcity and price increases.
4 There are barriers to flows of information about demand and supply factors, prices and rents. The property market can be particularly secretive.
5 In almost all 'market' economies, transactions in land and property are constrained by taxation structures and specific 'planning' or 'zoning' regulations concerning land development. These can arguably create scarcities, as discussed in Chapter 5.

These sources of economic inefficiency in the land market have three main effects upon property development. First, investment in property is regarded as inherently more 'risky' than investment in a very secure medium such as government stocks. This is taken account of in decisions on property investment. Second, it is possible for developers to make 'excess profits' from development, by withholding information from interested parties, or by taking advantage of any scarcity caused by planning restrictions, for example. Thus, the criticisms noted above have some grounding in fact. Third, it is also possible for even the largest developers to lose money, or go out of business through developing unsuccessful schemes. The recent failure of the massive Olympia & York property company has concerned the whole of the property market in Britain and elsewhere.

THE DEVELOPMENT PROCESS

Models of the development process

The process by which land and property is developed in a market economy has received considerable attention in the literature. Two recent review papers (Gore and Nicholson, 1991; Healey, 1991) have surveyed different 'approaches' to, or 'models' of, the 'development process'. These can range from simple descriptions of the development of a typical building on a typical parcel of land, to complex models of the ways in which development occurs over various types of land use and over a period of time.

Healey (1991) suggests that approaches to the study of the development process can be made from four different perspectives. First (altering her order of treatment), the *estate management* approach, in which the development process is presented descriptively through a series of 'stages' or 'events'. Second, the *behavioural social science* approach, in which attention is focused on 'actors' or 'agents' in the development process, and their interrelationships. Third, in the *neo-classical economic* approach, development is 'driven' by considerations of rent potential and calculations of yields from development. In other words, as argued above, development takes place to restore equilibrium to the land market. Fourth, the *political economy* approach examines broader structural influences and sees landowners as a separate class in opposition to both capitalists and workers (Sheppard and Barnes, 1990). The classification suggested by Gore and Nicholson (1991) is broadly similar.

In practical terms, it appears most sensible to view the neo-classical and political economy approaches as providing a broad understanding of the forces that drive property development in capitalist societies. The two viewpoints, although often said to be in opposition, can both offer important insights into property development, as discussed above. Models of the development process based upon these perspectives (e.g. Ambrose, 1986; Boddy, 1981; Harvey, 1985, which are discussed in both of the review papers mentioned above) are, however, too generalised to be easily applicable to particular examples. The first two approaches previously discussed, which Healey (1991) terms 'event-sequence' and 'agency' models respectively, while also being general in nature, can direct the researcher's attention towards specific information which should be sought to gain knowledge about particular developments. Therefore these two approaches are now described in more detail.

Event-sequence models

These models describe the various stages that occur when a development takes place. A very simple model, suggested by Cadman and Austin-Crowe (1978: 3) divides the development process into four stages:

1 evaluation;
2 preparation;
3 implementation;
4 disposal.

Although expanded to eight stages in subsequent editions (Cadman and Austin-Crowe, 1991: 2), the earlier model is appropriate here as a simple description of the stages involved in development. *Evaluation* involves, first, initiation of the development project in principle, either through 'a use looking for a site, or a site looking for a use' (ibid.). The evaluation stage proper involves financial assessment of the likely level of return from the project, and consideration of any physical and legal constraints that might arise. *Preparation* includes arrangement of short-term finance, acquisition of the site, design and costing, and obtaining planning permission. At the end of this process, the developer decides whether to proceed with the project: if so, contracts with other agencies are drawn up and signed (Cadman and Austin-Crowe, 1991: 4–9). *Implementation* involves construction of the project itself. *Disposal* involves letting the completed development to appropriate occupiers, and either managing the development or selling it to another company. This stage involves the acquisition of long-term finance.

Healey (1991: 224) criticises event-sequence models on grounds that they are descriptive rather than explanatory; and states that 'there is ample empirical evidence to demonstrate that there is no standard sequence of events for a development project'. Cadman and Austin-Crowe (1991: 2) do, however, point out that the 'stages do not always follow this sequence and often run in parallel'.

Agency models

Agency models concentrate on the various types of 'actor' (person, company or institution) involved in the development process. This approach is useful in drawing attention to the contributions from both private and public sector agencies that are necessary for development to take place.

Cadman and Austin-Crowe (1991: 10–18) describe the main types of actor involved in the development process. Figure 3.2 depicts these actors, and their relationships with the same authors' eight-stage model of the development process. Some of the relationships shown in this diagram are self-evident. However, three groups of actors – financial institutions, planners and occupiers – have more wide-reaching and complex effects upon development decisions than the diagram would indicate. These effects are of vital importance in the retail development process, and are discussed at length in later chapters.

The diagram indicates that, rather obviously, the 'developer' is involved throughout the development process. It is important to realise that the 'developer' is not necessarily a specialist individual or company, but can be any of the agencies shown in the figure. In later chapters we discuss how financial investors,

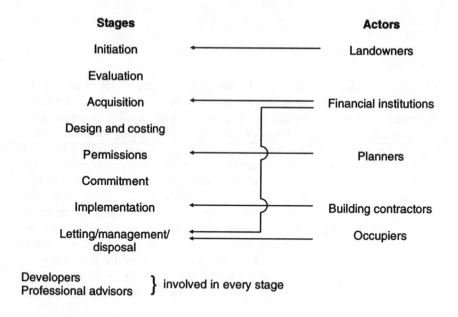

Figure 3.2 Stages and actors in the development process
Source: Based upon Cadman and Austin-Crowe (1991)

local government and retailers have become involved in retail development. However, specialist property development companies are also important in retail and other types of development.

In Britain there are several major 'property companies' whose rationale is commercial property development and which are large enough to be quoted on the Stock Exchange. These can be divided further into *property investment companies* and *property trading companies*. Both of these types develop properties, but the former retain ownership of the properties they have developed and receive rental income, while the latter make their profits from selling completed developments (Brett, 1992).

DEVELOPMENT APPRAISAL

In considering whether a prospective development is worthwhile financially, a developer should carry out an appraisal. This is similar to the behaviour of any investor faced with a decision about putting money into a scheme for which the benefits will arise at some time in the future. It is worth outlining first the position of the investor who is considering purchasing property, although this topic is discussed in more detail in Chapter 4.

Rates of return

Two measures are commonly used to determine the financial characteristics of a proposed investment. The first is the rate of return: this is defined as the amount of capital or rental increase over a period of time, expressed as a percentage of present value. Rates of return on property investment can be compared by analysts with those obtainable for gilts, equities and other forms of investment. No purchase is worthwhile financially if the anticipated rate of return is less than one could achieve by investing the same amount of money in some completely risk-free outlet, such as government gilt-edged securities. Investors expect a higher rate of return from property than from gilts, because there is always some degree of risk attached to property investment. A minimum premium of 2 per cent to take account of this risk is common (G. Brown, 1991: 4).

Rates of return from property development can be estimated in several ways, which are explained by many authors including Harvey (1992: 80–87) and Dubben and Sayce (1991: 119–125). Since developers often have to borrow money in order to carry out the development, the rate of return has to take into account the costs of borrowing money, and the time-lag between borrowing the money and getting the first year's income from the completed scheme. The calculation should take into account the estimated pattern of costs and revenues, year by year into the foreseeable future. More distant streams of net income (or 'net annual returns') are given less weight in the calculation than is more immediate income, a process known as 'discounting'. The *net present value* of a project can then be calculated. This is the sum of all discounted net annual returns, minus the capital cost of the project.

Investment yields

The second measure used in development appraisal is the *yield*: this is the current income from the property concerned, as a percentage of the property's freehold price. Yields tend at any point to be consistent across many properties of a similar type and location. Broadly speaking, the lower the yield, the more optimistic the market is about the long-term appreciation in value of an investment.

The inverse of the yield (property value divided by a year's rent) is known as the 'year's purchase' or 'capitalisation'. This is commonly used in valuations of property. It also makes explicit the view that land values and rents are formally related.

Methods of development appraisal

Figures 3.3 and 3.4, which are based upon the examples and discussion in Cadman and Austin-Crowe (1991: 41–50), show two types of development appraisal in common use. Each of these employs a comparison of Net Development Value (NDV) and Total Development Costs (TDC). The latter is

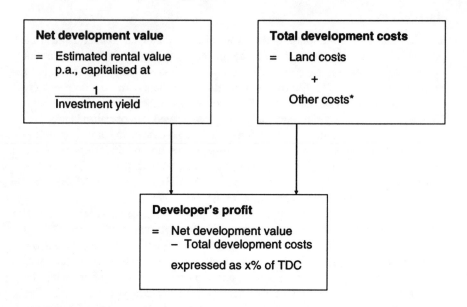

Figure 3.3 Development appraisal where land cost is predetermined

Note: *'Other costs' includes building costs, professional fees, finance costs, letting costs, etc.

self-explanatory. The NDV is the product of the first year's estimated rent from the completed development, and an estimated year's purchase (the inverse of the yield on the development). The year's purchase is estimated from knowledge of yields for the type of property and location concerned.

The two methods differ in their treatment of land cost. The first type (Figure 3.3) assumes that land costs are determined in advance, and calculates the developer's profit as a percentage of TDC. The second type of appraisal (Figure 3.4) assumes a given rate of profit and calculates the sum which the developer should offer for the site concerned in order to achieve that profit. This demonstrates the notion, that land value is related to expectation of future streams of rent income, under the highest and best use of the land.

The developer may wish to set a profit margin that is related to the degree of risk involved in the scheme. A conventional scheme in a good location, for which there is a known demand from reputable tenants, is relatively risk-free. Hence the percentage profit can be fairly modest, and indeed the market would expect this to be the case. On the other hand, a scheme that is unconventional or in a novel location for that type of development is seen as risky, and should only be carried out if the anticipated profit (given a successful outcome) is high.

In a perfectly operating land market, the price that the developer pays for the land required for development should reflect the degree of risk involved. It is also

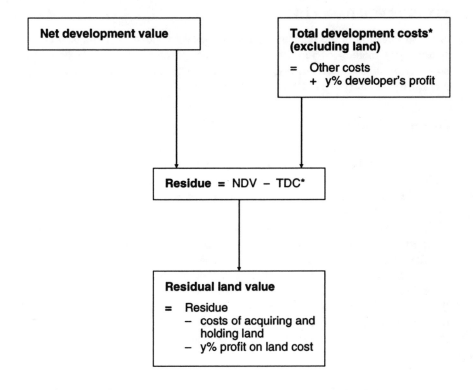

Figure 3.4 Development appraisal to determine land value

Note: *See Figure 3.3 for a more detailed treatment of Net development value and other costs

possible to distinguish 'existing use value' and 'development value' for the same property or piece of land. The former is related to the stream of incomes that derives from the property under its existing land use and physical condition. The latter is related to its maximum potential stream of incomes after (re)development. Developers can sometimes take advantage of this distinction, by purchasing land or property at existing use value, but then carrying out development. Here, the market is not working efficiently, and the developer is able to make an 'abnormal' or 'excess' profit. This may be done, for example, by purchasing separate properties that have little development value, so as to form a group that collectively does have development prospects. Thus, the developer in effect pockets the difference between development value and existing value. Another way of achieving this is to negotiate with local authority planners a larger amount of floorspace from the redevelopment than other actors considered feasible. In this way some British developers made very large amounts of money in the 1960s (Marriott, 1967).

FINANCE FOR DEVELOPMENT

A major question in the planning of any property development is the source of finance and method of repayment. A common distinction is made between short-term and long-term finance for development. The following account is summarised from Harvey (1992: Chapter 8).

Short-term finance

This is required to cover the developer's costs during the preparation and implementation periods (Figure 3.5). It is used to purchase land, and pay the building contractor and professional consultants. In some cases, finance is available from the developer's own resources. More often, a loan is negotiated over a period of between one and three years. In the case of very complex projects, long-term finance will probably be negotiated at the start of the project.

Short-term finance is normally obtained from banks: either clearing banks, or merchant banks, or subsidiaries of foreign banks. The situation is similar to that of any 'businessman' obtaining finance for short-term capital expenditure. A 'small' or novice developer may find it difficult to raise the total sum required for the development at a reasonable rate of interest. In contrast, established development companies can use existing holdings as collateral for loans, and will have less trouble raising short-term finance at reasonable cost.

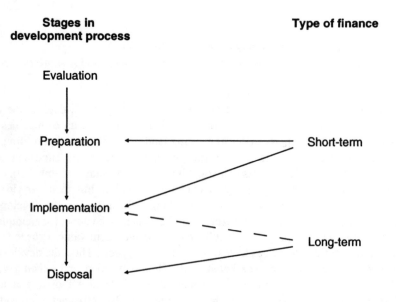

Figure 3.5 Finance for property development

Long-term finance

This is required to repay the capital costs of the development project, and is usually sought during the later stages of a project (Figure 3.5). If the developer has already taken out short-term finance, the capital costs can be repaid in two ways. The completed development may be sold to another company. Alternatively, the debt is transferred to another source, on a longer-term basis and at more favourable rates of interest. In this case, income from the development can be used to help repay the long-term loan, while the completed development itself provides security for the loan.

Long-term finance is generally provided by insurance companies, pension funds, charities and other trusts. These agencies have played a crucial role in commercial property development in Britain since the 1950s, although their role was to some extent displaced in the 'property boom' years of the 1980s by British and foreign banks (Cadman and Austin-Crowe, 1991: 74–77). This involvement of banks in long-term finance is thought unlikely to continue into the 1990s. The investment priorities and interests of the major financial institutions in retail development are discussed in Chapter 4.

In many cases, ownership of the completed development may be shared by the development company and the institution providing long-term finance. Here, the financial institution may enter a form of partnership with the developer, sometimes providing short-term as well as long-term finance. In return, it will impose conditions on the developer concerning the nature of the development, and will take a greater share of profits than it would if simply providing 'hands-off', long-term finance.

Disposal of completed developments

When a development is completed, the decision on what form of long-term finance to adopt is really equivalent to a decision on the method of disposal of the scheme. As discussed above, the developer may either sell the development to another company, or retain ownership, wholly or in partnership. Which action is taken may vary with the type of developer and the type of development.

In selling a completed development, the developer is in effect attempting to make a capital gain. The price obtained should allow an acceptable profit above the costs of acquiring the land, borrowing the money, and carrying out the development itself. Developers are likely to sell either to the occupier, or to a financial institution. The reward is money which can then be used to finance a new development, or be invested in some other medium. The penalty may be an immediate tax on capital gains.

This process of carrying out a development and then finding a purchaser is regarded as risky: there is no guarantee that the price offered will even cover the costs of development. Because of this, the established developer wishing to proceed in this way will identify, and try to agree terms with, potential purchasers during the evaluation or preparation stages.

If the decision is made to retain ownership, the developer then becomes a landlord and takes on a managerial function, being responsible for letting premises, marketing, security, maintenance, etc. Major developers who adopt this path become 'property investment companies', as discussed above. The financial objective is then to generate a stream of incomes that will allow an acceptable rate of return on the initial investment. A calculation of this type should be made before the company commits itself to the development. Companies who retain ownership may in fact be more centrally concerned with land ownership than development *per se*. These may include land users who carry out their own property development, or financial institutions who own properties as a long-term investment.

A developer who retains ownership also possesses a physical asset (the completed development), which may stand as security against loans for further developments.

RETAIL DEVELOPMENT

This section applies the principles established in previous sections to the process of developing specifically retail space. The treatment is very general at this stage: the models of the development process discussed above are reviewed, without reference to particular types of shopping centre or other retail development. It is easiest at this stage to think in terms of the 'retail developer' as a person or company which assembles land, researches demand, negotiates finance, designs and organises construction of one or more buildings which are intended mainly for occupation by retail firms.

Event-sequence models

An adaptation of the 'event-sequence' model is shown in Figure 3.6. The main characteristic that distinguishes retail development from other types is the need to lease all units in a centre to tenants before the centre is opened for trading. Building 'speculative' developments, which are intended to be let to tenants after completion, is unwise. A partially unlet shopping centre may not have sufficient variety of shops to attract customers, can rapidly become untidy or vandalised, and is hence seen by the market as a failure.

These considerations suggest that retail development incorporates two important stages that are sometimes absent from other types of property development. First, there is research on the demand for retail space in a particular location: many retail firms have very precise locational requirements (see Chapter 2). Not only does total demand have to be sufficient for a proposed scheme, but the nature of the scheme itself will reflect the level of demand from different types of retailer.

Second, negotiation with prospective tenants or long-term retail purchasers is a vital part of the development process. This usually occurs in two stages. First,

Decision to initiate a scheme

⎧ market surveys

  market research

  site survey

⎩ proceed?

Planning phase

⎧ Exploratory planning
   (feasibility)

  Preliminary planning
   (finance –
    tenant mix –
    design)

⎩ Final Planning
   (details)

Construction phase

Opening phase

Figure 3.6 An event-sequence model of retail development
Source: Based upon Dawson (1983)

one or more major tenants (or 'major space users') are sought at an early stage in the process. This is because shopping centres are felt to be more attractive to the shopper if they contain at least one 'anchor store'. Such a store, usually a supermarket, variety store or department store, owned by a well-known retail company, will be sufficiently attractive to generate shopping trips. Shoppers may then wish to visit the other stores in the centre during the same trip. Developers will not usually proceed further than the planning stage until they have agreed terms with the major space user(s). This is necessary to persuade other tenants that the centre will include a major retail outlet which will help attract shoppers into the development. Firms operating small units within the centre know that their own unit will not in itself be sufficiently attractive to entice large numbers of shoppers into the centre. They need a large store to provide that level of attraction; they may then benefit from the flow of shoppers thus produced.

This process puts prospective major space users into a powerful position. Since they are essential to the success of the scheme, they can use their power to bargain for favourable terms. Morgan and Walker (1988: 107) state that 'rents for department stores [in modern shopping developments within town centres] vary from nothing to about £5 per square foot'; rents for variety stores range from £4 to £10 per square foot. This compares with rents of up to £50 per square foot for small shops within similar developments. In other cases, the major space users have become part of the development team, again extracting favourable terms and probably sharing the income from other tenants in the centre. It also follows that major space users can require the developer to provide the best site within the scheme, regarding servicing or pedestrian access, for example; and can dictate the size and layout of their own stores. The developer then has to design the remainder of the centre around these requirements. These issues are discussed further in Chapter 8.

The second stage of attracting tenants occurs later, probably during the centre's construction. Publicity is aimed at firms that require small retail units. The developer likes to be able to agree terms with as many firms as possible, so that the centre is completely let when it opens. This ideal is often not achieved, and then the developer (or subsequent owner of the centre) has the task of letting units in the centre while it is trading. This can be difficult, because prospective tenants will naturally ask why there are still vacant units.

Agency models

In retail development, two 'agency' models are common. The first is development by the ultimate retailer, either of a free-standing store, or of a small centre in which the retailer concerned has the major unit. This model is discussed further in Chapter 7. The second model involves a developer organising the scheme and retailers acting as tenants. In this context, however, the 'developer' may be a specialist property development company, a financial institution, a local authority or other public agency, or any combination of the three.

In developing a shopping centre, a complex pattern of decision-making can occur, involving consultation and negotiation with a wide variety of 'actors'. The developer will use the services of consultant surveyors, who can act as advisers on the potential demand for a scheme, can specify precise costs for the construction phase, and negotiate the letting of premises. The developer will also employ architects for the design of the centre, and possibly town planning consultants to negotiate with the local authority. Other agencies involved in the development process include the construction company, anchor tenants and the local authority. Further details are provided in Northen and Haskoll (1977), Guy (1980a: 30–31), and Morgan and Walker (1988).

Finance for retail development

Morgan and Walker (1988: Chapter 11) list the six 'most common methods of financing retail development':

1 forward sale of the property to an institution;

2 by sale on completion, with interim finance provided by a bank or out of the developer's own resources;
3 by use of the developer's own money;
4 by long-term mortgage from a financial institution;
5 by sale of whole or part to occupiers;
6 by unitisation or securitisation.

Of these methods, 1, 3 and 5 appear to be the most usual. Relating these methods to the more general discussion above, method 1 is equivalent to involving the institution at the start, providing short-term as well as long-term finance. Often, the developer acts virtually as an agent for the institution, although if the initial yield is greater than expected, the developer may gain some of this excess income (Morgan and Walker, 1988: 93). Alternatively, the institution and developer may take shares in a financial partnership, sharing costs and revenues on some agreed basis. Criteria applied by institutions in evaluating proposals for such developments are discussed in Chapter 4.

Method 3 is most relevant in the case where a retail firm develops its own stores. The money required will come from normal cash flow, or from share issues.

Method 5 is used in the case of developments of single large stores for particular clients. It can also be used in developing larger centres, if the anchor store is sold on a long leasehold interest. This is common in the United States, where department store chains are in effect co-developers of shopping malls, but more rare in Britain (Morgan and Walker, 1988: 100).

Of the other methods, 2 is judged to be risky for shopping development, although it may be the only one available for a firm developing a centre in a situation which does not meet the criteria of the financial institutions. Mortgages (method 4) are common for shopping centre development in the United States, but are rare in Britain, because initial repayments are likely to exceed the yield possible in the short term (Morgan and Walker, 1988: 100). Finally, unitisation and securitisation, methods that enable investors to buy shares in a single property, have been much discussed in recent years (see Howells and Rydin, 1990; Dubben and Sayce, 1991: Chapter 12), but have not yet been applied to retail development in Britain, to the author's knowledge.

Rent setting

Unless carried out for owner occupation, retail development has to be justified initially by a calculation that the rents obtainable from the scheme represent an acceptable level of yield; and that the realisation of this market price, compared with costs of development, represent an acceptable level of profit for the developer. However, rents have to be related to what the tenants are actually prepared to pay, and are thus assessed on comparative bases, either with existing rents for prime locations in the same town, or rents in new developments elsewhere. Morgan and Walker (1988: Chapter 12) discuss rent setting in more detail.

Generally, rents charged (per sq. ft. per annum, in Britain) vary according to the relationship of retail space to shopping frontages. 'Zone A' rents, for the space extending 20 ft. back from the frontage, are usually twice as high as 'Zone B' rents (the next 20 ft. depth), and four times as high as 'Zone C' (the next 20 ft.).

As explained above, space is usually let to anchor stores at an early stage in the centre's development. In some cases a long lease of 99 or 125 years is taken by the anchor retailer at a very low 'peppercorn rent'. Other retail space is usually let on 21- or 25-year leases, with the tenant taking responsibility for insurance and repairs (Morgan and Walker, 1988: Chapter 13; Dubben and Sayce, 1991: Chapter 8). Rents are usually reviewable every five years, often on upward-only terms. This arrangement, which is very common in British retailing, is known as the 'institutional lease'.

An alternative method of charging rents is to base them on the tenant's retail turnover. 'Turnover rents' are common in American shopping centres but relatively rare in Britain. Where used, they are usually charged in addition to a proportion of the rack rent which would have been charged in the normal way. This proportion is typically 75–80 per cent (Brewer, 1990). Saunders (1990) and Kaye (1990) present, respectively, views against and in favour of turnover rents.

Management

An unusual feature of retail, compared with other types of property development, is that completed schemes are often 'managed' by the ultimate owner of the scheme. Management is necessary to maintain the high standards that help to attract customers, and to provide common services in centres where there may be many different tenants. These common services include security, cleaning, maintenance of pedestrian areas, lighting, air conditioning, landscaping, etc., and the promotion and marketing of the centre as a whole. These services are paid through 'service charges', which are demanded from tenants. Retailers often complain that, while rents are normally fixed for five-years, service charges rise from year to year. Towards the end of the five-year period, it is possible for service charges to approach or even exceed the rent itself.

CONCLUSIONS

This chapter has given an account of property development as practised in countries such as Britain. The emphasis has been on commercial development and, briefly, some particular characteristics of retail development and the retail property market.

The point has been made that rent, land value and land use are intimately related to one another. The theoretical arguments of neo-classical economists are seen to be reflected in the methods of land valuation, development appraisal and rent setting that are commonly used in professional practice. Practice also reflects some of the propositions of political economists. That landlords can act as a monopoly force, and set rents instead of simply responding to market forces, seems to be echoed in much of the practical and empirical literature on property valuation and development.

The neo-classical economists' charge that the land market is 'inefficient' has also been discussed. The inevitable risk involved in development is habitually translated into expectations of increased profits. It was also shown that developers can take advantage of market imperfections to make 'excess' profits. However, any tendency to do so has been reduced over time by the increasing involvement of financial institutions in property development. Examples of this tendency, and discussion of its implications for retail development, are presented in later chapters.

Retail development is seen to correspond with general models of development, but features of special importance also emerge. These include the need for careful site selection involving market research, and the need to negotiate with prospective tenants during the planning and construction periods. Typical sources of finance and ownership patterns tend to vary from one type of retail development to another, and are considered in more detail in Chapters 7 and 8. Finally, institutions, both private and public, have important control and influence on shopping centre development characteristics. These issues are discussed in the next two chapters.

Chapter 4

Institutional finance and retail development

INTRODUCTION

This chapter explores the relationships between retail development and the property investment policies of major financial institutions, including insurance companies and pension funds. It is shown, in this and subsequent chapters, that these institutions have a crucial role in determining not only the land value structure that gives rise to property development in the first place, but also the volume, location and nature of major retail developments themselves.

The special characteristics of property as a form of financial investment are discussed first. This leads to a discussion of the role of properties within an investment portfolio. The following sections review the main types of institution that seek to invest in commercial property, and their record of investment in recent years. The institutions' criteria for and record of investment in retail development are then discussed. Finally, some conclusions are drawn about the institutions' influences on the pace and location of retail development in the recent past and the immediate future.

PROPERTY AS AN INVESTMENT MEDIUM

Nabarro (1990: 47) outlines the nature of the property investment market. It is one of three linked markets. In *user markets*, firms buy and sell space. In *development markets*, new buildings are produced. In *investment markets*, rented buildings are traded between investors.

Ownership of rented buildings conveys two types of financial reward. First, the rents paid, less any management costs, constitute an income from the building concerned. Second, the building may appreciate in value over time. At the very least, land and buildings are regarded as a 'hedge against inflation'. As discussed in Chapter 3, rental income and capital value of property are linked through the notion of the investment yield and its inverse, the 'year's purchase'.

In Britain, an important category of owner of commercial property is the financial institution. Such institutions exist largely to manage and generate financial capital. Ownership of commercial property is an important way of achieving these aims, but the ownership is motivated by financial considerations rather than an interest in the retail or other processes taking place within the property itself.

Institutions are typically in receipt of very regular flows of money: the insurance company receives premiums or life assurance payments; the pension fund receives superannuation payments from participants. While some of this income needs to be spent on operating costs and payments of various kinds, some of it is not needed immediately and can be invested. The intention of investment is to provide a source of finance to cover future liabilities; investing money should ensure that at least the costs of monetary inflation are met, and it is hoped that a rate of return on investment can be achieved such that capital appreciation occurs.

An important characteristic of major institutions is that they choose what appear to them to be *safe* investments. This is because they are under obligation to guarantee future payments to claimants or beneficiaries. This aversion to risk-taking has had major effects upon the course of retail development in Britain in the last two decades.

Land tenure

Land and property can form a suitable investment medium: it can provide a regular income from tenants, and it can also provide capital appreciation, although the likely extent of capital appreciation is to some extent taken into account in the price of land. Commercial property itself can be classified into various types: as well as retail, office, etc., it can take freehold or leasehold forms. Freehold property is bought mainly to provide an income from tenants, and for long-term capital appreciation; but it may incur the need to manage the property, providing rent collection services, marketing, cleaning and maintenance, etc. These costs can obviously be heavy in the case of a shopping centre, and require expertise in property management. Leasehold property (where held on long lease) also provides an income from tenants on short leases, but similarly incurs management costs. In addition, long-term capital appreciation is less likely, because the property will eventually revert to the freeholder with no compensation. Third, it is possible to purchase freeholds of properties that are already assigned on long leases. In such cases there is a much lower income from freehold ground rents, but long-term prospects of capital appreciation because the property will eventually revert to the freeholder.

Which of these forms of investment is most suitable will reflect the combination of income and capital appreciation that is seen as most desirable. There may also be tax advantages in one type of investment rather than another. Whereas in the past the balance in this respect has shifted between income and capital appreciation, the taxation system in Britain at present does not generally favour either one or the other (Dubben and Sayce, 1991: 65).

The most common form of commercial property purchase amongst major financial institutions appears to be the outright freehold. This allows a regular income from tenants, who usually occupy premises on 'full repairing and insuring' leases with regular and upward-only rent reviews. Thus, there is a stream of incomes which is likely to rise in future years. In addition, the property in the long term will have development value, at which time it can be sold to a developer or redeveloped while still in the financial institution's ownership.

Financial criteria for investment

As discussed in Chapter 3, financial investment is judged by rates of return and yield. These two measures are to some extent inversely related. A high rate of return is obviously desirable. However, a low yield is also considered a desirable feature of an investment. It is an indication that the investment is in heavy demand: this demand is heavy because the long-term growth prospects are very good. Putting it another way, the price of the property is affected by expert estimates of the extent to which rent incomes will increase in future years. If a steady increase is judged to be likely, then the property is worth more than might be apparent simply from examining present income from tenants. If, however, the long-term prospects are poor, then the price should be low in relation to income. In another words, a high yield indicates a high risk that long-term prospects are poor, and that these have to be compensated by short-term profits.

Levels of yield are continually being set by the market's pattern of property transactions, but for particular types of property they tend to be consistent over the short term. Typical levels of yields for different land uses are discussed later in this chapter. Rates of return are more volatile, reflecting short-term variations in supply and demand.

INVESTMENT PORTFOLIOS

'Risk' and property investment

Investing money in any single property is always risky. It is not possible to determine precisely the stream of future incomes, nor the development value of the site in the far future. All that can be achieved are unbiased and informed estimates, which, as we have seen, rely partially on comparisons with what are thought to be similar properties.

This inherent riskiness of property as a medium of investment is resolved in two ways. First, properties are typically combined together in a portfolio to reduce the effect of untoward events in relation to any particular property. Second, a premium (typically 2 per cent) is added to the rate of return currently available from 'riskless' investments such as gilt-edged stocks. This is despite recent claims that gilts are actually more volatile over time than property portfolios (Fraser, 1985; Howells and Rydin, 1990).

G. Brown (1991: 19) classifies the risk associated with property investment into two types. *Systematic risk* affects all properties of a particular type, and includes general economic factors, taxation and finance changes in general. *Specific risk* relates to individual properties and includes tenant effects, location effects, structural effects, building quality, legal effects and depreciation. While these matters ought to be taken account of in the process of valuation, not all future events are predictable.

These effects can be incorporated into valuation through use of quantitative techniques. Typically, net present values (NPVs) are calculated to incorporate the effects of various possible combinations of rent levels, costs, etc. at future dates. An 'expected' net present value is then calculated by taking a weighted average of the NPVs, the weighting reflecting the set of probabilities estimated for the various outcomes. This and more complex methods are discussed in Dubben and Sayce (1991: Chapter 6).

Property investment portfolios

An investment portfolio for a large financial institution will consist of several types of investment, probably a mixture of property, equities and gilts. This is because medium-term trends in capital growth in these three types of investment have not in the past been strongly associated with one another. For example, in the early 1980s in Britain, equities performed well in the Stock Exchange while growth in property values was sluggish. In addition, G. Brown (1991: 16–17) shows that a portfolio which mixes risky investments (i.e. property or equities) with riskless (gilts) is more efficient than one totally based upon risky investments ('efficiency' being defined as achieving the maximum rate of return for a given level of risk).

Within a property portfolio, it is desirable to combine, say, retail with industrial property, because demand and supply factors for these two different types are unlikely to change in tandem. Thus, 'new assets should be considered not on their individual risk-return profile but on their implications for the risk profile of the portfolio' (McNamara, 1990: 103–104). Specific risk can be minimised by including many properties of each type within the portfolio. Systematic risk, however, will not be completely eliminated, hence the conventional 2 per cent premium on rates of return, discussed above. The three main types of property – retail, office and industrial – have varied over the years in typical rates of return, and this has led to varying patterns of institutional investment.

INSTITUTIONAL INVESTMENT IN PROPERTY IN BRITAIN

This section describes the main institutional investors in property in Britain, and the criteria which they normally apply in appraising potential developments.

Sources of finance for development

In principle, property development can be financed by any company that provides loans or wishes to invest capital in a development project. The major companies of this type are generally known as 'financial institutions'. A distinction is usually drawn between institutions that mainly provide loans, and those that mainly wish to invest long term in the developments themselves. The former includes banks and building societies, whereas the latter includes insurance companies, pension funds, property investment companies and property unit trusts. In addition 'traditional institutions', such as the Crown Estates, educational establishments and the Church of England, may invest in property.

Of the sources of loans, *building societies* have been traditionally non-profit-making and exist primarily to provide finance for private house purchase. They are not normally empowered to provide finance for commercial property development, although recent legislation has given building societies the opportunity to compete directly with the clearing banks. Whether this will lead to involvement in commercial property development remains to be seen.

Banks have long been the main source of short-term finance for commercial property development. However, during the 1980s, banks also became the main providers of long-term finance to the commercial property sector as a whole (Darlow, 1989; Nabarro, 1989). The 'big four' clearing banks in Britain were augmented by investment banks and foreign banks in this respect.

Conventional mortgages are generally unsuitable for commercial development finance because the interest payments for the first few years after completion of the development are likely to exceed rental income (Thompson and Wythe, 1988: 154). This is because yield percentages are usually well below typical interest rates, reflecting the assumption that rental incomes will increase over time. Some ingenious methods of financing were used during the 1980s to overcome this problem, in which the security for the loan tended to be either the development itself, or promised shares in the property company concerned (Dubben and Sayce, 1991: 246–247; Cadman and Austin-Crowe, 1991: 74–77). In each case, with the onset of the property slump at the end of the 1980s, these normally respectable arrangements became insecure, and banks became exposed to risk to an unprecedented extent. In May 1992, outstanding loans by property developers to banks in relation to UK developments amounted to some £40 billion. Of this total, about £17 billion had been lent by foreign banks (*Investors Chronicle*, 1992a). Several major property companies, with debts totalling £4.7 billion, were either in administration or receivership, or were attempting to reschedule loan payments (*Sunday Times*, 1992). The outcome is that banks are likely to be very much more cautious in lending to property developers in the 1990s.

In contrast with insurance companies and pension funds, banks have only rarely become long-term partners in property development. Indeed, one reason why many developers have preferred to borrow money from banks has been the latter's 'hands-off' approach to development. This may itself now change, after the unfortunate events of the late 1980s.

The financial institutions' property holdings

The institutions, in contrast to banks, tend to benefit from steady streams of income, such that surpluses can be invested on a long-term basis. Cadman (1984) and Nabarro (1990) describe the enormous increase in money saved with the institutions, and how much of this became invested in land and property in the 1970s. The net inflow into life assurance and pension funds continued to increase during the 1980s, reaching £41.6 billion in 1991 (Central Statistical Office, 1992: Table 7.1), although a relatively small proportion was invested in land and property.

By the end of 1989, the insurance companies held some £39 billion worth of 'UK land, property and ground rents' in their long-term funds, amounting to nearly 16 per cent of the total invested. The pension funds held £27 billion; amounting to 8 per cent of their total investments (Central Statistical Office, 1992a). Ownership of property amongst all financial institutions amounted to around £90 billion at the end of 1991 (see Table 4.1).

While the insurance companies and pension funds are the principal institutional investors in property, other institutions are also important. Property investment companies own at least £20 billion worth of property, and the traditional institutions around £7 billion. Of the traditional institutions, the Crown Estates (£1.8 billion) and the Church Commissioners (£2.7 billion) are the most significant property owners, although the latter have suffered substantial

Table 4.1 Institutional property ownership in the UK, 1991

Institution	Value of property owned (£ billion)
Insurance companies and pension funds	57
Property unit trusts	0.8
Property companies	20–23
Overseas investors	5.5
Traditional investors	7
Total	around 90

Source: Investment Property Databank (1992)

capital losses in recent years and are now attempting to dispose of some of their commercial property holdings (*Shopping Centre*, 1992; Mortishead, 1992).

McNamara (1990) and Schiller (1991) have pointed out that institutional investment decisions are increasingly made by professional fund managers. The largest of these in 1991 was Prudential Portfolio Managers, which manages some $57 billion on behalf of approximately forty different funds. Several of the largest institutions are now either merchant banks or investment management companies.

Criteria for investment

The institutions have traditionally seen property as a 'safe' vehicle for investment, which should remain stable in value over the short term and appreciate in the long term. Property is 'purchased for its stability and certainty, and not as a speculation' (Nabarro, 1990: 57).

The institutions apply quite strict criteria to their selection of property for investment purposes. Ideally a property acquisition, or proposed development, should possess the following characteristics (Cadman, 1984: 78):

* be modern, freehold or long leasehold premises;
* be located in the best areas;
* be of the best design and specification;
* be let to tenants of unquestioned covenant on full repairing and insuring leases that allow for frequent, upward-only rent reviews.

Nabarro (1990: 57) adds that there should be a good secondary market so that properties can be resold; and that buildings should be 'non-specialist'.

Properties that fulfil the above criteria are usually known as 'prime' and will support the lowest yields. Properties that lack some of these characteristics but which still attract investment are known as 'secondary'. These will support yields of at least one and a half times the prime yield for the type of property in question (Cadman, 1984: 80).

While it is often stated that institutional investors will only accept prime properties, there is evidence that their portfolios contain substantial amounts of secondary properties. This may be partly because prime investments can become secondary over the course of time, particularly in the office market where obsolescence is rapid.

A further limitation on investment may be the size of the development in question. Most institutions wish to see property comprising no more than 15 per cent of their total portfolio, and any one property taking up no more than about 10 per cent of their total property investment (Thompson and Wythe, 1988: 152). If these estimates are correct, in 1991 none of the pension funds would have been prepared to invest in a single property worth more than £180 million (see Table 4.2). While most commercial properties are obviously worth far less, some major office blocks and shopping centres would exceed this figure. Only twelve

Table 4.2 Hypothetical maximum single property investments for the largest pension funds, 1991

Pension fund	Size of fund (£m)	Maximum single investment (£m)*
British Coal	12,000	180
British Telecom	12,000	180
Electricity Supply	8,500	127.5
Post Office	7,750	116.2
British Rail	7,000	105
Universities Superannuation Scheme	5,800	87
British Gas	5,750	86.2
Barclays Bank	5,198	78
Imperial Chemicals	4,131	62
National Westminster Bank	4,050	61
British Steel	4,046	61
British Petroleum	4,000	60

Source: Thompson and Wythe (1988: Table 8.1), and *Investors Chronicle* (18 October 1991)

Note: * Assumes 1.5% of total fund

funds were likely to wish to purchase properties worth more than £60 million. Proposals for unitisation and securitisation of property investments have been designed to overcome this problem (Dubben and Sayce, 1991: 278–284; Howells and Rydin, 1990). The implications of these trends are discussed further in Chapter 8.

CYCLES OF DEVELOPMENT AND INVESTMENT

This section examines cycles of development and investment in Britain, from the mid-1960s to the early 1990s. As well as describing the very important 'property booms' of the early 1970s and late 1980s, and the successive property 'slumps' or 'crashes', some more general points are established regarding the roles of the financial institutions as property investors.

Development cycles

Many authors including Harvey (1985) and Whitehand (1987) have discussed long-term 'building' or 'development' cycles. A cycle spans the period between successive troughs (or successive peaks) of property development, and have been measured since the early nineteenth century. Typically a cycle appears to last some fifteen to twenty years.

Two main forces appear to generate development cycles. First, demand for property may increase over a number of years, because of growing economic activity generally, or because of changes in commercial or social behaviour. This leads to price or rent increases, and thus to perceptions amongst suppliers of space that new development is likely to be profitable. This is the 'boom' part of the cycle. Eventually the demand is satisfied, but because of time lags, new space keeps appearing. This new space is unwanted and hence land values fall, leading to the 'slump' part of the cycle.

A second force is related to switching of capital to and from land and property. In the early stage of the cycle, shortages in supply create a rapid increase in land and property values, allowing high rates of return on capital investment. The boom in values may be enhanced by forward investment in development projects: Harvey (1985) writes of economies 'awash' with surplus capital which seeks projects in which to invest (see also Healey *et al.*, 1992: Chapter 2). Later on in the cycle, land and property values stagnate and eventually decline, so that capital is withdrawn and invested in equities or other more profitable media.

The most recent cycles in British property development peaked in about 1973 and 1989, maintaining the approximately fifteen-year periodicity noted above. These years marked the highest levels of rents for prime space (Figure 4.1), and were followed by several years of falling land and property values. Vacancy rates increased as more and more developments which had been started at the peak

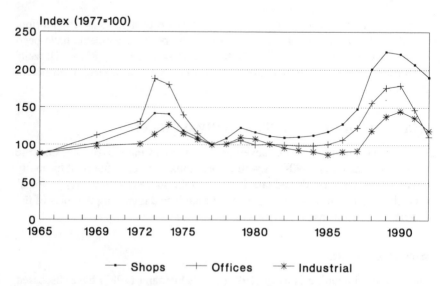

Figure 4.1 Prime rents 1965–1992, adjusted for inflation

Source: Hillier Parker, ICHP Rent Index

became completed at a time of falling demand. The events which led to these two peaks, and the trough in the late 1970s, are discussed by Dubben and Sayce (1991: Chapter 4), Key *et al.* (1990) and Nabarro and Key (1992), amongst others. The more recent slump in values is not fully dealt with in these texts but has been discussed exhaustively in property and investment journals and reports (e.g. Brett, 1991, 1992; *Investors Chronicle*, 1992c; Investment Property Databank, 1992).

The 'slump' stage of development cycles poses serious problems to the property development industry. While demand is growing in the 'boom' stage, rents increase but yields remain stable, in the expectation of further rental growth in the future. When demand falls, landlords may have to accept lower rents than had been anticipated. This, in itself, will lead to a reduction in land and property values, but the situation is exacerbated by an increase in yields, as prospects for the future become more uncertain. Thus, capital values typically fall more rapidly than prime rents. This has particularly serious implications for property investment companies. At a time of slump, their fixed assets decline rapidly in value while they may also be faced with debt repayments resulting from developments carried out during the boom. Hence, several important property companies have gone into receivership since 1990, echoing events during the mid-1970s.

The property boom in the late 1980s appears to have been on a larger scale than that of the early 1970s. The rise in rents was greater and lasted longer (Figure 4.1), and the extent of debt to property companies reached over £40 billion in 1991, compared with less than £15 billion (reflated to 1992 prices) in

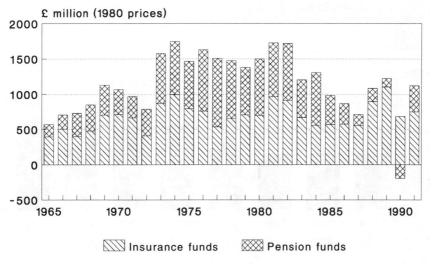

Figure 4.2 Net institutional investment in UK property

Source: Cadman and Austin-Crowe (1991); IPD (1992)

1974 (Debenham Tewson Research, 1992b: 4). It is possible therefore that the 1990s slump may be longer lasting and more severe than that of the late 1980s. The implications of this for retail development are discussed in later chapters.

Changes over time in institutional investment property

Figure 4.2 shows long-term trends in the amount invested in land and property in the UK, corrected for inflation. It will be noted that investment in property was particularly important in the ten years following 1972. This was associated with rapid growth in personal savings during this period, through life assurance and pension schemes, favoured by the tax system (Cadman, 1984).

The two boom periods of the early 1970s and late 1980s were marked, however, by a low level of property investment by the institutions (Figure 4.2). This may partly have reflected their suspicion of over-heating in the property market, but was mainly due to decisions to invest in equities rather than property. During most of the 1980s, equities showed more rapid gains in capital value than was the case for property. The pension funds in particular made very small net investment in property after 1984. By 1990, property accounted for only 8 per cent of pension funds' assets, a reduction from the 20 per cent figure at the beginning of the 1980s (*Investors Chronicle*, 1991c: 11). The insurance companies, however, have generally maintained an annual net investment of a little under £1 billion (in current values) since 1980 (Darlow, 1989).

Investment in new building, rather than purchases or sales of existing land and property, is of particular significance to the development industry. Figure 4.3

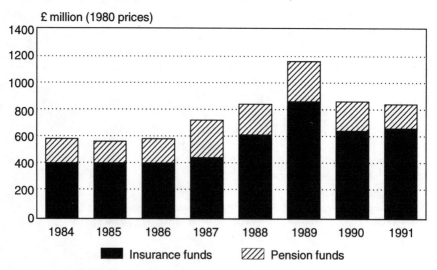

Figure 4.3 Investment in new buildings by institutions
Source: Central Statistical Office (1992b)

shows that, after 1983, investment by pension funds has remained roughly constant (taking inflation into account) while that by insurance companies has tended to increase. This investment in new building has accounted for most if not all of the institutions' property interests during this period, since in several years the pension funds became net sellers of existing properties. In 1991 both types of institution became net purchasers of existing properties, albeit on a modest scale.

Changes in time in investment yields

As explained in Chapter 3, the yield expresses the relationship between the annual rental income and the capital value of a property. Yields for prime commercial properties are in effect set by the market on the basis of experience and comparisons. Figure 4.4 shows trends in prime yields since 1971. Three features should be noted. First, yields show considerable constancy over time when compared with the rapidly fluctuating bank lending rate or the yield on government gilt-edged securities. This gives confidence to developers in appraising future development possibilities. Second, industrial yields have throughout the period been higher than office or shop yields, reflecting the generally weaker demand for new industrial space in the British economy. Third, the property slumps of 1974–1976 and 1990 onwards have, as we have seen, both been characterised by higher yields than normal.

INSTITUTIONAL FINANCE AND RETAIL DEVELOPMENT

This section reviews the major institutions' recent history of investment in retail property. Prime retail property possesses the general characteristics noted above. Location is particularly important for retail premises: the data for retail rents (Figure 4.1) and yields (Figure 4.4) relate to shops in '100 per cent trading positions'. Ideal locations for prime shops or shopping centres of various types are discussed in later chapters. Secondary retail properties may be of good design, etc., but may be in a less perfect location; or in a very good location but with some design or structural problem.

Methods of investment

The institutions can invest in retail property in three ways, although distinctions between these ways may become blurred in practice. These are:

1 Purchase of existing retail properties, either singly or in groups. Such purchases may be from other institutions, landowners or retail firms themselves.
2 Purchase of recently completed retail developments, from the developer. This is the main method by which the developer obtains capital gain from the development process, otherwise known as 'long-term finance' (see Chapter 3).

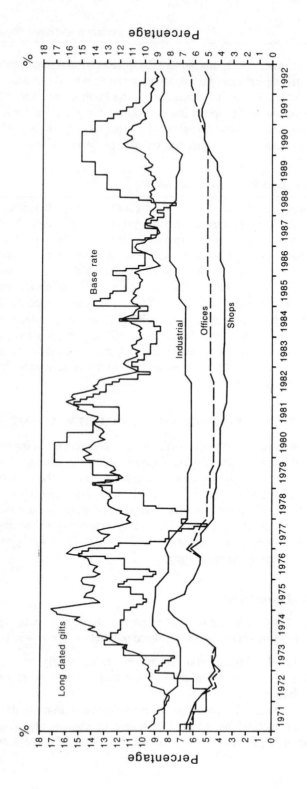

Figure 4.4 Prime commercial property yields

Source: Healey & Baker

3 Development of new shopping premises, in partnership with a property developer, or acting as the developer.

The last of these methods of investment became important in the 1960s. Financial institutions had for some time provided long-term finance to developers. However, the institutions were not always satisfied that developers had carried out the best possible development for the location concerned; and institutions also felt that an opportunity to increase profits from property investment lay in participating in the development itself, at the cost of some additional risk. For these reasons, insurance companies and pension funds became increasingly involved directly in retail development during the late 1960s and 1970s. In Chapter 8 it is shown that among the 'top twenty' retail developers in Britain, three have been financial institutions, even though this analysis excludes institutions involved simply as long-term financiers (Table 8.1). By contrast, none of the 'top ten' retail developers in the United States are financial institutions (Carlson, 1990), although long-term finance is often provided by financial institutions (Carlson, 1991).

Trends in retail investment

The relative importance of retail investment has varied over time. Between 1978 and 1985, retail property increased its share of institutional property holdings from 22.4 to 35.3 per cent (Investment Property Databank, 1986: Table 2.1). This reflected increasing demand for prime retail properties, and an indication that the market believed that these properties had very good long-term prospects for growth, shown in the very low yields of 4 per cent (Figure 4.4). In the mid- and late 1980s, institutional ownership of retail stabilised at around 35 per cent of the capital value of all property owned (Figure 4.5). Expenditure on retail (including purchases) stabilised at around 40 per cent of all expenditure on property (Figure 4.6), while receipts (mainly from sales of property) were around 30 per cent (Figure 4.7). Thus, the institutions consolidated their reliance upon retail property. The absolute increases in both expenditure and receipts on retail during this period appear to reflect the increased volume of activity generally in the property market. More recently, institutional expenditure on retail has fallen sharply, probably reflecting current uncertainty in the market.

Expenditure on retail property can be subdivided further into purchase (of existing property), development and improvement. During the 1980s, expenditure on purchase and development rose steadily in real terms, as did improvement expenditure after 1986 (Figure 4.8). The picture since 1989 has been somewhat confusing, although all three types of expenditure have declined substantially from their peak: purchases were the first to decline, not surprisingly, since development and improvement expenditure would reflect commitments made in previous years whereas purchases can react more quickly to changed market conditions.

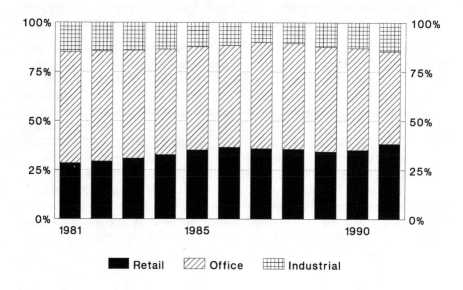

Figure 4.5 Proportions of capital value of institutional property
Source: Investment Property Databank (1992: Table 4.11)

Figure 4.6 Institution expenditure on retail property
Source: Based upon Investment Property Databank (1992: Table 4.1)

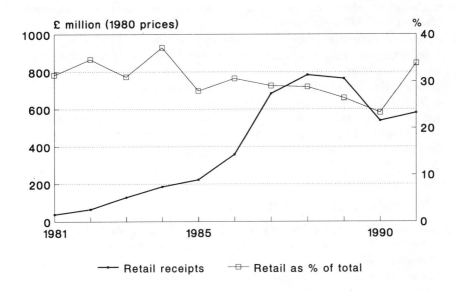

Figure 4.7 Institutional receipts for retail property

Source: Based upon Investment Property Databank (1992: Table 4.1)

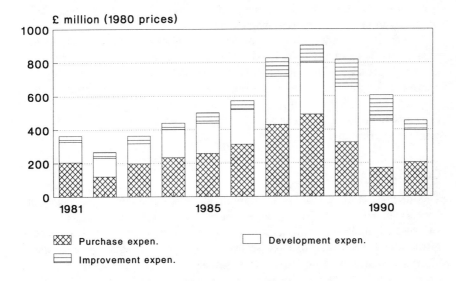

Figure 4.8 Institutional retail expenditure by component

Source: Based upon Investment Property Databank (1992: Table 4.2)

In financing retail developments, institutions are as subject to conservative notions about prime retail property as they are when purchasing existing shops. Many of the retail development proposals of the 1980s were in locations not normally regarded as 'prime' by the development industry. Thus, they aroused little interest from the institutions, who saw no need to take risks developing novel types of centre in new locations, while safer forms of investment were readily available. This theme will be discussed in greater depth in Chapters 7 and 8.

Within these general trends, some differences have occurred between types of institution. Insurance companies were more likely to invest in property generally in the 1980s than were the pension funds, and some insurance companies such as the Prudential and Norwich Union have major interests in enclosed and other shopping centres.

Letting and management policy

Providers of long-term finance may find themselves in the position of managing a completed development. Those property investment companies that specialise in retail are, of course, experienced in this function. However, several financial institutions have large retail portfolios and the question of management arises. The institutions generally prefer a 'hands-off' style of management, in which as much responsibility as possible is passed on to the tenants through full repairing and insuring leases (Dubben and Sayce, 1991: Chapter 8). However, with the realisation that active management and marketing of centres is important, shopping centre management teams are increasingly being employed by the institutions, and the role of shopping centre management is increasingly being distanced from that of portfolio management.

The institutions are cautious by nature and prefer to let retail units to tenants regarded as being totally reliable. This means that planned centres, and the prime parts of unplanned centres, are dominated by multiple retail firms operating on a national or regional basis. Turnover rents are frowned upon, since rental income is difficult to predict from this source (Thompson and Wythe, 1988: 158). This contrasts with the situation in the United States where rents based fully upon turnover are the norm.

CONCLUSIONS

This discussion of the role of institutions in retail development has been very general in nature: specific cases are discussed in later chapters. Four main conclusions can be drawn from the discussions in this chapter. First, the financial institutions have helped to increase the demand for good quality retail space. Their abundance of money requiring a 'safe home' has arguably supported high prices and rents for the best quality retail space, although it is also the case that the institutions can perform a useful function in purchasing retail space at a time when demand and prices are relatively low.

Second, the conservative policies of the institutions have strengthened the position of the more successful shopping centres. Prime retail areas and properties are defined quite narrowly in Britain, and this has augmented land values and has in effect created very large sums of fixed capital within our town and city centres. Institutions have joined most of the major British retailers in supporting further investment in central areas, a situation much in contrast to that in the United States, for example. But it can also be argued that the conservatism of the institutions has restricted the development of new forms of retailing or new retail locations.

Third, the reduction in involvement in property development by the financial institutions during the 1980s has concerned many commentators. This gap in financing was met by the banks, but at the cost of subsequent difficulties both for lenders and debtors. Despite recent increases in yields, there remains a gap between yields, meaning that a return to straightforward mortgage financing is unlikely. This is especially the case in respect of retail development, for which yields are traditionally among the lowest. The outcome of these problems for the 1990s is not clear. Securitisation and unitisation may become the solution to financing large-scale developments that the market regards as essentially sound. However, it is not clear whether the institutions will increase their support for retail or other property development to the extent shown in the 1970s.

Fourth, many institutions perform a vital function as owners and managers of prime shop units and shopping centres. Some commentators feel that they can take an oligopolistic position, determining rents in an arbitrary manner and dictating terms to retail tenants through the 'institutional lease' with its upwards-only rent review clauses. It has been claimed that:

> UK commercial property rents are effectively set in a market composed of two distinct sectors. In the small market for new lettings (comprising about 4 per cent of the total in any year), rentals are responsive to market forces, although even in this sector the market is made opaque by confidentiality clauses in leases and by other factors. The remainder of the overall market, accounting for the bulk of rentals, constitutes a rent-administered sector, in which rents are dictated by legal and institutional factors and procedures, including 'upwards-only' clauses and 'comparables'.
>
> (Burton, 1992: 81)

The institutions will argue that such procedures are necessary to maintain the long-term appreciation in property values which are required for their own clients' funds. But it has to be questioned whether the retail industry always benefits from the heavy involvement of the institutions in development and property ownership.

Chapter 5

Land use planning and retail development

INTRODUCTION

This chapter examines the importance of the public sector, and particularly land use planning, in regulating and otherwise affecting retail development. In the British context, the focus of attention is mainly the statutory system of land use planning enacted in the various Town and Country Planning Acts, and implemented by local authorities. The chapter explains the way in which this system operates, and ways in which it has influenced retail development. The discussion includes positive aspects (land assembly and the promotion of development) as well as negative ones (the control of proposals for development). Two particularly important aspects – support for retailing in town and city centres, and opposition to off-centre development – are discussed in detail. The final sections widen the perspective, making international comparisons and discussing relationships between land values and planning control.

THE BRITISH LAND USE PLANNING SYSTEM

The British system of land use planning arose largely through a series of reactions to the effects of rapid and unregulated urban development during the nineteenth century. Initially, concern was mainly to ensure adequate public health and a pleasant physical environment, following the excesses of Victorian industrial cities (Ashworth, 1954; Cherry, 1988; Cullingworth, 1988; Hall, 1988). The development of low-density 'urban sprawl' in the 1920s and 1930s led to an emphasis on the containment of urban areas and the preservation of open countryside (Hall et al., 1973). The system of planning control which became established in the 1947 Town and Country Planning Act, and which has survived in essence since then, is designed to 'regulate the development and use of land in the public interest' (Department of the Environment, 1992a). This echoes the conclusion of Lichfield and Darin-Drabkin (1980) that Britain's system of governmental land policy is essentially 'regulatory' rather than 'developmental' or 'financial' (see also Healey et al., 1988).

The planning system

The system itself is essentially negative: development may not be undertaken without first obtaining planning permission. Permission for development is usually granted by a local planning authority. The term 'development' refers to almost any type of construction, redevelopment or change of use, and this means that planning control is comprehensive and affects all types of retail development. Local planning authorities also have responsibility for preparing development plans. These set out the patterns of land use and related policies which the local authority wishes to see take place over the next few years.

The Town and Country Planning Act of 1947 linked the two elements of the planning system by stating that when a planning authority is deciding whether to approve an application for development, they must 'refer to the provisions of the development plan'. However, other 'material considerations' may also be taken into account by the authority. These may range widely, but should 'be related to the purpose of planning legislation' (Department of the Environment, 1992a: para. 23). Thus, the British system is rather more flexible in its operation than land use planning systems in many other countries (Department of the Environment, 1989a; Wakeford, 1990). In particular, (a) an application which is contrary to the provisions of the development plan can still be approved; and (b) an application which fits in with the development plan can still be turned down on other grounds. In each of these cases, this should only happen if 'material considerations' convincingly outweigh the provisions of the development plan. In this context, government 'advice' to planning authorities is a 'material consideration'. Thus, discretion lies with the local planning authority to approve, attempt to modify, or reject any planning application, but central government attitudes are also important.

The relative importance of these three matters – the development plan, other 'material considerations', and central government 'advice' to planners – have varied over time. This has been of central importance in mediating the effects of the land use planning system on patterns of retail development. The following three sub-sections examine each of these matters in turn. The detailed discussion relates mainly to England and Wales, but major differences pertaining to Scotland are mentioned where necessary.

The development plan

The current system of development planning in Britain, following amendments made in 1991 to the legislation, is as follows. County councils or (in Scotland) regional councils are responsible for the preparation of *structure plans*. These plans set out the authority's view of the most desirable pattern of land use within its area over the next fifteen years. They are intended to be fairly broad brush and act as a general guide to development control rather than a detailed pattern of recommendations for specific parcels of land. According to government advice, their principal functions are to:

- provide the strategic policy framework for planning and development control locally;
- ensure that the provision for development is realistic and consistent with national and regional policy;
- secure consistency between local plans for neighbouring areas.

(Department of the Environment, 1992b: para. 3.4)

Structure plans have met with substantial criticism from both public and private practice (Healey, 1983: Chapter 3; Cross and Bristow, 1983). They have been seen by many planners and developers alike as too vague to serve as a useful guide to the appropriate scale and location of new development. However, their strategic role in regulating the amount of development over a period of time is widely acknowledged.

The second part of the development plan system comprises the *local plans* which are prepared by district councils. These, as with structure plans, present the council's view on the most appropriate pattern of land use within its area, usually over a ten-year period. Compared with structure plans, however, the focus is much more local and specific. Local plans should:

- set out the authority's proposals for the control of development; and
- make proposals for the development and use of land and . . . allocate land for specific purposes.

(Department of the Environment, 1992b: para. 3.8)

Local plans should also be 'in general conformity with the structure plan' (ibid.).

The current position is that each district council must prepare one local plan covering all of its area. Many existing approved local plans were, however, prepared under previous government advice and apply to just part of the district concerned, and many settlements are not yet covered by a local plan. The government expects there to be complete coverage of England and Wales by local plans by the end of 1996. Scotland is already almost completely covered by local plans, although not necessarily at district-wide scale (Mackenzie, 1989; Begg and Pollock, 1991).

In the London boroughs and Metropolitan districts of England, areas which belong in the major conurbations, a third type of development plan is prepared: the *unitary development plan*. This type of plan was devised to combine the functions of structure and local plan, following the demise of the Metropolitan Counties and Greater London Council in 1986. The unitary development plan comprises two parts: the first is analogous to a structure plan, describing the authority's 'general policies for the development and use of land' (Department of the Environment, 1992b: para. 3.10). The second part is analogous to a local plan, containing 'proposals for the development and use of land' (ibid.).

In England and Wales, one type of area is specifically exempted from the development plans system. *Urban Development Corporations* (UDCs) were set up in 1980 to accelerate the process of urban renewal in a number of run-down, 'inner city' areas. The best known and most successful, in terms of private sector investment, has been the London Docklands Development Corporation (Brownill, 1990). The corporations, which are appointed by Secretaries of State rather than elected, have substantial powers to purchase land and carry out infrastructure works, so as to make land suitable for development by the private sector. At the time of writing, twelve Urban Development Corporations exist in England and one in Wales.

Development control and 'material considerations'

Planning permission must be sought in Britain for any type of development. 'Development' is defined in the Town and Country Planning Act of 1990 as 'The carrying out of building, engineering, mining or other operations in, on, over or under land, or the making of any material change in the use of any buildings or other land.' However, many minor types of development have been given what amounts to an automatic planning permission through the Town and Country Planning General Development Order, a Statutory Instrument last revised in 1988. Changes of use are only defined as 'development' if they are between the 'classes' defined in the Town and Country Planning Use Classes Order of 1987.

Planning permission has to be sought from the district council concerned. A fee is payable. Councils can approve a proposal, reject it, or approve it subject to certain conditions. The applicant for planning permission can appeal against refusal, against conditions attached to a permission, or against failure of the council to determine the application within a period of eight weeks from submission (Telling, 1990).

One of the distinguishing features of the British planning system is the degree of discretion allowed to local authority planners in making decisions on applications for development. Flexibility can be shown towards what type of development is acceptable within a particular area. However, a proposed development which is acceptable in general land use terms may be deemed to be unacceptable for other reasons, which may or may not relate to development plan policies. Research (e.g. McLoughlin, 1973; H.W.E. Davies et al., 1986) has shown that planners often find approved development plan policies of little relevance when considering applications for planning permission. 'Other material considerations' thus inevitably take precedence in influencing decisions.

Research by H.W.E. Davies et al. (1986) established that the considerations taken into account by development controllers can be categorised into 'strategic' and 'practical'. Broadly speaking, the strategic considerations relate to the volume, location and timing of development, and are likely to be the subject of specific policies in development plans. These considerations vary substantially in nature from one district to another. The practical considerations relate mainly to 'amenity' and the form and layout of development. Any coverage in development plans is likely to be very broad in nature, and the development controller will need to use more judgement and initiative in applying these considerations. On the other hand, there is widespread agreement amongst planners about the nature of these considerations.

Areas do exist in which the normal development control restrictions and procedures are relaxed. *Enterprise Zones* were established in 1980 and have been designated in over twenty areas of Britain. Relaxation of planning control is one of several incentives designed to attract private investment: the zones are typically derelict former industrial areas. In these areas, certain prespecified types of development are in effect given automatic planning permission, while other types of development remain liable to control in the usual way. The Enterprise Zone incentives last for only ten years and the 'first round' zones designated in 1981 have thus reverted to normal planning control.

Simplified Planning Zones, established in 1986, are similar in nature, although they do not bear the financial incentives which add to the attractiveness of Enterprise Zones.

Finally the question of *'planning gain'* should be mentioned. The town planning legislation allows a developer to offer some extra facility, as part of the planning application, which would be advantageous for the local authority concerned. A 'Planning Obligation' can be offered by either side in order to provide such extra facilities. This replaces the 'Section 106 Agreement' (formerly Section 52 Agreement) sanctioned in the Town and Country Planning Acts. This process is usually termed 'planning gain' and is thought by many to represent a 'price' which developers often have to pay in return for obtaining planning permission. Government advice (Department of the Environment, 1991) is that the extra facility must have some clear relationship with the main development proposed.

Central government advice and intervention

Central government has played a vital part in the British planning system. It initiates and provides planning legislation, both through Acts of Parliament and the Statutory Instruments such as the General Development Order (see above). It also provides 'advice' to local authorities on ways in which they should prepare development plans, consider applications for development, and interpret and apply the planning legislation generally. 'Advice' is supplied formally to all planning authorities through circulars, and series of Planning Policy Guidance Notes (in England and Wales) and National Planning Guidelines (in Scotland).

In addition, the content of development plan policies, and decisions on planning applications, are both subject to a degree of control by central government departments. Until very recently, structure plans had to be submitted to central government for approval, and central government still retains powers to 'call in' development plans for alteration in what it considers to be exceptional circumstances. In addition, both structure and local plans are usually debated at a public inquiry, chaired by a government-appointed inspector. Central government also retains the right to make decisions on planning applications, following an appeal against refusal or the conditions attached to a planning permission. Central government may also 'call in' an application for its own determination, before it has been considered by the local authority concerned. This procedure is invoked only for large-scale and controversial applications, or for applications that involve more than one local authority. Decisions on appeals and call-ins are widely regarded as indications of government policy where this is not made clear through formal advice.

LAND USE PLANNING AND RETAILING IN BRITAIN

The course of retail development in Britain since the 1940s has been massively influenced by the land use planning system. This has occurred partly through the processes of control over development, outlined above. But the planning system has also encouraged retail development where this has fitted in with its overall objectives. This has led in particular to substantial growth of retailing in town and city centres. This section outlines some typical elements of land use planning policies in so far as they affect retail development. Later sections enlarge on two main aspects of these policies – support for town and city centres, and policies for the control of off-centre or 'out-of-town' retailing.

Planners' attitudes to retail development

Town planners have, since the 1940s, had considerable influence over the location and scale of new retail development in Britain. This is a topic about which many planners hold strong views, and have been prepared to attempt to impose them upon retailers and developers. Before examining the detailed nature and effects of planning control, it may be useful to summarise the basic standpoint of many town planners to issues concerning retail development. Planners have justified what amounts to their intervention within the land market for the following reasons:

1 Planning intervention is beneficial to the market because it can improve the efficiency of its operation. This is particularly the case where strategic land use planning can reduce uncertainty about future patterns of population and employment change within specific areas (Healey *et al.*, 1988). Another example would be the use of land purchase powers by public bodies, to accumulate sites for major retail schemes.

2 Planners also justify intervention where they feel that the operation of an uncontrolled market is likely to lead to inequities in the level of service to the local population. In particular, the decentralisation of food retailing since the late 1970s (see Chapter 7) has caused concern for the 'disadvantaged consumer' living in inner urban areas (Royal Town Planning Institute, 1988: Chapter 6; Westlake, 1993). Multiple-owned supermarkets have been closed down, or replaced by limited-line discount stores, while the local population

has been unable to reach the new superstores in more suburban locations (Guy, 1987; Rees, 1989). Planners have used such arguments as support for restrictive or interventionist stances (Montgomery, 1990).

3 The most frequent reason for intervention is, however, that a retail proposal may have 'external' effects that are unrelated to the commercial success or failure of a scheme: these effects can be positive or negative, or both, but do not enter the retailer's balance sheet. Positive effects can include the attraction of other land uses into an area that requires new investment; or environmental improvements to untidy or derelict areas. Negative effects at a scale local to the development itself can include traffic noise and visual intrusion. More generally, any development that may be likely to increase the amount of car travel by the local population may be opposed as wasteful of energy and harmful towards natural resources. Finally, a particularly important negative effect, which at times has tended to obsess planners, is the competitive impact of new developments upon existing retailing. This issue is discussed later in this chapter.

Two general observations should be made at this stage. The first is that – to some extent – the arguments above are supported by sections of the retail and development industries (Oxford Retail Group, 1989; 1990). This is partly because owners of existing shopping centres may wish to enlist the help of planners in protecting their centres against competition from new development. The more general argument that the planning system reduces uncertainty as to the future state of the built environment also tends to be supported by established interests.

The second qualification is that central government ministers and civil servants have often appeared to see their function in terms of mitigating some of the more zealous anti-development attitudes amongst local authority planners. The role and influence of central government 'advice' is discussed later in this chapter.

Retail policies in development plans

Given the belief amongst planners that it is necessary to intervene in the market where retail development is concerned, it is not surprising that local authority planning policies have tended to be quite heavily interventionist. At times they have sought at a strategic level to control the overall rate of growth in retailing, and the locations for new development. More recently, policies to set overall rates of growth in retail floorspace have been discouraged by central government (Department of the Environment, 1988: para. 8), but locational policies are still common.

Most structure plans have contained proposals for retailing, although central government advice did not until the late 1980s specify retailing as a topic which *must* be included in structure plans. The present situation (mid-1993) is that among the nine 'Key Strategic Topics for Structure Plans' is included 'The urban economy, including major industrial, business, retail and other employment-generating and wealth-creating development' (Department of the Environment, 1992b: para. 5.9; 1992c: 40).

It will be noted that retail development appears to be considered worthy of attention in development plans because it can generate employment and create wealth; not in its own right as a service to the local population.

Similarly, there has been no obligation to include policies for retailing in local plans, although the above statement appears to apply also to local plans. However, local plan policies are likely to be of considerable importance in the 1990s in controlling the pace, location and nature of retail development. This is because the Planning and Compensation Act of 1991 made clear the primary role of statutory development plans in determining applications for development (Mynors, 1991). It inserted a new section 54a into the 1990 Town and Country Planning Act:

> Where, in making any determination under the planning Acts, regard is to be had to the development plan, the determination shall be made in accordance with the plan unless material considerations indicate otherwise.

This altered the previous situation in which the development plan had been regarded as equal in importance to 'other material considerations'. Mynors provides a useful example:

> One potential effect of the new section 54a is to place greater emphasis, and hence increased pressure, on the plan-making process. Thus, instead of a sequence of inquiries each concerning a particular proposal for a superstore on the edge of a town, there may now be a major inquiry into the local plan, deciding how many superstores are needed for that town over the next ten years, and where they should be.
>
> (Mynors, 1991: 7)

Most of the research literature on retail planning policies in Britain has concentrated on structure plans, probably because of their more 'strategic' emphasis and their more comprehensive coverage of the country. Reviews (e.g. Barras and Broadbent, 1982; Davies, 1984: Chapter 5; Sparks and Aitken, 1986; Gibbs, 1987) have noted that policies have been dominated by assumptions about the existence, and adequacy, of retail 'hierarchies' in the plan area. The hierarchy is essentially a descriptive device used by geographers to classify shopping areas in terms of their physical size and relationship with their catchment areas, and is discussed further in Chapter 6. Planners, however, have tended to use the hierarchy in a normative fashion, specifying systems of retail concentrations within urban areas which appear to satisfy consumers' requirements for access to shopping (Burns, 1959). This specification usually involves an intimate relationship between the size of a shopping area and the extent of its catchment. Most shopping areas are seen as drawing custom from local residential districts. Thus, modern shopping centres that rely on custom drawn from a wider area are not easily fitted into a hierarchy of centres. Delineation of a hierarchy within any area has thus tended to become a device for presuming against new 'off-centre' retail development.

Two other principles that have tended to dominate plan-making have been the desire to enhance and protect existing town centres, and the desire for containment of urban areas. The former principle is discussed below; the latter, which has influenced attitudes to edge-of-town retail development, is discussed further in Guy (1980a: Chapter 6).

Typical planning policies for retailing

Taking the two types of plan together, local authority policies for retailing can now be summarised. They tend to include the following elements:

1 Regulation of total retail floorspace

This type of policy, common in structure plans in the 1970s, sought to forecast 'shopping needs' of the local authority area as a whole, at some future date. The resulting total floorspace estimate would then give rise to a limit on new retail development. This approach has been criticised for failing to recognise the dynamic nature of retailing or to understand the requirements of retailers for new shopping space. It assumes essentially that 'floorspace provision and consumer requirements are in some sort of natural equilibrium' (Teale, 1989: 78), and that the market will respond to population change and other factors through an incremental growth in floorspace. Teale (ibid.) comments that 'The nature of existing floorspace – its type, age, configuration, use in terms of space allocation, let alone its actual business efficiency – is ignored. All floorspace is treated as equal.'

2 Allocation of new retail floorspace

This type of policy arose from policy 1 above. The assumed amount of new floorspace required in the future was allocated either to geographical sub-regions of the local authority area, or to various types of centre, or some combination of the two. In the early structure plans, alternative policies of this nature were exhaustively tested using gravity models and other techniques (Davies, 1984: Chapter 5). Typically, policies for increasing floorspace in existing centres were compared with policies for developing new centres. Such exercises can be criticised for failing to examine *qualitative* differences between existing centres, and deficiencies in existing retailing (ibid.).

3 Plans for specific new retail development

Perhaps as a result of the analyses described above, or for other reasons, proposals for new centres, or expansion of existing centres, have often been a feature of development plans. Here the local authority has identified a 'need' for retail development of a specific type: for example, a retail park, or additional floorspace in a town centre, or a speciality development. In some local plans, specific sites have been identified (Royal Town Planning Institute, 1988: 40).

4 Conditions for the development of 'new' retailing

More debate in retail planning has focused on this issue than on any other. Market pressures for development of new free-standing stores outside existing shopping areas first arose in the late 1960s. Policies in the early structure plans attempted to define conditions under which such developments could be permitted. These conditions were often so wide-ranging and restrictive that they amounted virtually to a complete ban on such development. Following a succession of public inquiries, in which approved plan policies were often overturned in favour of developers, policies appear to have become more liberal. Such policies are discussed in more detail in a later section.

5 Protection and improvement of existing shopping areas

Policies that seek to 'protect' or 'safeguard' retailing in existing town and suburban shopping areas are characteristic of almost all development plans. These take two forms. First, it is hoped that existing shopping areas can be protected through restrictions on off-centre development. Second and more positively, attention is given to deficiencies of existing shopping areas, particularly unplanned parts of town centres and inner suburban areas. Here there can be an important role for local authorities in co-ordinating and managing improvements to the infrastructure of such areas, such as car parking, landscaping, shop fronts, etc. Policies of this type, often found in local plans, are described further in Chapter 6.

6 Development control policies

The types of policies listed above all imply some form of control over development. Many plans include development control policies that relate specifically to retail development. These may include more general policies aimed at maintaining and improving the environment, related to the 'considerations' in development control discussed earlier in this chapter.

Retail policies in development plans have tended to change in nature during the last twenty years or so. Structure plan policies in the 1970s were generally very supportive of existing centres, relying on arguments about the merits of sustaining retail hierarchies. A restrictive attitude was taken towards 'new forms of retailing', at that time comprising superstores and retail warehouses. These were seen as either generally unwelcome, or acceptable only within existing shopping areas. Since the early 1980s, however, many counties have generally adopted a less restrictive stance with respect to retail growth and change. For example, Cambridgeshire County Council moved from a restrictive stance towards an acceptance that some off-centre retail development would benefit the major town centres (especially Cambridge) through relieving traffic congestion. Similarly, Essex County Council anticipated the need for off-centre development and saw the proposed regional shopping centre at Thurrock as an opportunity to improve retail facilities in that part of the county (Building Design Partnership, 1992; see also BDP Planning, 1992: 110–114). However, some other authorities have remained generally hostile to off-centre development during the 1980s.

During this latter period, central government ministries have sometimes deleted or modified structure plan policies which they have considered to be too restrictive on retail interests. Examples of such policies might be a blanket prohibition of new shopping centre developments above a certain size, or restriction of new developments to certain existing centres only. The condition that structure plans must be approved by central government before they become statutorily effective was, however, removed in 1991. It is possible thus that policies may become more restrictive in the 1990s.

Local plan policies are more difficult to summarise. Recent research suggests that district councils tend to emphasise the importance of existing retail hierarchies and may be more restrictive towards off-centre development. The main emphasis is on protecting and enhancing existing central shopping areas, and (in some cases) identifying sites for new retail development, usually in relationship to new residential areas (BDP Planning, 1992: 114–115).

Two very common themes in development plans emerge from this brief review: (a) protection and support for existing town and city centres, and (b) restriction of off-centre development of any retailing larger than the purely local facility. These broad policies are discussed in more detail in later sections, although it should be remembered that they are closely related to one another.

Central government attitudes

Central government attitudes have also been of considerable importance in affecting the course of retail development. This has occurred in three ways. First, policies in structure plans which are regarded by central government as being too detailed or too restrictive on new development have been amended or deleted. Second, some decisions of local authorities to reject applications for new development have been overruled, permission having been granted by the Secretary of State (for the Environment, in England; or for Wales, or Scotland, as appropriate), following an appeal by the applicant. Third, local authorities' decision-making on retail applications has been influenced by the criteria drawn up by central government regarding proposals for retail development. Local authority planners and councillors are heavily influenced in their decision-making by central government views, both as expressed in advice notes, and from evidence of past appeal decisions. Most local authorities will not refuse an application for retail development if it appears very likely that the application would be approved on appeal. Apart from the wasted time and effort, the local authority can under certain circumstances be required to pay the costs incurred by the applicant in fighting the appeal.

Government attitudes can be summarised under two headings: retail planning in general; and criteria for major retail development.

Explicit government criteria for *retail planning* in general do not exist as such (Davies, 1986). (The two guidance notes which are discussed below relate specifically to 'major retail development' (Scottish Development Department, 1986; Department of the Environment, 1988, 1993)). The various local authority policies mentioned above have all received support from government, but in some cases have subsequently been frowned upon. In particular, policies that attempt to estimate future floorspace needs and then allocate retail growth between geographical areas were recommended in early advice on structure and local planning (Ministry of Housing and Local Government, 1970). Later, however, this advice was replaced by the following, in the Department of the Environment's Planning Policy Guidance on Major Retail Development:

> When preparing plans it will be appropriate for local planning authorities to take account of forecasts of retail expenditure over the plan period and the possible implications of these forecasts for the location of different types of retail development. However, policies should not attempt to prescribe rigid floorspace limits for new retail development, either overall or in specified localities, since this would impair the ability of developers, retailers and the planning authority to respond to changing market conditions and the demands of customers.
>
> (Department of the Environment, 1988: para. 8)

The revised Guidance (Department of the Environment, 1993) largely retains this statement, but also suggests that:

> Development plans should make adequate provision for retail developments, including a choice of sites for different types of retail development.
>
> (Department of the Environment, 1993: para. 47)

The notion of forward planning by local authorities of specific retail developments, through acquisition of sites and agreement with developers, appears, however, to be frowned upon by central government, although there is no specific comment on this in the Guidance. The government's view is that retail development should be driven by the market's interpretation of the shopping needs of the local population. The planner's role is seen as regulating development, largely by prohibiting or modifying proposals which 'would cause harm to interests of acknowledged importance' (Department of the Environment, 1992a: para. 5), and accepting proposals that do not cause such harm.

Proposals in development plans for improving existing centres would normally be welcomed by central government. The Guidance welcomes proposals for the 'modernisation and refurbishment of town centres ... especially where it involves the use of derelict or unused land and it brings about environmental improvement, including the careful treatment of historic buildings and townscape' (Department of the Environment, 1988: para. 13). The revised version of the Guidance (Department of the Environment, 1993: para. 14) is similar.

Criteria for development control in development plans are also welcomed, particularly in view of the recent emphasis on local plan policies as the main consideration in development control. However, specific criteria that seem too restrictive may be frowned upon.

Government criteria on *retail development* are stated explicitly in the Guidance Note (Department of the Environment, 1988, 1993). The criteria can also be gauged from analyses of appeal and call-in decisions by Secretaries of State (e.g. Lee Donaldson, 1986, 1987, 1991; Gibbs, 1981, 1986).

The major criterion discussed is the possible effect upon existing town centres. The 1988 Guidance reproduced advice first given in 1985, that:

> Since commercial competition as such is not a land use planning consideration, the possible effects of a proposed major development on existing retailers is not in this sense a relevant factor in deciding planning applications and appeals. It will be necessary, however, to take account in exceptional circumstances of the cumulative effects of other recent and proposed large-scale retail developments in the locality and to consider whether they are on such a scale and of a kind that they could seriously affect the vitality and viability of a nearby town centre *as a whole* – for example, whether they seem likely to result in a significant increase in vacant properties, or a marked reduction in the range of services the town centre provides, such as could lead to its general physical deterioration and to the detriment of its future place in the economic and social life of the community.
>
> (Department of the Environment, 1988: para. 7)

This advice, while retaining the consensus view that town centre retailing should be supported by the planning system, was widely criticised by commentators as being insufficiently restrictive of new development. The test for effects upon town centres was seen by many as, first, too vague, and second, weighted in favour of the developer. However, following recommendations in the Department's commissioned study (BDP Planning, 1992), the revised Guidance takes note of these criticisms. It indicates what might be regarded as significant 'economic, social and environmental impacts' on a town centre. These include:

- the likely effect on future private sector investment. . . in that centre. . . .
- the extent to which the [competing] development would put at risk the strategy for the town centre set out in the local plan. . .

- changes to the quality, attractiveness and character of the centre, and to its role in the economic and social life of the community;
- changes to the range of services that the centre will continue to provide; and
- likely increases in the number of vacant properties in the primary retail area.
                    (Department of the Environment, 1993: para. 36)

The guidance, however, concludes that:

> local planning authorities should not refuse permission for development on the grounds of the effect on a town centre, unless there is clear evidence to suggest that the result would be to undermine the vitality and viability of that centre which would otherwise continue to serve the community well.

(ibid.: para. 37)

The other major criterion discussed in the 1993 Guidance is 'accessibility and transport':

> Retail development should be sited where it is likely to be accessible by a choice of means to transport, and to encourage economy in fuel consumption.

(ibid.: para. 38)

Other criteria, which may include the need to avoid development in green belts or other open countryside, the need to protect land required for other uses such as industry, and the need generally to avoid significant environmental effects, were specified in the 1988 Guidance. These criteria appear now to have been subsumed in the general advice that 'Local planning authorities should also take account of all other interests of acknowledged planning importance' (ibid.: para. 31).

The Department has introduced some procedural requirements for consideration of 'major' retail applications (those of over 20,000 sq. m. gross floor area, or possibly 10,000 sq. m. in urban areas not previously developed for retail purposes). The developer should in all cases submit to the local authority a statement of the likely impact of the development upon other retail locations. In some cases an Environmental Assessment may also be required. Finally, local planning authorities in England and Wales are obliged to notify the Department of the Environment (or Welsh Office, as appropriate) of any proposals for major retail development. In certain circumstances, smaller proposals might also need to be notified (Department of the Environment, 1992d; Unit for Retail Planning Information, 1992a). In Scotland, the lower limit for notification is 40,000 sq. m. of gross retail floorspace.

The experience of public inquiry decisions, from both appeals and 'call-ins', confirms broadly the criteria listed above, while adding detail to some of them. Since the research on such decisions relates almost entirely to off-centre development proposals, this question is discussed further in a later section.

Development control

The development control process is the interface between the developer and the local authority. Development control decisions depend upon development plan policies, as discussed above, but also a variety of other 'material considerations'. In the retail context, 'development' can mean:

- the construction of new shops or extensions to shops;
- changes of use of non-shop buildings to shops, and in some cases, change from one type of shop to another;
- carrying out other works, such as building a car park;
- altering the appearance of a shop, by providing a new shop front or with certain types of advertisement.

(Thomas, 1990: 17)

Many parts of Britain are still covered by development plans which are seriously out of date, and which do not reflect the growth of new types of shopping centre during the 1980s. This has led to a high degree of reliance upon 'other material considerations' in the development control process.

H.W.E. Davies *et al.* (1986: Figure 2.1) list eighty-seven different considerations used by planners in development control. Those frequently used by their sample of planners to appraise retail applications are shown in Figure 5.1. In considering just one hypothetical 'major retail' application, planners interviewed in this study said that they would typically take around fifty-five separate considerations into account (ibid.: Table 2.3).

A survey of local authority councillors and planners by J. Sainsbury plc (1990) indicates that government advice on major retail development is a less important determinant of decision-making than the views of local residents. The majority of planning committee members (elected councillors) approached in this survey felt that 'regulating the number of retail units could, in itself, be a valid planning consideration'. This view is, according to current government advice, incorrect, and would make the local authority vulnerable to defeat at appeal, and possibly faced with an award of costs to the appellant.

Retail planning in urban development corporations and enterprise zones

As explained above, these areas lie outside the conventional planning system: Urban Development Corporations are not necessarily covered by local plans, whilst Enterprise Zones are not necessarily subject to normal development control procedures. In both types of area there is a very strong emphasis on attracting private sector investment. It is not surprising therefore that there has been considerable pressure for retail development in some of these areas. Urban Development Corporations are generally seen as more sympathetic to off-centre retail development than are conventional local authorities.

Enterprise Zone designation has had the more important impact upon retail development. Although in most of the zones retail development is subject to normal planning control, in a few zones permission has been allowed either for any type of retail development or for any development below a certain size limit

Amenity	Site characteristics	Topography Landscape Historic buildings Archaeology
	Design (visual)	Architectural style Scale, Mass, etc. External spaces
	Physical impact	Daylight Sunlight Hazardous uses
	Operation	Hours of operation Litter Obsruction
	Relation to surroundings	Impact on buildings Impact on protected land Non-conforming use
Arrangement	On-site layout	Roads: layout Roads: capacity Parking: layout Parking: capacity Pedestrian movements New pedestrian routes Disabled persons Refuse collection Backland development Security
	Off-site relationships	Incompatible uses Highways: proximity Highways: capacity Utilities: proximity Utilities: capacity
Efficiency	Resources on-site	Sub-surface conditions Condition of buildings Conversion potential Vacant land/buildings
Coordination	Phasing on-site	Links with other uses Interim measures
	Phasing off-site	Other linked proposals
	Operation/time	Temporary uses
Quantity and distribution	Quantity	Loss of existing use Increase in use Expansion of premises Employment generation Impact on uses off-site
	Distribution and location	By sub-areas
Other considerations		Planning gain Applicants' needs Site assembly Precedent

Figure 5.1 Planning considerations used in development control

Source: H.W.E. Davies *et al.* (1986).

Table 5.1 Planning gain related to superstore development in Plymouth

Developer	*Planning gain*
Sainsbury	Provision of alternative employment land Park-and-ride scheme Crèche facilities 'Per cent for art' contribution Tourist information centre Highway works associated with the development itself
Tesco	Crèche facilities Facilities for the disabled Nature conservation areas 'Per cent for art' contribution Highway works
Plymouth and South Devon Co-operative Society	Provision of three areas of open space Community buildings

Source: *Planning* (19 February 1993:10)

(Sparks, 1987; Thomas and Bromley, 1987). This has led to development of retail parks and regional centres in Enterprise Zones (see Chapter 8).

Planning gain from retail development

As discussed in the previous section, developers may offer benefits to the local community in return for permission to develop. An acceptable example of planning gain, in the retail context, would be financial support by the developer for improvement of a road junction in the vicinity of the development, needed partly to accommodate the extra traffic generated by the development itself. Indeed, developers of schemes generating 250 or more vehicle movements a day are likely in future to be required by the Department of Transport to pay towards such road improvements where these involve a motorway or trunk road (Department of Transport, 1992).

Another acceptable example of planning gain would be the provision by the developer of a multi-storey car park in a town centre shopping scheme. An obvious example of 'planning gain' which would be unacceptable to the development industry and to central government would be the construction by the developer of a leisure centre, to be presented free to the local authority, at some distance from the proposed retail development. However, the dividing line between 'acceptable' and 'unacceptable' planning gain is not easy to define. Table 5.1 lists examples of planning gain accepted by developers and considered by the High Court as 'lawful' in a recent case. Further examples are discussed by Debenham Tewson (1988) and Peart (1989).

It is hoped that during the 1990s, the increasing coverage of the country by local plans, and the emphasis on the development plan as the primary consideration in development control, will lead to a more orderly and transparent approach to retail development, in terms both of criteria for granting permission or refusal, and opportunities for planning gain.

LOCAL AUTHORITY SUPPORT FOR TOWN AND CITY CENTRES

As mentioned above, a major component of planning policy in Britain has been support of retail activity in town and city centres. This is part of a wider commitment to the town centre as a whole, but it is recognised that retailing is usually the most important economic activity in the town centre.

Support for town centres arises from a variety of largely social and cultural reasons. The central area is a major focus of employment and of public offices and entertainment facilities. It is the most accessible part of the town so far as access by public transport is concerned. It often contains the major landmark and historic buildings and spaces by which the inhabitants of an area secure their identity (Holliday, 1983).

Development plan policies almost invariably support retail development within town and city centres, although often subject to overall limits on size, and criteria related to environmental and traffic impacts. However, local authority support for town centres has not been demonstrated simply through the wording in planning policies, or by attempts to restrict off-centre development. More positive policies have been practised, leading to important effects upon retail development processes. These policies are described in the remainder of this section.

Land acquisition and partnerships

Many authorities have actively supported retail development schemes through land acquisition and/or joint development with private sector interests. Acquisition of land held to be suffering from problems of 'bad layout and obsolete development' was first authorised under the Town and Country Planning Act of 1944 (Telling, 1990: 9). This provision was intended mainly to allow local authorities to purchase, compulsorily if necessary, land which had been made derelict through wartime bombing. However, its use has extended well beyond this limited purpose. The Act allowed local authorities to delineate Comprehensive Development Areas (CDAs), through a procedure involving draft orders, receipt of objections from those affected by the order, and possibly a public inquiry. Approval had to be sought from the relevant central government ministry or department.

During the 1950s and 1960s, local authorities made extensive use of the 1944 Act provisions to acquire land in or adjacent to central shopping areas. The designation of a CDA often presaged large-scale development of retail and other uses appropriate to a town centre, together with improvements to vehicle access and car parking. This process was encouraged by a publication by the Ministry of

Housing and Local Government (1962), which praised comprehensive development of town centres and provided examples of possible schemes (see also Davies, 1984: Chapter 8). Braithwaite (1989) provides a case study of successive redevelopment plans for part of Dundee town centre, showing how the nature of the proposals reflected physical planning ideals of the period concerned.

Local authorities had two main reasons for acquiring central area land and entering into large-scale redevelopments. The first was to improve levels of access by public transport and (particularly) private cars, in the realisation that car ownership was rapidly increasing. The Buchanan Report, sponsored by the Ministry of Transport (Buchanan, 1963) encouraged councils to redesign their road networks so as to accommodate anticipated levels of traffic, rather than make the best use of existing space through appropriate traffic management and public transport policies. This led to proposals for new inner ring roads and multi-storey car parks.

The second reasons for acquiring central area land was to extend the main shopping area. Before the reorganisation of local government in England and Wales in 1974, many of the leading towns and cities were constituted as county boroughs, and enjoyed complete control over planning and transport decisions within their area, tempered only by central government limitations on expenditure. Councillors saw that expanding and 'modernising' the central shopping area, and improving vehicle access, was a way of enhancing the status of their town. From the late 1950s onwards, a number of private property developers saw opportunities to work with such councils. The developer would in effect design a scheme for new shopping development, possibly with office and/or leisure space, and present it to councillors, sometimes by-passing professional planners working in the same councils (Marriott, 1967). The developers could not, however, complete their schemes without the council's power to purchase all or part of the land required.

The results were a series of comprehensive redevelopments in town and city centres, involving new shopping space, other commercial uses, and improved car parking and road access. Councils were sometimes able to extract other 'planning gains', such as libraries, swimming pools and bus stations. Prominent among such developments were at least seventeen 'Arndale' centres built during the 1960s and early 1970s by Town and City Properties, of which the largest were in Manchester (1,189,000 sq. ft. gross retail area), and Luton (700,000 sq. ft.). Several of these new centres were co-developed by private companies and local authorities, but the latter's main role was usually in purchasing the freehold of the land required for the scheme (see Chapter 8).

In the case of partnerships, various arrangements were made. The most common appears to have been that the town or city council remained as ground landlord, and the developer (or institutional funder) became the principal lessee, taking a very long-term interest at a peppercorn rent. The various buildings and retail or service units within the development were then let to appropriate tenants, usually on conventional 'institutional' leases (see Chapter 4). These tenants might include the council itself for certain non-commercial uses. Hence the term 'lease and leaseback' is often used for such arrangements. Typically, there was an element of profit-sharing between private and public sector agencies. More information and suggestions for good practice are provided in Raggett (1984).

After 1973 fewer such schemes were initiated. The first immediate reason was the property slump of 1974–1976 which temporarily made large commercial developments unprofitable: the costs of repaying capital at a time of high interest rates outweighed the probable returns on such schemes (see the 'worked example' of such a development in Department of the Environment, 1975: 67). And after the passing of the Community Land Act by a Labour government in 1975, leases of more than 99 years to developers or institutions became unlawful. Of greater significance in the longer term, however, were changes in local government administration. First, the county boroughs were replaced by metropolitan or 'shire' districts, nested within a new set of county councils, in England and Wales in the Local government Act of 1972, implemented in 1974. This led to a weaker identification of towns with local authorities, and to a greater level of strategic control over large-scale retail development, in the new series of county structure plans. Second, while the powers to acquire land under the 1944 Act remained with district councils, greater restriction on local government expenditure during the late 1970s and (especially) the 1980s meant that large-scale purchasing of expensive central area land for what amounted to speculative development purposes became ever more unlikely. However, a few schemes contemplated in earlier years, such as the St David's Centre in Cardiff (commenced in 1977) were completed during the 1980s on land bought by councils under the 1944 Act powers.

Equally important in hastening the demise of large-scale joint public/private central area schemes, were changes in wider attitudes to central area planning. The 1960s schemes had often meant the demolition of historic areas of the town centre, and the replacement of intimate small-scale townscapes with 'brutal' modernist architecture. Books such as Amery and Cruickshank (1975) helped focus opposition against further such plans, sometimes winning over councils after they had initially accepted the scheme to be in the best interests of the town concerned. A well-known example was in Carlisle, where a scheme involving extensive demolition in the town centre was eventually rejected by councillors in favour of the more sympathetic 'The Lanes' development (Scott, 1989). Another well-known example – Chesterfield – is discussed in Aldous (1990). At the same time, concern grew over the domination of central areas by vehicle traffic. The solution to this problem became increasingly seen in terms of restricting traffic within central areas through pedestrianisation and 'traffic calming' (TEST, 1988; Hass-Klau, 1990), rather than providing sufficient road space to meet unrestricted demand for vehicle movements.

A final issue which led to a reduction in local authority involvement in town centre retail schemes was one of accountability. Marriott (1967) and Ambrose and Colenutt (1975) showed how certain councillors could in the early 1960s form alliances with developers to force through schemes which may have been contrary to wider public interest. Healey *et al.* (1988: 190) point out more generally that development projects promoted by the public sector – especially local authorities themselves – tend to receive less thorough scrutiny for environmental and economic impacts than would similar schemes proposed entirely by the private sector. There is little question that some town centre 'partnership' schemes were damaging in their environmental impacts, and possibly in their economic impacts upon other nearby town centres. For the reasons discussed above, this problem seems less likely to occur in the future.

Other local authority support for central areas

In recent years, local authorities' policies for central areas have concentrated more on environmental and, in some cases, management and marketing approaches for the town centre as a whole (Royal Town Planning Institute, 1988: Chapter 7). Development policies often recommend the improvement of car parking and public transport and pedestrian access to town centres: powers to carry out these improvements are vested in local authorities. For example, in the centre of Cardiff, the local authorities have carried out substantial improvements to infrastructure which have complemented the substantial private investment made by property developers and retailers (Guy and Lord, 1993).

A recent extension of local authority support for town centres has been in the setting up of town centre management schemes. These are partly a response to increasing competition from off-centre developments. As town centre management mainly affects the 'unplanned' retail parts of the town centre, discussion of this issue is deferred to Chapter 6.

PLANNING POLICIES AND OFF-CENTRE RETAILING

This section discusses local authorities' reactions to proposals for off-centre development in Britain, and ways in which attitudes have been modified through experience and by central government advice and decisions. The main physical and geographical outcomes of the tension between public and private objectives for off-centre retail development are discussed in more detail in Chapters 7 and 8.

Land use planning policy has generally been very cautious about allowing major off-centre retail development. The main reasons for this appear to have been a desire to maintain the existing hierarchy of shopping centres, and to protect central area retailing (existing or proposed schemes) from what is seen as unfair competition. In addition, assumptions are often made that off-centre retailing:

- favours car users over public transport users, and is thus wasteful of resources;
- is inaccessible to non-car owners, which is inequitable;
- is unrelated to other commercial and cultural land uses, and hence brings no

Table 5.2 Typology of local authority policies for off-centre retailing

Continuum	Category	Attitude displayed towards specified outlet types
Negative	1	Presumption against
	2	Generally not allowed
	3	Not on land zoned for industry/warehousing
	4	'On its merits'
Conservative	5a	Allowed in or adjacent to existing centres provided a specified list of criteria is satisfied
	5b	Allowed in or adjacent to existing centres (*no* criteria)
	6	Allowed on designated sites
	7	Allowed on fringe sites
	8a	Specific types of outlet allowed outside exisiting centres
Positive	8b	Allowed outside existing centres providing a range of criteria is satisfied

Source: Gibbs (1987: Table 5)

community benefits and does not encourage multi-purpose travel;
- can absorb land which is needed for other purposes, such as industrial development;
- can result in loss of open rural land.

These issues are explored in more detail elsewhere (Davies, 1984: Chapter 9; Gayler, 1984; Guy, 1980a: Chapter 8; Lee Donaldson, 1991).

Planners have used these arguments to justify planning policies that severely restrict the possibilities for new off-centre development. Gibbs (1987), in an analysis of structure plan policies, discerned eight categories of policy, which are listed in Table 5.2. Attitudes by development control officers in local authorities to off-centre retail development, also from Gibbs' (1987) study, are summarised in Table 5.3.

Gibbs' analysis relates mainly to the 'first wave' of structure plans, approved in the late 1970s and early 1980s. There is evidence that later modifications of structure plans have been more liberal to off-centre development, although policies still favour town centre retailing (Building Design Partnership, 1992). A further change in the 1980s was the increased role of district councils in considering applications for retail development. Under the Town and Country Planning Act 1971, 'major' applications could be regarded as a 'county matter' which had to be determined by county rather than district councils. However, these rules were changed in 1980, whereby all applications for retail development

Table 5.3 Justifications for planning policies for off-centre retailing

Justification	No. of citings
All off-centre outlets:	
Effect on other outlets	56
Need	44
Accessibility to community	28
Supply of industrial land	27
Supports the existing hierarchy	23
Conflict with amenity	21
Accessibility by public transport	21
Innovation	20
Traffic generation	20
Maintain the role of the town centre	15
Competition with the town centre	15
Employment	15
Retail warehouses:	
Supply of industrial land	16
Size of site required	11
Suitability to the town centre	8
Effect on other outlets	8
Competition with the town centre	6
Maintain the role of the town centre	6
Traffic generation	6
Directed to fringe sites	6
Employment	6
Accessibility to community	6
Innovation	6
Conflict with amenity	5
Supports the existing hierarchy	5
Sites on fringe of town centre	5

Source: Gibbs (1987: Table 7)

were to be determined by district councils. Although the districts are instructed in a general sense to conform with the provisions of approved structure plans, and are also obliged to inform the county concerned about major planning applications, there is evidence that in some cases off-centre retailing has been allowed which appears to contravene structure plan policies (Gibbs, 1987; Guy, 1988). There are two broad reasons for this. First, districts that do not possess a major town centre may wish to build up their retail function by allowing substantial new development (examples are discussed in TEST, 1989: Chapter 3). Second, districts have approved off-centre schemes in the belief that if refused, the schemes would be developed in a neighbouring district, and would still have economic impact upon the district's existing centres (Gibbs, 1987: 52–53).

A final aspect of local planning policy is related to the positive externalities derived from off-centre retail development. Two such advantages to a local council might be (a) the opportunity for environmental regeneration, and (b) employment opportunities in the new development. A typical grocery superstore would employ between 200 and 300 people, although many of these jobs would be likely to be part-time or casual in nature (Sparks, 1983). These benefits of new store development may outweigh the normal objections in areas where environmental degradation and/or job losses are significant.

Some commentators have derived from these arguments the notion of regional differences in the acceptability to planners, and hence rates of growth, of large new store and retail park developments. For example, the average population per grocery superstore ranged from 88,000 in Wales and the North of England, to 194,000 in Greater London in 1988 (Thorpe, 1990: 190). Generally, the least affluent regions have possessed the largest numbers of superstores relative to population, and it is likely that similar disparities have occurred for other types of off-centre retail development. This counter-intuitive phenomenon seems to have resulted largely from planners' greater willingness to accept off-centre development in the less

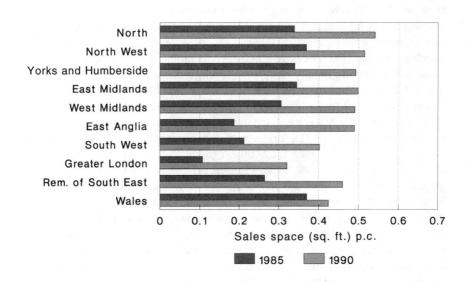

Figure 5.2 Grocery superstore provision by region in 1985 and 1990
Source: Lee Donaldson (1991: 2)

affluent regions, for reasons discussed above. B.K. Davies and L. Sparks (1989) confirm this view by showing that there was a higher proportion of planning refusals in the 'south' than the 'north', in the period up to 1986.

More recent analysis by Lee Donaldson (1991: 2) shows that regional disparities were less marked in 1990 than in 1985. Sales area per head of population is now at similar levels in most regions, the major exception being Greater London, where it is still much lower than elsewhere (see Figure 5.2). This suggests that the planners' resistance to superstore development became less pronounced generally during the late 1980s, a conclusion consistent with observations above on the relaxation of structure plan policies and the more liberal attitude of central government during this period.

Central government mediation

Local authority policies in the 1970s were usually very restrictive on off-centre development. A common tactic was to confine 'large new stores' to existing shopping centres, despite evidence that these locations were often unsuited to this type of development (Guy, 1980a: 148; Guy, 1980b). Many planning applications were refused, but on appeal, were given permission by the Secretaries of State for the Environment or for Wales or Scotland (Lee Donaldson, 1986, 1987, 1991; Gibbs, 1981). It became clear that central government was advising its inspectors to use rather more liberal criteria than local authority planners had done. Indeed, some appeals were allowed which directly overruled approved structure plan policies. In particular, arguments that there was 'no need' for a new store, or that the new store might take a modest amount of trade away from existing shopping centres, were unlikely to succeed. If, however, the new development would prejudice the success of a proposed town centre retail development, then the off-centre scheme would probably not be supported by the inspector at a public inquiry. Any new development which would occupy land under 'Green Belt' or other protection, or which was likely to be developed for industry in the near future, would also probably be unacceptable.

Central government advice, in the form of a Development Control Policy Note for England and Wales (Department of the Environment, 1972, 1977), and National Planning Guidance for Scotland (Scottish Development Department, 1978) aired the main issues for and against off-centre retail development. The generally cautious tone of this advice nevertheless was more liberal than most local authority planning policies. In the 1980s the Thatcher government became more sympathetic to private sector development in general, and retail developers felt encouraged to submit much larger schemes involving, first, clusters of large stores, and then complete regional shopping centre proposals. Official government advice was now out of date and eventually new Guidance was released (Scottish Development Department, 1986; Department of the Environment, 1988).

Ironically, by this time it appears that most local authorities had realised that the competitive effects of the first two 'waves' of decentralised retailing

(Schiller, 1986, 1987) were by no means as drastic as had been feared; and the release of town and district centres from heavy delivery vehicles and car-borne shoppers was to be welcomed (Royal Town Planning Institute, 1988; Distributive Trades Economic Development Council, 1988; BDP Planning, 1992). This point was reinforced in government advice (Department of the Environment, 1988: para. 18). More recently, however, political opinion appears to have swung back in favour of supporting town centres (Department of the Environment, 1993).

These variations over time in government attitudes to off-centre retailing are manifested in the statistics of appeals against refusal of planning permission. The number of such appeals related to applications for 'major retail' development in England rose from 124 in 1984 to 297 in the year ending March 1987, since when it has fallen again to 156 in the year ending March 1992. The rising trend probably reflected increasing pressure for retail development, rather than changes in attitudes of local planning authorities. Since the late 1980s, the fall in the number of appeals reflects the falling-off of development activity, and probably an increasing tendency for planning permission to be granted as policies become more liberal.

There has also been some variation in the proportion of appeals allowed by Secretaries of State, which rose from 35 per cent in 1984 to around 50 per cent from 1986/87 onwards. In a review of appeal decisions regarding applications for grocery superstores, Lee Donaldson Associates (1991: 13–15) distinguish three main criteria used by Inspectors to determine appeals: land use planning, shopping impact and traffic issues. 'Land use planning' includes environmental issues, such as the 'proper use' of the site, Green Belt and countryside policies, and the impact of the proposed development upon the environment. It also includes land supply issues, and alternative uses for the site. 'Shopping impact' includes the direct competitive impact of the proposed development upon the established retail hierarchy; and the impact upon alternative retail development proposals already supported by the local authority, such as town centre development. 'Traffic issues' include the effects of traffic generated by the proposed development on the existing road network; and the design of effective traffic access to the site.

Fitting off-centre schemes into the retail hierarchy

Another type of outcome from the tension between retailer and local authority objectives was the production of shopping centres that represented a compromise between the two sides. If the retail developer could produce a centre that seemed to fit into the hierarchy of shopping centres, then its competitive effects might seem more acceptable to planners, particularly where population growth created an increased demand for retail goods. Out of this compromise was born two types of shopping centre: the 'new district centre' and the 'retail park'. These are discussed further in Chapters 7 and 8.

INTERNATIONAL COMPARISONS

It is probably true to say that all developed countries possess some type of land use planning system, in order to regulate land transactions and development in the wider public interest. Concern over the environmental and economic impacts of retail development is widespread. However, different countries have formulated different types of planning control, and within some countries the system varies considerably from one state or province to another.

So far as retail development is concerned, there are two important aspects which differentiate the various national or provincial systems of land use control. The first is the extent of flexibility and discretion embodied in the system. The British system is unusually flexible: national and local planning policies are generally vague and allow considerable discretion to planning officials. In contrast, planning systems in most other European countries and North America are more precise, based around the principle of zoning ordinances which set out precise rules of land use and building design for specific areas (Department of the Environment, 1989a; Wakeford, 1990). The second relevant dimension of planning systems is the extent to which there is strategic control over retail development. Here, European systems generally impose such control (often through specific legislation rather than land use planning guidance as such), whereas most states and provinces in North America do not.

Zoning versus flexible policies

Little research appears to have been carried out on the effects upon development of different types of planning control. In Britain, it is possible for new retailing to be developed in areas where the preferred land use has been some other type; in countries where zoning systems predominate, this would not appear to be possible. In addition, zoning regulations might confer more strict control over size, layout and appearance of new development than in the British case, where these features are generally discretionary and negotiable. However, research into zoning systems suggests that zoning or other restrictions can be altered fairly easily in the developer's favour if a convincing case can be made; or if political pressure is applied; or if planning gains are promised by the developer.

Strategic control over retail development

This issue appears to have been much more important in establishing contrasts between countries in rates of retail development. The emphasis has generally been on limitation of retail development outside existing shopping centres.

In several countries in continental Europe, legislation has been introduced specifically to control the growth of off-centre retailing. The situations in France and Belgium may serve as examples. Following rapid development of hyper-markets and sub-regional centres during the 1960s and early 1970s, legislation was introduced under pressure from associations of independent shopkeepers. In France, following the 'Loi Royer' of 1973, large new stores of over 1,500 sq. m. sales area, or 1,000 sq. m. (in small towns) can be built only with the permission of a 'departmental commission of commercial planning', which includes local retail trade representatives (Delobez, 1985: 150). In Belgium, proposals for such stores or centres of similar size limits are subject to advice by the Social Economic Committee for Distribution and a Provincial Committee for Distribution (François and Leunis, 1991). The outcome has been a substantial reduction in the volume of new hypermarket development (ibid.).

In Germany, there is more variation as planning procedures are under the control of state rather than national government. However, restrictions on new development outside existing centres are common (for details see TEST, 1989).

On the other hand, the prime example of minimal strategic control over retail development is in the United States. Only in a few states is there any kind of land use planning control over location and rate of new retail development overall (Dawson and Lord, 1985). In cities with zoning regulations but no strategic control, such as Charlotte (Lord and Guy, 1991), shopping centre proposals often require applications for changes in zoning, to commercial from other uses. However, this is likely to receive support from those municipalities that seek to increase their income from sales tax.

Finally, the situation in Canada shows elements of both European and US examples. There has been variation in attempts to impose strategic limitation on new development, over space (the eastern provinces being more restrictive) and over time (greater restriction in the 1980s than in earlier periods). Further details are provided in Shaw (1985) and Hallsworth (1988).

PLANNING POLICIES AND LAND VALUES

The final issue examined in this chapter is the relationship between typical land values for retail areas, and the constraints imposed by land use planning policy. The argument is that land use planning policy acts to ration the amount of land available to developers, creating a form of scarcity (Teale, 1989). Although land price data are difficult to obtain and interpret, some evidence can be assembled to test this proposition.

Teale (1989) approaches this issue through a comparison of retail provision in the United States with that in the United Kingdom. He shows that, using 1985 data, Americans 'enjoy' twice as much floorspace per capita in 'traditional stock', and nine times as much floorspace in 'purpose-built shopping centres'. The major reason for the latter disparity is stated to be that 'the Americans started seriously developing large-scale purpose-built shopping centres almost 20 years before the British' (ibid.: 79). However, Teale claims that 'without planning controls, the per capita provision of shopping in southern Britain, especially, would clearly be far greater'.

A comparative study of two medium-sized cities in the US and UK gives support to this view. In Charlotte, North Carolina, suburban land zoned for retail development and in good locations would have sold in 1990 at between $75,000 and $150,000 per acre, whereas similar land in Cardiff, UK, with planning consent for retail development, would have sold at around £400,000 per acre (Guy and Lord, 1991). Thus, the British land was worth between five and ten times as much. Differences in shop rents are also substantial, with space in prime covered shopping centres charged at approximately four times as much in Cardiff (ibid.). Differences in rents for off-centre schemes appear, however, to be much lower. This indicates that yields are lower for this type of development in Britain than in the US, possibly because development in the US tends to be funded through mortgages, which require higher interest payments than the low institutional yields typically found in Britain.

Teale also claims that 'planning constraints are much stronger in the south [of Britain] than in the north' (Teale, 1989: 79). This recalls the disparities between regions in terms of provision of grocery superstores, discussed earlier in this chapter. There are conceivably two parts to this argument. The first is the familiar proposition that disparities in retail provision occur because planning permission is harder to obtain in some regions than in others. The second part is that new development is restricted not only by planning controls as such, but also by the increases in land values and rents created by planning restrictions and the resulting scarcities of developable land.

The evidence is less clear concerning the second proposition. Figure 5.3 indicates that rents are higher for off-centre retail warehouses in London and the south-east and south-west regions than elsewhere in Britain, using Valuation Office data of land transactions in 1990. However, rents for modern industrial units of around 1,000 sq. m., which are much less likely to be subject to planning-derived shortage, are also higher in these regions. In fact, there is a consistent difference of around £30–40 per sq. m. between the two types of property throughout the regions of Britain. Thus, it is not clear whether planning constraints have had substantial effects on shop rents: their effects appear to have been outweighed by more general regional variations in land prices, themselves reflective of the more prosperous economy of the 'south'.

CONCLUSIONS

This chapter has shown that land use planning policy can have major influences on retail development, in terms of both its volume and location. The main elements of policy in Britain have been to encourage retail development in town centres and restrict off-centre development. Those policies favouring central area retail growth have been broadly successful in achieving this objective. They have, however, led to a form of development (the large-scale enclosed centre) which is particularly common in town centres in Britain and much less so in town centres elsewhere. It appears also that this local authority encouragement and intervention led to developers obtaining excess profits, particularly in the 1960s

Figure 5.3 Regional variations in rent
Source: Valuation Office (1990)

when the full development value of central area land was not always realised by purchasers. This phase has ended and local authorities no longer possess the capital resources to purchase large areas of expensive central land.

British policies which restrict off-centre development have had mixed success. They have almost certainly slowed down the pace of development, and have led to the establishment of very high land values for suburban retail development (see Chapter 7). But the British experience has been at variance with several European countries and parts of Canada, in which controls over suburban retail development have been intensified as the implications of such development for existing town centres has become clear. In Britain, such controls were instead relaxed during the 1980s, partly for political reasons, although we may now be entering a more restrictive phase.

Finally, the flexible nature of the British planning system has often been criticised for leading to unsatisfactory compromises, inconsistent decisions, and substantial regional and local variations in rates and types of new retail development. While the 'guidance' from central government has been intended to relieve this situation, the new emphasis on development plan policies in the determination of planning applications may create a situation in which regional and local disparities are wider than ever.

Chapter 6

'Unplanned' retail development

INTRODUCTION

In this and the following two chapters the focus shifts to the products of the retail development process: shops, retail areas and shopping centres. These chapters draw upon the material already discussed in an attempt to explain how these various types of retail space have been and are being produced. While Chapters 7 and 8 deal with various forms of planned retail development, this chapter explores the development process for 'unplanned' retail areas.

Unplanned retailing is a neglected topic in the retailing and property development literature. It plays a prominent role in most developed countries, and yet there is little published material on its development history or its relationships with 'planned' development and institutional investment. In contrast there has been much geographical research into the location and retail characteristics of unplanned retail space, but this literature provides little information on the development process for such areas.

In Chapter 2, 'unplanned' retailing was defined as follows: 'an unplanned retail area is one which has evolved in a gradual and/or piecemeal manner, often through conversion of buildings originally designed for some other purpose. Its ownership is likely to be fragmented between several companies, including some of the retail occupiers'. The contrast is drawn with 'planned centres', which are developed in a co-ordinated manner and are usually under one ownership. Because the term 'shopping centre' is often used to denote planned centres (e.g. Dawson, 1983), this term is avoided in this chapter. S. Brown (1991) has used the term 'unplanned cluster', but this may suggest a degree of nucleation in the spatial arrangement of shops. Instead the term 'unplanned retail area' is used in this chapter to denote any group of shops that has arisen through piecemeal development processes. However, the commonly used terms 'town centre' and 'city centre', which refer to the geographically central areas of towns and cities, and which can include planned centres, unplanned retailing, and other uses, are retained in this chapter.

Unplanned retail areas can arise in two different ways. First, through *piecemeal development* of retail premises, usually by retail firms themselves. This topic is discussed in more detail in Chapter 7, although some mention of development by retail firms is made in this chapter. Second, unplanned retailing can arise through *conversion* of non-retail premises to retail. Many unplanned retail areas, particularly in town and city centres, contain both purpose-built and converted retail premises.

An important implication of this essentially piecemeal development process is that unplanned retail areas usually lack many of the features of planned centres, such as large, purpose-built car parking areas, separate vehicle and pedestrian access for customers and suppliers, and a unified and clearly delineated ownership and tenancy structure. Retail premises, especially where originally converted from residential units, are often too small for modern retail requirements. These issues will be discussed later.

This chapter explains first the processes by which unplanned retail premises and retail areas have originated. Characteristics of their present-day ownership patterns are discussed. It is shown that unplanned retail areas possess both problems and opportunities for land use planners. Thus, an underlying theme is the way in which unplanned retail floorspace is being accommodated within the increasingly organised and institutionalised pattern of retailing in Britain.

THE DEVELOPMENT PROCESS FOR UNPLANNED RETAILING

This section reviews some of the processes by which unplanned retailing has come into use and maintained its competitive position. The term 'development process' may refer to the change in use of existing premises, rather than construction of buildings in the first place. It can also refer to piecemeal redevelopment of premises for retail purposes, within what remains essentially an unplanned retail area. The following discussion, however, relates largely to conversion of buildings to retail use. The emphasis is on events in the nineteenth and early twentieth centuries, when the majority of unplanned retail space in Britain first came into use.

It is necessary first to recall the relationships between land value and land use, discussed in Chapter 3. It was stated there that in a market economy, land use is liable to revert to the 'highest' or 'best' use: that which generates the highest bids for price or rent. In central locations within urban settlements, it is generally accepted that retailing (or retail services such as banks) usually form the highest use, and hence tend to 'capture' these locations. This process of 'capture' can take two forms. In the modern economy, where commercial interests plan their requirements ahead of development, locations can be captured through purchase of land and deliberate development of suitable premises for retailing, as discussed in other chapters in this book. However, in past periods, commercial development generally was slower and less well organised: in particular, before the 1950s in most countries, property development and retailing were predominantly managed in a rather unco-ordinated manner by local property and retail interests. The commercial property development company as such appears to have become important in Britain only in the 1950s (Marriott, 1967).

Conversion of residential space

Much unplanned retail development arose then through the process of conversion of residential or other property to retail use. This process could occur either through a retailer buying residential premises freehold, or (probably more often) through the ground landlord seeing potential for retailing in a particular location and offering retail premises to rent. Until 1948 in Britain, change of land use from residential to commercial would not generally have required planning permission from the local authority. Thus, conversions could occur quickly in response to perceived demand.

The result of this conversion process in Britain was typically a mixed-use building, with the ground floor used for retail sales and the upper floor(s) for residential. In some cases only the front room on the ground floor would be retail: the rear rooms would be family accommodation, with other families living upstairs. This pattern can still be found in small shops in the older urban residential areas of Britain. In other cases, the rear ground floor might be used for storage, repairs or even manufacture of retail goods.

As trade grew, more and more of the building could become used for retail purposes. Upper floors might be used for storage, or even as an extension of the sales area. Where shops coalesced to form a recognisable group, 'shop fronts' were often built out towards the road, occupying part of the former front garden. This pattern is common in the surviving Georgian streets of inner London: in 1849, an architect complained that 'one by one each house casts a proboscis forth in the shape of a long, low, narrow shop, covering the dull patch that once was dignified as the front garden' (quoted in Dyos, 1966: 148). Another solution to the problem of overcrowding was to rent or buy adjoining premises.

A further essential stage in the growth of specialised retail areas was the development of the 'lock-up shop' (Carter and Lewis, 1990: 94). For the first time, retailing was separated from residential use. By 1911, 172,000 shops in England and Wales (28 per cent of the total) were in buildings which were not used as dwellings (Jeffreys, 1954: 15). Shop premises which had no other use could more easily be bought and sold, demolished or renovated.

Central areas

The town centre is a point of maximum accessibility and contact, usually where roads leading to other settlements meet. Town centre retailing in Britain originally took the form of periodic markets: visiting farmers and traders would bring goods into the town on a regular basis for selling to the town's population, and might also buy goods made within the town itself. The first permanent shops appear to have been sited around markets, with their proprietors frequently also owning a market stall (Wild and Shaw, 1979). Such shops became common in the eighteenth century in market towns (Phillips, 1992), although records suggest the conversion of properties around market places as early as the sixteenth century

(Conzen, 1960). As the demand for retail goods grew, shops would be developed, mainly through conversion, in streets adjoining the market place. During the nineteenth century, the demand for retail premises in town centres grew rapidly, especially in towns of rapid population growth.

Local government action was also important in the development of specialised central area retailing. First, many municipal corporations (the predecessors to local authorities) set up local boards with responsibilities for lighting and paving during the first half of the nineteenth century. The work of these boards created secure and attractive areas which customers would be prepared to visit for purposes of shopping (Carter and Lewis, 1990). Second, many private parliamentary acts were passed during the century to enable street realignment and widening, and provision of market halls. In England and Wales there were nearly 400 bills passed for the latter purpose alone, with the greatest number in the 1850s (Shaw and Wild, 1979; Shaw, 1992). Market halls were necessary particularly in the new industrial towns which lacked traditional market places, and remained the principal point of sale for perishable foodstuffs well into the twentieth century (Carter and Lewis, 1990: 94).

This resulted in further consolidation and extension of the town centre, and rapid increases in rental values in the central area itself (Wild and Shaw, 1979; Shaw and Wild, 1979). Towards the end of the century, covered arcades were developed in several towns to utilise space between major shopping streets (Mackeith, 1985). These may be seen as the forerunner of the planned 'shopping precinct' of the 1960s, or even the more recent enclosed developments within town and city centres. In some cases, whole streets were redeveloped in order to provide additional space for retailing. For example, in Glasgow:

> A street of mainly two- and three-storey buildings, comprised of both Georgian town houses with shop-fronts inserted and elegant small-scale Regency shop-front buildings, often with private gardens at the rear and some with their upper floors still in residential use, was transformed by 1894 into a street of mainly four-storey Victorian buildings. These had continuous shop-fronts, almost entirely commercial use of their upper floors, approximately treble the floor-space concentration of the buildings they replaced (since the whole of plots were built over) and even greater increases in cubic capacities, since ceilings were higher.
>
> (Whitehand, 1987: 121)

The middle of the nineteenth century saw the beginning of two very significant developments in retailing: the department store and the multiple retailer. Developments by both of these organisations were important in giving the town centre much of its present-day appearance and character.

Department stores were particularly important in reshaping major town and city centres. The department store originated in the middle of the century, in two ways (Jeffreys, 1954; Shaw, 1992). First, the 'bazaars', covered areas in which many different types of goods were sold by separate independent traders, became consolidated under one ownership. Second, 'monster stores', selling mainly drapery goods in the early nineteenth century, extended their range into clothing, furnishings, grocery provisions and other goods, often building up an important mail order trade in addition to their business at the store itself. The space requirements of the department store were much greater than the average shop building could supply. Hence, department stores established suitably large premises in two ways (Shaw, 1992). First, they expanded through the purchase of adjoining retail or residential premises, without total redevelopment. Second, they bought up neighbouring premises and demolished them, building a brand new, large store. In some cases, this involved a movement from the original location, as in the cases of Marshall and Snelgrove in the West End of London, to an 'island site' which maximised the street frontage of the store (Shaw and Wild, 1979).

Multiple retailers also originated during the late part of the nineteenth century. The number of multiple firms in the grocery and provisions trade increased from 14 in 1880 (owning 108 branches) to 114 in 1900 (3,444 branches) (Fraser, 1981: 116). Other multiples grew in footwear retailing, and then clothing. Jesse Boot began selling proprietary medicines in 1874; by 1900 there were 181 branches, and by 1914, there were 560 (Carter and Lewis, 1990: 92). The early locational policies of such firms do not appear to be well documented, but it might be supposed that, apart from some of the grocery stores, branches were almost entirely in town and city centres.

Suburban retailing

The nineteenth century also marked the beginnings of retail development outside town centres, serving the needs mainly of the local population. A typical location for early shopping development was the major road, either on the fringe of the town centre or within residential areas. This would provide good access for both suppliers of goods and customers. In addition, the initial residential development was often to a grander scale along major roads than in the side streets behind, allowing more potential for retail conversion. It is possible that this latter reason may be more important in explaining the widespread development of 'ribbon' shopping areas along major roads in British towns, than the advantages of access.

Although the vast majority of suburban shops were (and are today) owned by small independent firms, the growth of grocery multiples such as Lipton's and Home & Colonial (Jeffreys, 1954; Mathias, 1967), and the many co-operative societies (Jeffreys, 1954; Purvis, 1992) also enhanced the development of suburban convenience retailing. In contrast to independent retailers, who would be expected to rent or purchase converted houses, the better capitalised multiples and co-operatives were likely to develop their own stores.

In many residential areas, covenants attached to individual houses prevented the establishment of any form of 'trade': an attempt by the original landowner or builder to preserve the social status of the residential area. Hence, development of retailing (as well as public houses and other forms of trade) may have been restricted to the less well-off or more haphazardly developed areas of a town.

An additional case of conversion from residential was the 'corner shop'. This was usually converted from residential use, and served the community with routine consumer goods such as groceries or cooked food to take away. Such shops may have started with the residential tenants selling goods from the front room on a casual basis, and the rear of the ground floor and the upper floor(s) were likely to remain in residential use.

The urban retail hierarchy

These various types of unplanned development form parts of the so-called 'hierarchy of shopping centres' familiar to any geography student. Originally developed from observation of settlement sizes in southern Germany (Christaller, 1966), the idea of the hierarchy was adapted in an attempt to explain the location and size distribution of business centres in several American cities, of which the most detailed case study was Chicago (Berry, 1963; Simmons, 1964). Further discussion and critical reviews of central place theory can be found in several texts (e.g. Berry and Parr, 1988; Beavon, 1977; S. Brown, 1992; Carter, 1981; Davies, 1977a; Jones and Simmons, 1990; O'Brien and Harris, 1991).

A fourfold classification of 'town centre', 'district centre', 'neighbourhood centre' and 'local centre' was suggested by Burns (1959) and was frequently applied in British planning practice. This classification is usually applied to unplanned retail areas and planned centres alike. Typical sizes and catchment areas for these types of retail area are shown in Table 6.1.

Table 6.1 Characteristics of traditional shopping areas in British towns

Shopping area	Catchment area	Shop numbers and types
Central area	Whole town, plus surrounding suburbs and rural areas	Usually over 200; mainly comparison and specialist goods
District centre	Inner urban or suburban area of 20,000–50,000 population	Around 100; convenience and comparison goods
Neighbourhood centre	Surrounding residential area of about 10,000 population	20–40; mainly convenience goods
Local centre	Immediate surrounds; 500–5,000 population	1–10; Convenience goods

Source: Guy (1984: Table 1)

A much discussed question in retail geography has been the nature and function of urban 'ribbons'. This term refers to the linear arrangements of shops along urban streets. In Berry's (1963) classification of retailing in Chicago, ribbons were separated from 'nucleations', not simply because their spatial form is different, but also because in the American situation their function is usually different from that of nucleated retail areas. The American ribbon exists essentially to serve motorists, providing a mixture of motor accessories, fast food and other requirements for 'passing trade'; whereas the nucleated centre essentially serves the surrounding residential population. In British towns, however, ribbons of retail and business use arose during the nineteenth century for reasons both of access and availability of premises for commercial use, as discussed earlier in this chapter. Studies of retailing systems in British cities (e.g. Davies, 1974; Guy, 1976; Potter, 1982) have shown that some shopping areas that physically have the appearance of ribbons do, in fact, function partly as neighbourhood or district centres for the local population, rather than simply supplying goods for 'passing trade' using the highway. For this reason, classifications of shopping areas in British cities have either included ribbons in the conventional hierarchy of 'centres', or have described them as ribbons but have also indicated their central function for the local population (e.g. Davies, 1974). S. Brown (1991), however, in attempting a classification of retail areas that does not rely upon hierarchical notions, makes a basic distinction between 'unplanned clusters' and 'linear locations'.

Competition in unplanned retailing

The development of the retail hierarchy in urban areas represented a mixture of two familiar economic processes. First, each retail area possessed a degree of monopoly, conferred by its location. Local retailing grew up in response to local demands for everyday goods and services. Before the establishment of car ownership amongst most urban households, consumers were limited to shopping in retail areas within easy reach: for routine shopping, this could mean centres within walking distance (Guy and Wrigley, 1987). Thus, many unplanned retail areas would to some extent hold monopoly positions based on their location with reference to a catchment population. Indeed, central place theory is based upon the premise that consumers will normally visit the nearest centre that offers them the goods and services that they require.

However, within these retail areas, the second economic process – competition – would often exist between retailers selling similar goods or services. Without the types of regulation normally found within planned shopping centres, which limit the range of goods and services which shops can sell (Savitt, 1985), competition was much more likely to arise. Despite the supposed advantages to the consumer of competition between retailers, it can be argued that competition inhibited the growth of individual retail outlets. They would be less likely to be able to grow to a size where economies of scale would begin to take effect (McClelland, 1966).

In practice, competition also existed between retail areas themselves. Survey evidence shows that consumers often do not visit their nearest shopping centre for routine goods and services, even when shopping on foot (Guy and Wrigley, 1987). This apparently irrational behaviour recognises that shops have attributes other than location; a longer journey offers more utility to the shopper if it allows greater choice or lower prices, for example.

The effects of competition have been to bring failure as well as success. Thus, unplanned retail areas have contracted as well as expanded: either through a reduction in spending power in their local catchment area, or through increasing uncompetitiveness with other shopping centres, planned or unplanned. The most dramatic reduction in numbers of unplanned retail premises has been in areas of slum clearance and population loss, most typically the inner areas of industrial conurbations (Shepherd and Thorpe, 1977). However, in many other urban areas there has been a steady fall in numbers of retail units, particularly 'corner shops' and within inner urban shopping ribbons. Retail premises have been converted to other commercial uses, or in some cases back to residential use. Thus, the cycle of unplanned retail development has almost been completed.

OWNERSHIP PATTERNS AND INVESTMENT IN UNPLANNED RETAILING

The distinguishing characteristic of unplanned retailing is that it has become established in a piecemeal manner rather than through a series of co-ordinated investment decisions. Nevertheless, much unplanned retail space is owned by large multiple retail concerns, property companies and financial institutions. This section attempts to quantify the extent of this interest, and discusses some implications.

Ownership patterns in unplanned retail areas in Britain have been a poorly investigated topic. Only recently have ownership records for land and property become accessible to the general public via access to Land Registry records (on payment of the appropriate fee).

In smaller unplanned retail areas it may be assumed that most retail premises are owned either by descendants of the original builder/landowner concerned, or by the retail firm itself. To complicate the issue, many premises are probably owned on long leasehold by the retailers concerned. In larger unplanned retail areas, where multiple retailers, banks and so on are important, the pattern of ownership is likely to be more complex. First, the national companies may own at least some of the premises from which they trade. Second, some premises are likely to be owned as investment properties by financial institutions. Third, in some cases properties may be owned by property companies, either as a prelude to redevelopment, or for other reasons. Table 6.2 shows that, in a small sample of major town centres in Britain, financial institutions and developers/property companies owned in 1987 about three-quarters of the retail properties, and retailers only one-tenth of the total. However, these estimates will have included

Table 6.2 Ownership of sample of retail properties in six prime shopping areas, 1987*

Property owners	No. of outlets	%
Financial institutions	64	40
Developers/property companies	57	36
Retailers	16	10
Local authorities	14	9
Others	9	6
Total	160	100

Source: Bernard Thorpe (1990: Table 8)
Note: * Centre sample: Cardiff, Chester, Lancaster, Milton Keynes, Oxford and Peterborough

properties within planned shopping centres. In unplanned retail areas, the proportions owned by retailers and by other agencies may be much higher. These issues are examined in the remainder of this section.

Ownership by multiple retailers

The extent of freehold or long leasehold ownership in unplanned retail areas by multiple retailers and service providers is very difficult to establish. A few indirect indicators can be used. The Retail Inquiry shows that in 1988 the 835 'large multiple' retail organisations, each with at least ten outlets, operated from 63,900 premises. However, some of these would have been located in planned developments; others would be in unplanned areas but held on short leases. Table 6.3 shows that in a sample of ten medium-sized town centres surveyed during the mid-1980s, between 11 per cent and 55 per cent of premises operated by large multiple retailers were located in planned centres opened since 1965, the remainder being in the largely or wholly 'unplanned' remainder of the shopping centre.

This still does not reveal whether premises in unplanned retail areas are owned by the multiples or simply leased by them. Another clue lies in the declared property assets of the firms themselves. Freehold and long leasehold ownership by major retail firms is discussed further in Chapter 7. Generally, operators of large department and variety stores tend to own their premises freehold, having often organised their development to a particular specification in the first instance. However, more specialist multiples that trade from smaller premises are less likely to own the premises. Table 6.4 shows that, at one extreme, Great Universal Stores appear to own all their premises, while at the other, companies that expanded rapidly in the 1980s, such as Tie Rack, Sock Shop, Next and Burton, are paying relatively high amounts of rent and therefore would appear to own few of their premises' freehold.

Table 6.3 Multiple firms' representation in town centres

| Town centre | No. of multiple owned units in: | | Planned as % of all multiple units |
	Planned centres	Rest of town centre	
Aylesbury	42	34	55
Derby	46	95	33
Dudley	24	65	27
Eastbourne	43	53	45
Gloucester	43	78	36
Kidderminster	27	50	35
Macclesfield	22	32	41
Sunderland	38	67	36
Worcester	12	95	11
Yeovil	32	59	35

Source: *Newman's Retail Directory* (1988)

It is not necessarily the case that owning the bulk of one's outlets is an advantage for the retailer. First, freehold ownership may disguise the true costs of using property in expensive city centre locations. It has been argued that some of the major UK retailers would appear less successful financially if they had to pay market rents for their high street premises (Richards and MacNeary, 1991). Second, ownership of valuable freeholds may give rise to threats of takeover and 'asset stripping' by other, more aggressive companies. For this reason, and to gain an injection of capital, it may be advantageous for retail companies to sell their freeholds to property companies or institutions, and lease their premises from them. These issues are discussed further in Chapter 7.

Institutional ownership of retail premises in unplanned retail areas also appears to be widespread, though detailed estimates are not available. In 1985, it was estimated that nearly 55 per cent of the retail 'units' owned by a sample of institutions were of the 'standard single' variety (Investment Property Databank, 1986); and over a quarter of these retail units were built before 1940. This suggests that shop premises in unplanned retail areas form a significant part of many investment portfolios. The standard single units comprised about 54 per cent of the capital value of institutions' retail holdings in 1981; by 1991 this proportion had fallen slightly to 47 per cent (Investment Property Databank, 1992: 131). The number of such properties had fallen from 4,210 to 3,607 during this decade, indicating either the effects of redevelopment or some sales to non-institutional interests.

Premises in good condition and let to reputable tenants are, of course, characteristic of 'prime' investments (see Chapter 4). Indeed, it can occur that the 'best pitches' in a town centre lie in the unplanned part of the centre rather than

Table 6.4 Rent as a percentage of sales, 1989–1990

Store	Rent as % of sales
GUS	Nil
Marks & Spencer	1.1
Argos	2.1
Boots	3.2
Kingfisher	3.4
Sears	4.1
Dixons	4.2
W.H. Smith	4.3
Storehouse	6.0
Laura Ashley	6.3
Ratners	7.1
Pentos	8.2
Burton	8.4
Etam	9.5
Next[1]	10.0+
Tie Rack	11.2
Sock Shop[2]	11.3

Source: Richards and MacNeary (1991: Table 2.6)
Note: [1] 4.4% for company as a whole
Note: [2] Based on 1988–1989 figures

in any planned area. Thus, purchases of single retail premises in prime locations are generally acceptable to institutions, although it is more likely that retail premises are acquired in 'bundles' – from landowners, multiple retailers, property companies, or other financial institutions.

The 'secondary' retail market, most of which is composed of premises in town centres but outside the best locations within the centre, probably consists almost entirely of older properties in 'unplanned' areas.

The outcome can be a very fragmented pattern of ownership, both with respect to any particular institution, and within any shopping centre. This contrasts strongly with planned centres, which are normally under one ownership.

The commitment of institutions to the more successful unplanned retail areas also has implications for future possibilities of redevelopment. Much of the planned shopping centre development of the 1960s and early 1970s was carried out by developers who were able to accumulate sites by purchasing individual properties piecemeal at use value rather than development value, as discussed in Chapter 3. At that time, many owners were not aware of the potential for redevelopment, and thus sold their properties at what appeared in hindsight to be low prices. This is less likely to happen in the future, where premises are owned by large financial institutions, who will be more aware of development possibilities as well as existing use values. Indeed, the assembly of sufficiently large sites for redevelopment could be problematic if their ownership is split between several major institutions, none of whom may wish to see land with potential for redevelopment passing to a rival institution.

Major *property companies* also own parts of unplanned retail areas, either as a prelude to redevelopment, or through purchases of bundles of property. One example is the ownership of 270 Stead & Simpson shoe shops by Clayform Properties. Following takeover of Stead and Simpson in 1989, Clayform closed twenty-nine units in 'prime town centres and high streets' and had let nine units at 'considerably enhanced rents' by the end of the year (Clayform, 1989). It is intended, however, to retain the units in 'market towns and local suburban centres' as a viable retail operation.

UNPLANNED RETAILING AND RETAIL PLANNING

In many developed economies, particularly in Western Europe, unplanned retail areas comprise the majority of retail space. In Britain it is possible to make a rough estimate of the proportion of total retail and service floorspace occupied by unplanned retail areas. This can be done through deduction: in England, in 1986 there were some 837 million sq. ft. of 'retail space' as assessed by the Inland Revenue Valuation Office (Hillier Parker, 1988; Schiller and Boucke, 1989). From this total should be deducted about 80 million sq. ft. of space in shopping centre developments in England (Hillier Parker, 1987), and perhaps 60 million sq. ft. of free-standing planned development of grocery superstores and retail warehouses. This leaves about 700 million sq. ft. of unplanned retailing, representing around 80–85 per cent of the total retail area in England. Its share of turnover would of course be lower, as planned centres include shops that are larger and that trade more efficiently than the average for unplanned retail areas. Nevertheless, unplanned retail space is of great importance in most local property markets, and its condition and potential has wider economic and social implications. This section explores these issues, concentrating particularly on implications for the local retail economy and the built environment.

Retail planning problems in areas of decline

A substantial amount of unplanned retail development lies within successful town and city centres, or in other areas where retailing is well supported by the local population or by visitors and tourists. The opportunities and problems that this creates are discussed later in this section. It is likely, however, that most unplanned retailing lies within retail areas that are of marginal viability overall. These may include town centres that have suffered severe competition from new retail development elsewhere, or that are in areas of economic and population decline. They also include a very large number of suburban retail areas, particularly shopping ribbons developed initially in the nineteenth century.

One of the most serious problems in retail planning at present is the management of decline in these retail areas. Decline can manifest itself in increasing vacancy rates for commercial buildings, culminating in physical deterioration and sometimes structural collapse. There can also be changes in the nature of shopping facilities, from standard provision of routine goods needed by local people, to 'twilight' premises selling goods and services of a dubious nature to passing trade (Davies, 1977b). Older, unplanned retail areas are often characterised by heavy traffic owing to their location on major roads, but it is loss of trade and physical decline which is generally held to be the major problem.

Research has shown that injection of public sector capital, usually in the form of grants to shopkeepers to maintain the physical structure of the shops, may give temporary benefits; but it may only delay the inevitable decline of shopping centres in areas where the local customer base is in decline (Department of the Environment, 1989b).

One solution sometimes suggested for declining unplanned retail areas is to carry out 'renewal' in the form of a planned scheme within the centre. Whether this is appropriate or not may depend upon the nature of the unplanned retail area. Any planned development involves heavy 'up-front' costs, which are normally reclaimed through suitable levels of rent. These levels are likely to be higher than those charged for unplanned retail premises in the same location, whose rents partly reflect historic costs of development. Thus, new retailing has of necessity to be more efficient (in terms of sales per unit of floor area) than the norm for older, unplanned development. This means that unless the new development succeeds in attracting more spending into the retail area as a whole, the planned scheme will, in effect, be replacing a larger amount of unplanned retailing. Hence, the development of new retailing in a declining shopping retail area can hasten the decline of the remainder of the centre. A detailed account of such a process is provided in a report by the Benwell Community Project (1979) (see also Davies, 1984: 232).

Management of retail decline is still an unfashionable topic in retail planning circles, but one which local authorities and other public sector agencies will increasingly have to tackle. King (1987) discusses the future of retail areas that are suffering from competition from new development, population loss in catchment areas, physical obsolescence or some combination of these problems. He concludes that the less successful areas should be seen by planners as locations for a mixture of small-scale economic activity, rather than primarily as retail centres.

Retail planning problems in town centres

The legacy of unplanned retail development in more successful locations, mainly town centres, can also be problematic, although some of these 'problems' can also be seen as opportunities. Problems are of two types. The first is where retail change is inhibited by characteristics of the properties available. The small size of most unplanned retail properties, and the fragmented pattern of ownership often found in such retail areas, means that retail premises cannot easily be enlarged to improve efficiency. Retailers wishing to take up retail space within existing shopping centres may be inhibited from so doing by a lack of sufficiently large available retail units, or by peculiarities of land ownership. To take two examples from the author's recent research in retail patterns in small towns in Wales:

1 Multiple retailers have from time to time expressed interest in opening stores in a town centre. A typical requirement would be a sales area of at least 22 ft. by 80 ft. (1,760 sq. ft.), but most of the retail premises in the prime retail area of the town were built in the nineteenth century and offer a sales area of between about 150 and 600 sq. ft.
2 Local businessmen would like to open a new store in the town centre, but prefer to buy premises' freehold. At the time of the study, shops becoming vacant were always offered on short leases.

A lack of sufficiently large premises can be overcome in the longer term by planned development of new retail space. However, rents required from new space may be much higher than that quoted for existing space, thus deterring potential tenants. Problems related to ownership structures are also difficult to overcome in the short term.

The second set of problems in unplanned retail areas lies in the adverse environmental effects which existing retail activity and new retail development can create. First, unplanned retail areas are usually in formerly residential areas and occupy frontages along major roads. This generally means that individual stores have no car parking space for employees and customers; access to the store may be confined to the front of the shop. This creates inconvenient working conditions in the shop itself, while outside the shop, delivery vehicles block main roads and customers drive around in search of a parking space. This leads to traffic congestion, danger for pedestrians, and environmental pollution.

Second, problems arise concerning the use of upper floors. Unplanned shop premises in town centres often comprise at least three floors, with retailing simply on the ground floor. The highest rent-paying use for upper floors is likely to be offices, but problems of limited space and access can mean that these premises are not easily let to office users. Hence, upper floors are often left vacant, to the detriment of the environment in general. In recent years in Britain, a movement to encourage the (re)establishment of residential uses on upper floors has grown (Walker, 1990; Petherick, 1992). This is argued partly from a perceived need to make use of upper floors, to help maintain buildings of architectural interest, and partly to increase the number of people living in town centres, an objective which is held to extend use of the centre throughout the week and add atmosphere and variety to the centre (Civic Trust, 1989).

These problems in town centres have led to much discussion amongst both retailers and land use planners. The favoured solution in the 1950s and 1960s was to seek a partial replacement of existing retailing by enclosed shopping centres (Ministry of Housing, 1962). This phase is discussed in more detail in Chapters 5 and 8. A reaction eventually arose to such proposals: partly because of the loss of areas of historic and architectural interest, and partly through the perceived poor quality in constructional and architectural terms of some of the new development. This reaction led to the notion that modern retailing should be accommodated within the existing built environment as far as possible, and that if new development was desirable in order to maintain a centre's competitive position, it should respect the scale and character of the existing environment (Royal Town Planning Institute, 1988: Chapter 7). It was also realised that the advantages to the retailer of a well-organised and managed environment, found in planned shopping centres, could also to some extent be created in the unplanned retail area. Two concepts are now prominent in retail planning in town centres: environmental improvement (including traffic-calming and pedestrianisation) and town centre management.

Environmental improvement

Investor confidence in town centres is strengthened when it is perceived that the local authority is taking meaningful steps to make the centre more attractive in appearance. Such measures can range from extensive repaving and landscaping schemes, which might or might not embrace pedestrianisation measures, to small-scale maintenance works on Council property, such as public conveniences or tourist information kiosks. A co-ordinated approach to shopfronts, street furniture and signing also assists. The local authority also has an important role in ensuring public car parks are clean and tidy, well maintained and inviting to shoppers.

(Royal Town Planning Institute, 1988: para. 7.48)

Pedestrianisation is perhaps the most important of these improvements. It involves ideally the removal of all traffic from the shopping street, turning it into a pedestrian way. This can bring major environmental benefits at relatively little cost. In most cases, it has been found that retail turnover improves after pedestrianisation, despite retailers' common fears that it will inhibit trade (Hass-Klau, 1988). This appears to be because the pedestrianised street is itself more attractive to shoppers, and possibly also because retailers can place goods or advertising material outside the store without seriously obstructing pedestrian flow. In many cases, however, full pedestrianisation is difficult to achieve, because there is no alternative to the street itself for access for delivery vehicles. The usual solution here is to restrict delivery to (say) before 10.30am and after 7.00pm, and to limit vehicle access to delivery vehicles during these times, so that the street does not become a thoroughfare at night. A more flexible compromise is *traffic-calming*, in which vehicles requiring access to the shops are generally allowed but have to give way to pedestrians. Special forms of street paving are often used to make it clear to vehicle drivers and pedestrians that the latter have priority (TEST, 1988).

The ultimate objective of a pedestrianisation scheme should be to allow pedestrians priority throughout the whole of the shopping centre. This objective has been virtually achieved in many German cities (Hass-Klau, 1988). The British practice appears generally to fall short of this ideal, although some good examples can be found.

The other methods of environmental improvement listed above are to some extent consequent on pedestrianisation or traffic-calming, such as the use of traditional materials and designs for paving and street furniture. A largely separate issue is the improvement of shop fronts, which has become a common exercise in towns of historic interest. Here, grants are usually made available to retailers to encourage projects ranging from provision of hanging flower-baskets to complete renovation of a building, involving removal of unsympathetic accretions to the original structure.

Town centre management

Town centre management is an attempt to replicate some of the advantages of planned shopping centres in the whole of a town centre. These advantages include regular cleaning and litter removal; maintenance of pedestrian routes, vehicle access and car parking; promotion and marketing of the centre; and organisation of special events and entertainments to help attract custom. It is felt that these techniques should be applied to the unplanned areas of town centres, in the interests of the centre as a whole.

Town centre management appears to have been suggested initially in Britain in the early 1980s, by leading retailers and other private sector interests (e.g. Spriddell, 1980; see Wells, 1991 for a detailed discussion). The concept arose through awareness that many town centres were increasingly being seen by the public as disorganised, badly signposted, dirty and polluted, and sometimes physically dangerous places (Bowlby, 1987). With increasing competition from off-centre retailing, and the threat of regional shopping centres, the established town centres needed to take positive steps to maintain their competitive position.

Town centre management usually involves three types of activity:

- *development* – making capital improvements;
- *management* – keeping it running efficiently; and
- *promotion* – creating an image and climate of success.

(Baldock, 1989: 53)

It has become an established feature in Britain, with the appointment of over fifty town or city centre managers by the middle of 1993. In several other towns a management initiative has been set up without employment of a town centre manager as such. A typical arrangement in either case will include two types of committee. The first is a steering group, composed of representatives of sponsoring organisations, such as local authorities, retailers, the chamber of trade, the police, etc., and intended to guide the broad direction of the town centre management initiative. Second, a working group with similar representation organises more detailed action programmes (Association of Town Centre Management, 1992).

Stansbury (1993) classifies town centre managers as 'enablers' or 'doers'. The enabler takes a strategic role and relies on other actors to carry out agreed tasks. The doer takes direct responsibility for such tasks, including street cleaning, other environmental improvements and promotional activity. However, success to date appears to have been modest, partly because the level of financial participation by the private sector has been disappointing. However, two major companies, Boots and Marks & Spencer, have contributed both financial and human resources to town centre management schemes (Hollins, 1993).

In the absence of a unified ownership structure in town centres, there is only a limited number of ways of improving the functioning and status of their retail areas. Town centre management has the potential to remove some of the more unpleasant and inefficient aspects of unplanned retail areas, and to make some improvements to the overall retail performance of a centre through development and promotional activity. However, individual retailers, particularly where they own premises' freehold, have freedom of choice as to whether or not to improve their premises in the public interest.

It can be claimed that this state of affairs is in fact desirable: where allowed to compete with each other, retailers may become more efficient, widen product ranges, and generally provide a better service. The fragmented ownership structure of unplanned retail areas is valuable in allowing relatively easy access into retailing by independent businessmen/women: independents often find it difficult or impossible to convince the owners and managers of planned centres that they are sufficiently credit-worthy to be allowed access to retail units. The result tends to be that planned centres (especially where located within older town centres) are characterised largely by multiple retailers, trading from standard facias and selling standardised ranges of goods, whereas the unplanned parts of town centres are much more varied in type of retailer, style of facia and window display, and variety of goods sold.

CONCLUSIONS

This chapter has shown that unplanned retail areas are, because of their sheer volume of retail space, a very significant part of the retail scene in Britain. In addition, many of the most popular and valuable retail areas are unplanned: their architectural and environmental qualities have increased their popularity. The characteristic mixture of multiple and independent retailers in the more successful unplanned retail areas is also an attractive feature, which tends to be missing from the more successful planned centres.

The old concept that unplanned retail floorspace is inefficient and should be replaced by planned centres is thus no longer held in planning circles. Some unplanned retailing, particularly where located on major roads, still provides unsatisfactory conditions for both retailers and shoppers, and undesirable external effects. However, the variety and continuity with tradition provided by unplanned retail space within town and city centres is now highly valued. It could be argued that the onus is on planned centre developers to show that their proposals can fit into the existing pattern of retailing, in terms of both physical appearance and pedestrian and traffic access routes.

Chapter 7

Development by retailers

INTRODUCTION

Much retail development is carried out by retail firms themselves, usually for their own use. This chapter deals mainly with development by retailers over the last thirty years or so. It concentrates on two main topics. The first of these is the development by retailers of so-called 'large new stores' in locations outside major shopping centres. These have comprised some of the largest construction programmes ever associated with retail companies. The second topic is the property development, investment and disposal activities of major retailers in Britain. This little-researched area is shown to have major implications for profitability of retailers themselves, as well as for the built environment.

Development by retailers is one of the main modes of development discussed in Chapter 3. In some ways it is a very simple model of development, and could be summarised (ironically for retailing) as 'cutting out the middleman'. A major development project involves, however, the skills identified in Chapters 2 and 3, no matter who carries them out. Therefore a retail firm carrying out development on its own behalf must either buy in, or internalise, the skills and expertise required. These include site identification, demand estimation, design of the development, land purchase, and negotiation with town planners. Only a very large company with a co-ordinated programme of store development is likely to possess all of these skills in-house. Smaller companies will need to 'buy in' whatever skills are necessary.

Retailer development has been important over a long period of time. In Chapter 6, it was shown that development of large new department stores contributed much to the growth of town centre retailing in the nineteenth century. The stores were important in their own right, and also enhanced the status of the town centre, thus attracting further growth of 'unplanned' retailing. In the first half of the twentieth century, the variety store chains of F.W. Woolworth, Marks & Spencer, British Home Stores and Littlewoods expanded rapidly. By 1939, these chains had expanded their coverage to around 1,200 stores in Britain, and commanded nearly 20 per cent of the total sales achieved by multiple retail organisations (Jeffreys, 1954: 69–70). Most of the new stores were purpose-built for the retailers concerned: Woolworth and Marks & Spencer both developed characteristic architectural styles to facilitate immediate recognition, irrespective of location.

During the 1950s and 1960s there may have been less development by retailers than in the periods before or since. The major department and variety stores had by that time reached capacity coverage, and town centres were beginning to undergo the more integrated shopping developments or redevelopments discussed in other chapters. The 1970s, however, saw the growth of development of large new stores in off-centre locations, mainly by a small number of major food retailers. This contributed to an estimate that by 1986, some 32 per cent of the new retail floorspace in Britain was developed by retail firms (Thompson and Wythe, 1988: 154). The pace of development of large new stores has increased since then, while the latter part of the 1980s also saw increasing involvement of 'high street' retailers in property development.

This chapter proceeds with a discussion of the motivations for development, and property investment and disinvestment, by retail firms. This is followed by a review of the recent store development programmes of major grocery retailers in Britain, including superstores, supermarkets and 'district centre' schemes. This topic is given detailed treatment because of its intrinsic importance and interest. After a brief discussion of recent and current store development programmes amongst other types of retailer, the final section examines the recent moves into other property development programmes by some of Britain's major 'high street' retailers.

PROPERTY DEVELOPMENT, INVESTMENT AND DISINVESTMENT BY RETAILERS

This section discusses the motivations for property development, investment and disinvestment by retail firms. Reasons why a firm should wish to develop its own retail outlets are first discussed. The focus then turns towards the substantial property portfolios held by major retail companies. These represent opportunities for participating in further property development, and for raising finance through disposal of selected properties to property companies or financial institutions. These two types of opportunity may be termed property investment and disinvestment. The section discusses these issues in general terms: detailed examples are given later.

Development by retailers – the preconditions

It may seem natural that a retail firm wishing to relocate or expand its network of shops would wish to carry out development itself. However, development requires an array of special skills which are unlikely to be in the possession of most retail organisations. A second factor is that many retailers will wish to locate within larger retail complexes, to benefit from the power of the whole centre to attract customers. In these circumstances, it makes sense to seek premises within a shopping centre, planned or unplanned, rather than construct one's own premises.

This means that programmes of store development by retailers are likely to take place only under certain conditions. These relate to the type of goods being sold and the particular site and location requirements of the firm, as well as its ability to organise the development process effectively. The following four conditions appear to be important:

1 A programme of expansion is necessary to generate demand for new stores. This expansion may be geographical, with the firm moving into new market areas, or an expansion in merchandise, requiring larger stores.
2 Existing retail premises available on the market are unsuitable for the firm's purposes, usually because of physical or site problems. These can include inadequate size, inappropriate internal layout, or poor vehicle access and parking.
3 The firm prefers its stores to be free-standing: competition with other retailers locally is not welcomed. The firm thus avoids conventional shopping centres that are developed by property companies or financial institutions.
4 Financial institutions are unwilling to provide long-term finance for free-standing store construction. This makes such development unattractive to property developers.

While it is not essential for all four conditions to apply, experience shows that in practice they have tended to.

Finance for development by retailers

A major issue, as with any type of property development, is the raising of finance for development. Retailers in carrying out development require short-term finance to pay land and construction costs, like any other developer. However, the issue of long-term finance may not always arise. Frequently, the retailer retains free-hold ownership of the completed scheme for purposes of retailing, although in some cases, retailers have subsequently used sale and leaseback arrangements to raise further capital. The following discussion concentrates on methods of raising short-term finance.

Four methods are generally used to provide short-term finance:

1 Use can be made of cash generated by retail sales. Profit not issued to shareholders in dividends can be used partly to finance new store development. Retailers of fast-moving consumer goods may at any time have substantial cash reserves, especially if suppliers of retail goods are paid in arrears.
2 Loans can be provided, usually by banks.
3 Property companies and/or financial institutions can be invited to participate in the development. This amounts to a mixture of short-and long-term finance, and is less commonly used for retailer development than for other forms of retail development.

4 The firm can raise money from shareholders and/or financial institutions, by
   making a rights issue or other form of share offer.

The case studies discussed below demonstrate all these methods. However, loans
and share issues have tended to be the main methods used for financing major
store development programmes in Britain. Share issues to finance retail expansion have a long history. Jeffreys (1954: 26) states that, at the end of the
nineteenth century, multiple retailers could not continue financing their expansion beyond about fifty branches simply through use of retained profits. At
this stage, it became necessary to become a public limited liability company and
to raise capital on the public market. In contrast, involvement of institutions,
either in joint ventures to develop new properties or in sale and leaseback
arrangements, is relatively recent and became important only in the 1980s.

Property management and investment by retailers

The major retail firms in Britain are substantial property owners in their own
right. Table 7.1 shows that sixteen of the leading firms claim to own nearly £17
billion of property overall, of which nearly £12 billion is owned freehold. This
total is probably an underestimate, because many of the land and building values
incorporated into these estimates are based upon historic costs or out-of-date
valuations. Calculations made by Goldman Sachs (1989a: 7) indicate that the
open market value of the property owned by thirteen leading 'high street'
retailers at that time may have been around £7.9 billion instead of the £6.2 billion
'net book value' shown on their balance sheets. These totals do, however, include
relatively small proportions of non-retail space (head office, warehousing, etc.)
as well as, in some cases, property owned outside the UK.

During the 1980s, retail firms came under increasingly rigorous scrutiny from the
stock markets, and property values began to rise rapidly after several years of
stagnation. These circumstances led several firms to take a more questioning stance
towards their considerable property holdings (Goldman Sachs, 1989a; Kleinwort
Benson, 1989). One product of this was an increase in disposals, particularly sale and
leaseback schemes. Another product of these pressures was the formation of
property-owning and/or property-developing subsidiaries of retail organisations.

A more cautious approach has been to form joint companies with property
developers or financial institutions. This approach has been used mainly for
one-off schemes involving property previously owned by the retailer concerned,
but some joint companies have continued to produce further schemes.

Property disposals and disinvestment

A common reaction to the identification of massive property assets has been to
dispose of some freeholds and long leaseholds. Goldman Sachs (1989a) identify
three reasons for such behaviour on the part of major retailers:

Table 7.1 Ownership of land and property by sixteen major retail companies

Company	Year	Net book value [1] of land and property [2] (£m)		
		Freehold	Long leasehold [3]	Short leasehold
Argyll Group	1992	962.1	147.7	135.0
Asda Group	1992	982.5	550.7	162.0
Boots	1992	801.8	162.9	31.1
Burton Group	1991	289.3	163.9	323.8
Co-operative Retail Services	1992	283.7	30.7	3.3
House of Fraser	1991	494.4	85.3	42.6
Kingfisher	1992	392.6	91.9	37.3
Kwik Save	1991	186.6	21.2	39.5
John Lewis	1992	356.2	276.7	60.0
Marks & Spencer[4]	1992	1,402.6	797.3	159.1
MFI	1991	99.2	38.7	27.7
J. Sainsbury	1992	2,451.9	502.1	146.1
Sears	1991	673.5	126.2	68.6
W. H. Smith	1991	184.2	8.2	15.8
Storehouse	1992	84.9	122.4	99.0
Tesco	1992	2,300.5	372.5	99.2

Source: Company reports

Note: [1] This does not usually represent a fully comprehensive up-to-date valuation of each company's land and property holdings
  [2] Totals include some non-retail properties although these are usually insignificant
  [3] Fifty years or more to run from date stated
  [4] Includes overseas properties

1 *By sale of retail branches on the open market.* Some branches may be seen as unprofitable, or may not correspond with the company's future plans, and are closed down. It is then natural to dispose of them on the open market, either individually or as a 'package'. Disposals, when on a large scale, may be seen as ways of raising capital (or reducing debts) rather than simply as rationalisation of operations.

2 *By sale (or lease) and leaseback.* A package of freehold properties is sold, either freehold or long leasehold, to a property company or financial institution. The company then leases the stores it wishes to continue operating on normal 'institutional leases' or on some other arrangement. The motive for this type of disposal is usually to raise finance for further expansion of operations. Alternatively, the money obtained may be invested to produce a short-term profit, since the rate of interest available from banks and other institutions is almost always higher than the yield obtainable from prime retail

property. This is known as the 'yield gap', and arises because the yield takes long-term growth prospects into account.

3 *By sale to a property-owning subsidiary.* This method can be used in order to make the opportunity costs of retail property ownership transparent to the firms itself and to shareholders. It may also be used as a cosmetic exercise to take debts off the balance sheet.

The results of programmes of store disposal have been to weaken significantly the value of property portfolios held by retail firms. Goldman Sachs (1989a: 9) estimate that between 1979 and 1989, their sample of major retailers disposed of £2.3 billion worth of property, at 1989 open-market values, some 22 per cent of the 1979 total.

These devices, aimed at either financing new expansion or improving a company's financial standing, were commonly used in the 1980s in both food and non-food retailing, and specific examples are discussed in later sections. While the focus of discussion here is upon their implications for retail development, one further effect should be noted. Any decision that involves diluting a company's property holdings, or raising new finance, alters the company's asset base and debt structure, making it possibly more vulnerable to short-term speculation and fluctuation in share values. The stock markets take in any case a notoriously short-term view of a company's prospects (Wrigley, 1987; Hallsworth, 1991; Myers, 1992).

LARGE-STORE DEVELOPMENT IN THE UK GROCERY INDUSTRY

Most development by retail firms has in recent years been in the form of large stores built outside traditional retail locations. Prominent among this movement has been a small number of grocery retailers. This section describes and explains their programme of new store development since the mid-1960s. The discussion concentrates on issues such as the competitive environment, criteria for size and location of superstores, and sources of finance for store development programmes. Other aspects of this programme, particularly the geographical spread of large grocery stores, and the town planning issues, are discussed in Chapter 5 and elsewhere (e.g. R.L. Davies, 1984; B.K. Davies and Sparks, 1989; Gayler, 1984).

The competitive environment

The retail grocery industry in Britain is, as in other developed countries, polarised between a small number of very large firms and a very large number of small firms. While the number of firms in all size categories has tended to decline (Figure 7.1), the market share has become more concentrated amongst the 'large multiples': firms that own at least ten shops. Figure 7.2 shows that these firms now take at least three-quarters of total turnover in food. In fact, firms with more

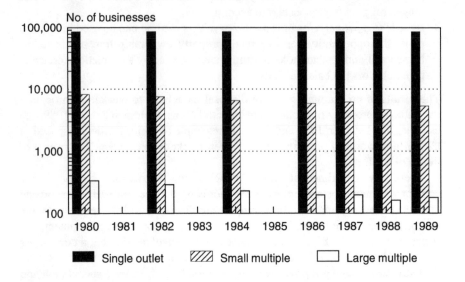

Figure 7.1 Food retail businesses, by ownership type
Source: Central Statistical Office (1992: Table 2 and Appendix A)

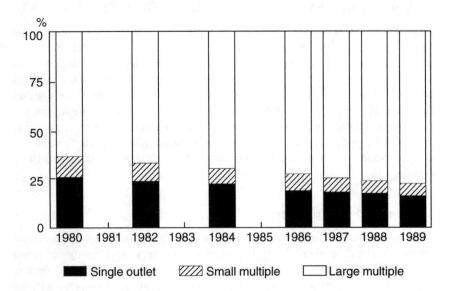

Figure 7.2 Shares of total food turnover, by ownership type
Source: Central Statistical Office (1992: Table 2 and Appendix A)

than one hundred shops (0.03 per cent of the food retailers) took over 60 per cent of sales in 1989 (Table 7.2). These statistics, which describe all retailers selling mainly food, probably underestimate the power of the large multiple grocery firms within the more narrowly defined grocery trade.

One feature that distinguishes grocery from other areas of retailing in Britain is that overall expenditure by consumers on food and related products has tended to remain almost constant over the years when monetary inflation is taken into account (Figure 2.2). This means that in order to grow, firms have had to attempt to increase their share of the market. This has occurred at aggregate and individual level.

At aggregate level, the multiples as a whole have greatly increased their share compared with both independents and co-operatives (Figure 7.2). This reflects the economies of scale available to larger firms, and particularly the ability to negotiate favourable bulk purchasing arrangements with suppliers. This has led to multiples showing consistent price advantages over independents over a wide range of grocery products (Guy and O'Brien, 1983; Guy, 1991a; McGoldrick, 1987, 1988). In addition, the multiples can raise capital much more easily than independents. This has proved necessary in order to build new stores, improve existing stores, introduce mechanisation and communications equipment, develop new distribution methods, and so on.

The leading multiples have also been in competition with one another to improve their share of the market (Table 7.3; Figure 7.3). This natural inclination of any major company has been magnified by pressure exerted by institutional shareholders: large grocery companies have until recently been considered to be very safe investments, because the consumer demand for groceries remains steady in time of recession. Firms are expected to perform well, increasing market share, profits and dividends from year to year.

Table 7.2 Concentration in food retailing, 1989

Size of business	Percentage of total:		
	Businesses	Outlets	Turnover
1 outlet	90.60	68.2	17.3
2–9 outlets	9.12	18.2	6.7
10–99 outlets	0.25	5.4	13.1
100–499 outlets	0.02	3.0	39.2
500++ outlets	0.01	5.2	23.7
Total	100	100	100

Source: Business Statistics Office (1992: Table 3)

Table 7.3 Market shares of major grocery retailers, 1992

Company	Share of sales through food and drink shops (%)
J. Sainsbury	11.7
Tesco	10.9
Argyll	7.1
Asda	6.2
Gateway	4.1
Kwik Save	3.6
Wm Morrison	1.8
Waitrose	1.6

Source: *The Grocer* (23 January 1993: 10)

Market share can be improved in three ways. First, a retailer can take over other grocery retailers and operate from all or some of their stores. This device was used in the 1980s by the Dee Corporation (subsequently Gateway, now Isosceles) and by Argyll Stores to build market share (Table 7.4). Tesco also used this device in 1987, taking over Hillard's to establish a strong base in Yorkshire without the expense of building new stores in an area already heavily developed.

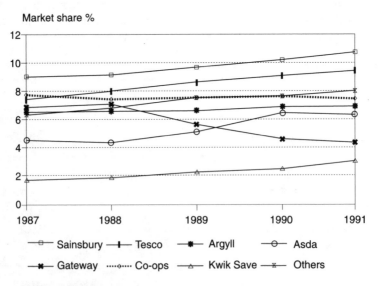

Figure 7.3 Market shares of major grocery retailers
Source: *Grocer* (5 Dec. 1992h)

Table 7.4 The rise of the Dee Company, 1979–1986

Year		Progress
1979		Alec Monk joins Linford (Carrefour)
1981		Renamed 'Dee Corporation'
1983	(June)	Takes over: Key Markets
	(Dec.)	Takes over: Wellworth
1984	(Sept.)	Takes over: Lennons
	(Oct.)	Takes over: International
1985	(Oct.)	Takes over: Lonsdale and Thompson
1986	(March)	Takes over: Herman's
	(April)	Purchases: Woolco stores from F.W. Woolworth
	(June)	Purchases: Fine Fare and Shoppers Paradise from Associated British Foods
	(Aug.)	Purchases: Medicare chemists from Reed International
	(Sept.)	Plans to convert all 1,100 grocery stores to Gateway format

Source: Guy (1987)

Second, the firm can attempt to increase turnover in existing stores, thus attracting custom from stores owned by rivals. Third, the retailer can build new stores, which attract custom in areas where shoppers may previously have visited the rivals' stores.

Recent research has suggested that the search for new store sites is a crucial element of competition between the major firms. In Britain, just five major firms take around 40 per cent of the food retail market (Table 7.3), and possibly up to 60 per cent of the grocery market (Nielsen, 1992: 45). Many observers have found an apparent lack of price competition between these firms, with many prices for commonly bought groceries being almost identical. The large stores owned by these companies also sell very similar assortments of products and offer a broadly similar shopping environment. Under these conditions, each new store can establish a loyal market of shoppers living closer to that store than to other stores, owned by other companies. Thus, the monopoly conferred on retail stores by their location, important in past times where shoppers could only travel short distances to shop, may have re-established itself under what amounts currently to monopolistic competition (Moir, 1990; Wrigley, 1991, 1993). The former author states:

> significant competition in the retail grocery trades, among the largest busi-
> nesses, is far from ubiquitous and does not affect all aspects of trading policy
> and behaviour. Competition takes many forms and varies in intensity. It is
> greater when retailers are seeking sites for new store development. It then falls

away after stores are built and trading. It is almost non-existent once a shopper is captured in a store.

(Moir, 1990: 116)

Smiddy (1991: 38) concurs, stating: 'Competition within the [retail grocery] industry has not been very evident on the trading front. It has, however, been acute in the quest for sites.'

In recent years, the largest firms have found that one of the most important means of improving market share is to open new stores. Since 1987, Tesco and Sainsbury have both increased their pace of store openings, while Safeway's rate has remained roughly constant and Asda's gone into sharp decline (Figure 7.4). In 1990–1991, for example, Tesco improved sales on the previous year by 17.5 per cent, of which 8.5 per cent represented takings from new stores and 9 per cent represented increased takings from existing stores (Tesco, 1991). By spring 1993, about a quarter of all Sainsbury's and Tesco's floorspace is likely to be in stores built within the previous three years (Table 7.5). Competition between the 'big five' in recent years is discussed in more detail later in this section.

This process of expansion is most effective if the new stores are built in areas where the firm does not yet operate stores. Geographical expansion was feasible and effective for all the major grocery retailers during the 1970s and 1980s. Each company started from a fairly narrowly defined geographical base, and during this period attempted to extend its operations through most of urban Britain, as exemplified in a study of Asda (Jones, 1981). Treadgold and Reynolds (1989) provide further examples.

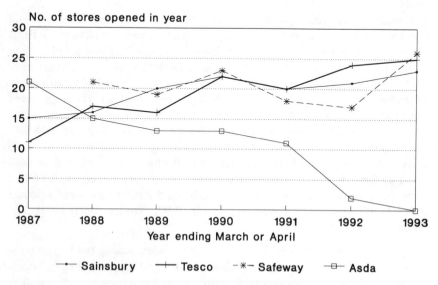

Figure 7.4 New large grocery store openings, 1987–1993
Sources: Company reports

Table 7.5 Modernity of grocery floorspace (in '000 sq. ft. sales area)

Company	Total space	Space opened 1991–1993	
Sainsbury	8,885	2,340	26%
Tesco	11,050	2,790	25%
Argyll	9,060	1,915	21%
Asda	8,645	980	11%
Gateway	6,350	300	5%

Source: Credit Lyonnais Laing (1991: 10)

Building new stores in areas already served by the firm may be less effective, because the new store will compete with existing stores. In some cases, the existing store(s) will be closed down. Figure 7.5 shows a steady trend of replacement of small supermarkets by superstores and large supermarkets during the 1980s.

Thus, a store development programme is crucial to the largest grocery retailers. Pressure to maintain such a programme has resulted in the companies using unusual methods to raise capital for store development. Another effect may have been inflation in land prices. These issues are discussed later in this section.

Another outcome of this competitive process is that smaller grocery firms find it very difficult to develop large new stores (McClelland, 1990). They can instead attempt to expand through buying existing (probably smaller and not optimally

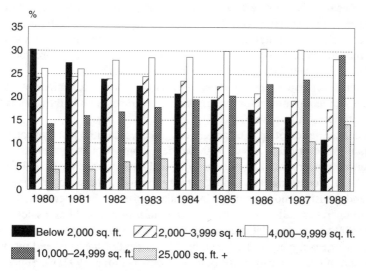

Below 2,000 sq. ft.   2,000–3,999 sq. ft.   4,000–9,999 sq. ft.
10,000–24,999 sq. ft.   25,000 sq. ft. +

Figure 7.5 Store size profiles, multiple grocery stores
Source: IGD Research Services

located) stores, or through reorientating their 'offer' to the consumer (Duke, 1991). One smaller firm – Kwik Save – has, however, followed a successful programme of new store development in the 1980s, albeit stores of a smaller size and in different types of location (Sparks, 1990).

Grocery superstore size

The largest grocery firms in Britain have mainly used the superstore to establish their presence in new areas of trading. The grocery superstore is usually defined as a single-level, self-service store of at least 25,000 sq. ft. sales area, selling a wide range of foods, and supported by car parking. The Unit for Retail Planning Information uses a slightly different lower size limit of 2,500 sq. m. (26,910 sq. ft.). This type of store offers advantages in terms of delivery access, car parking for staff and shoppers, flexible internal layout, and sufficient space to display the 20,000 food and grocery lines which a typical large store will carry.

The superstore can in fact be regarded as a scaled-down version of the *hypermarket*, a single-level store of at least 5,000 sq. m. sales area selling a wide variety of both convenience and comparison goods. The hypermarket appears to have originated in France in the early 1960s (Dawson, 1983: 89–92), and the first example in Britain (the Gem store at Nottingham, with 55,000 sq. ft. of sales area, built in 1964) preceded the development of grocery superstores in Britain. However, superstores rapidly became more popular among the major retailers. There appear to be two main reasons for this: first, the greater acceptability to town planners of a large store selling convenience goods rather than comparison goods; and second, the early experience of operating hypermarkets in Britain, which indicated that comparison goods were not selling successfully from the hypermarket format. However, most Asda and some Tesco and Co-operative stores continue to sell significant proportions of non-food items. It should be added that the French hypermarkets have established a much more successful record of selling non-foods, such as clothing and furnishings.

The term 'superstore' is now commonly used in Britain to include stores that fulfil the size requirements for hypermarkets. The discussion in the remainder of this chapter uses this convention.

The concentration of up to 60 per cent of grocery sales into just five companies in Britain is inextricably linked with the development of the superstore. Asda commenced grocery retailing only in 1965, and have established their 9 per cent share of the grocery market almost entirely through superstore retailing. Both Tesco and Sainsbury now regard their 'standard' offer as the superstore, although they still operate smaller units. The Tesco 'conforming store' has a sales area of over 35,000 sq. ft., and flat, free surface-level parking. These accounted for 62 per cent of the company's sales area, but 72 per cent of the sales and just under 80 per cent of the operating profit (Credit Lyonnais Laing, 1991: 6). Superstores also offer economies of scale to the operator, principally in wage costs (Shaw *et al.*, 1989), as exemplified in Table 7.6.

Table 7.6 Comparative wage costs, sales intensity and operating margins by size of store

Store size group (sq. ft. sales area)	Wage costs	Sales per sq. ft.	Operating margins
< 15,000	124	95	66
15,000–25,000	102	95	96
> 25,000	91	108	114
Company average	100	100	100

Source: Richards and MacNeary (1991: Table 2.8). Data are for J. Sainsbury plc and for 1990

The use made of superstore floorspace has changed since the 1970s. At that time, a typical superstore would include around 20,000 sq. ft. of food and grocery sales, and substantial areas of non-food sales, including clothing, electrical goods, and do-it-yourself and other household items. By the end of the 1980s, the food and grocery space had typically expanded to around 30,000 sq. ft., to include fresh fruit and vegetables, fresh fish and large ranges of frozen foods and delicatessen items. In Sainsbury's stores, non-foods typically include toiletries and cosmetics, and a few items of stationery and kitchenware. Asda and Tesco still sell clothing from their larger stores, but not electrical goods.

Relationships between gross floor area and sales area have also varied over time. The early superstores tended to rely upon direct deliveries of goods in bulk from individual suppliers, and hence required substantial storage areas. More recently, the major companies have developed their own distribution networks, or used a small number of 'third party' carriers (McKinnon, 1989). Goods can be sorted and prepared for shelf display in company warehouses, thus reducing the need for storage space in the superstore itself. The difference between gross and sales area is largely, in recent stores, space devoted to staff facilities. There are also consistent differences between the major companies, related partly to differences in definition of 'sales area'. Broadly, Tesco and Asda include all areas accessible to customers, whereas Sainsbury and Argyll do not (Table 7.7).

Grocery superstore location

In choosing whether to develop a superstore in a particular location, the fundamental rule is that the store must produce an acceptable rate of return on the initial investment. In estimating rates of return, the company concerned will need to make an estimate of annual sales from the proposed store. Tesco and Sainsbury expect their sales estimates to be accurate to within 10 per cent of the actual figure (Kleinwort Benson, 1991). The method used by Tesco is a version of the

Table 7.7 Proportion of sales area to gross area, major grocery retailers

Company	Sales area as % of gross area
J. Sainsbury	53
Tesco	67
Argyll	70
Asda	54

Source: Kleinwort Benson (1991: 14)

well-known 'gravity model' (Penny and Broom, 1988; see also Wilson, 1988; Guy, 1991b), which predicts the retail sales at a location, given information on population characteristics, travel times on the road network, and the attractiveness of rival stores in the area. Potential locations for superstores are evaluated using this type of model. It should be noted, however, that this method was developed by Tesco only during the 1980s; before 1981, the company had no store location unit and appears to have assessed the potential of new store locations in a less rigorous manner. It should be assumed that other major firms use similar methods, although definite information on this is hard to establish.

Despite the complexities of store location assessment and sales forecasting, it is possible to discern some fairly consistent relationships between superstore location and catchment area size. In the 1970s, Asda made use of simple requirements, variously described as a minimum of 80,000 population within 3 miles of the store (Jones, 1981: 198), or 70,000 population within 10–15 minutes' drive time (Unit for Retail Planning Information, 1977: 35). At that time, the likelihood of significant competition from other superstores close to the proposed store was much less than it would be today. Despite this fact, the necessary population catchment for superstores appears to have declined since the 1970s. Research by Thorpe (1991, Table IV) shows that travel-to-work areas of over 60,000 population are more likely than not to have at least one grocery superstore; areas with over 200,000 population are likely to have at least three. Commentators have claimed recently that a population of under 50,000 should be sufficient to support a single superstore (Brown, 1988, cited in BDP Planning, 1992: 23). Approximate calculations based upon 1989 data show that a superstore of 25,000 sq. ft. sales area trading at £600 per sq. ft., with a population catchment of 50,000, would absorb at least 40 per cent of the total amount of money available for spending locally in food shops, although a small proportion of sales would be in other product groups such as alcoholic drinks or cosmetics.

Siting within urban areas

The early days of hypermarkets and superstores saw a number of experiments at store development, with operators taking opportunities to either build new stores or adapt old industrial or warehouse buildings (Guy, 1988). In hindsight, it seems that the first large store in an urban area would inevitably attract large numbers of shoppers, and precise location within the area was not an important issue. In some cases, stores were developed where it was thought that town planners would acquiesce. In other cases, planning permission was refused, and the developer would appeal to the Secretary of State concerned (see Chapter 5).

Disputes with planners arose because the retailers' requirements for superstores were different from those for conventional shops; in particular, the conventional requirements that shops should be close to other shops, and within walking access of the local population, were now almost irrelevant. In addition, the large site requirements for superstores (up to 10 acres including access and car parking) ruled out location within most traditional shopping centres, which were often hemmed in by residential areas. It became clear in the late 1970s that the grocery companies preferred to develop in edge-of-town locations, which were cheaper to purchase than central sites, and were easily accessible by road. Other possible locations incurred greater costs to the firm, even though their social and planning benefits might be stronger (Guy, 1980a, 1980b). Chapter 5 discusses town planning policies, and the crucial role of central government guidance, in more detail.

The mid-1970s also saw the emergence of the new 'district centre', developed by retailers themselves, as a compromise means of developing superstores. These centres are discussed later in this chapter.

In the 1980s, the off-centre superstore became the norm, with other sites including town centres and 'purpose-built centres' decreasing in importance (Figure 7.6). Unfortunately, the data upon which this figure is based do not distinguish between in-town, edge-of-town and out-of-town locations, and the term 'purpose-built centre' appears to include both 'district centres' as discussed later in this chapter, and shopping malls built within unplanned town centres (Thorpe, 1991: 366). However, more detailed research in south Wales also suggests a trend towards development in free-standing, edge-of-town sites (Guy, 1988). This appears to have arisen partly from dissatisfaction by retailers with town centre and district centre locations; and partly from more tolerant attitudes of town planners. It became accepted that grocery superstores were unlikely in most circumstances to harm materially the established town centre; that they generated substantial volumes of traffic which could best be handled in off-centre locations; and that central government was placing increasing pressure on local authorities to accept superstore development proposals where these did not threaten 'material harm to interests of acknowledged importance'.

The pace of development

The early years of superstore development are associated with Asda and the Yorkshire company Wm Morrison, together with some of the Co-operative societies. It was not until the mid-1970s that Tesco and Sainsbury became heavily

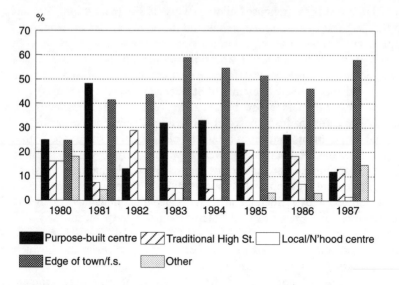

Figure 7.6 Type of site, new multiple grocery superstores
Source: IGD Research Services

involved (Davies and Sparks, 1989). Rates of development accelerated during the 1970s and early 1980s (Figure 7.7). Actual numbers built lagged behind the companies' interest in development, because of the time necessary to purchase the land and develop the store, and because of the high proportion of planning refusals encountered during this period (Davies and Sparks, 1989). These data also underestimate rates of new grocery store development, because Sainsbury and Safeway in particular have often built stores which are technically too small to be classified as superstores, but are generally over 15,000 sq. ft. in sales area (Treadgold and Reynolds, 1989).

The late 1980s and early 1990s have seen the most rapid rates of development so far with over fifty superstores opened each year (Figure 7.7). During this period the programmes of store development closely reflected the fortunes of the large companies in the Stock Market. Sainsbury and Tesco performed success-fully, increasing sales and profits from year to year, and maintained a steady expansion in superstore development (Figure 7.4). Two other companies of the successful 'big five' of the mid-1980s, however, began a decline in new store openings and financial success generally.

Asda, which had been by far the leading superstore developer up to 1980, began to find its growth in profits slipping away, and then made what has since been seen as a major error of judgement, purchasing sixty-one large stores from the Isosceles company (formerly Gateway) in 1989 for £705 million. Although purchasing these stores was much cheaper than building new stores, many of the stores were found to be undertrading, or duplicated existing Asda stores.

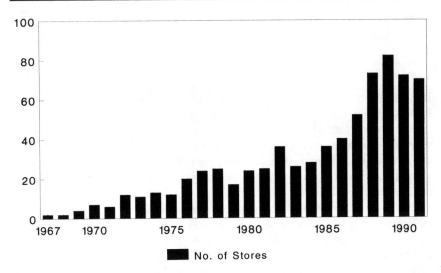

Figure 7.7 Hypermarkets and superstores opened in year
Source: Unit for Retail Planning Information (1992b)

A revaluation of these properties in 1992 led to the company writing down £320 million (*Grocer*, 1992f; see also Hallsworth and McClatchey, 1993). The need to service the debt associated with this purchase further reduced the opportunity for major new capital expenditure. The outcome was that Asda's programme of new store development was severely cut back (Figure 7.4), and eventually the company, under new management, announced in 1992 that no more new stores were to be built for the time being. The company is now repositioning some of its existing stores to emphasise low prices.

The Isosceles company was formed by some of the senior management of Gateway with backing from various financial institutions and acquired the company in 1989 through a heavily leveraged buyout. Isosceles was thus under obligation to repay over £2 billion of debt and immediately withdrew from the superstore development race, following sale of many of its superstores to Asda. This company's trading performance is still regarded as poor, and its debt provisions have virtually wiped out any trading profits since 1989 (Economist Intelligence Unit, 1991; Hallsworth, 1991). The company's present development plans are discussed in the next section.

These withdrawals from superstore development were, however, matched by an increased store development programme by the Safeway arm of Argyll Stores. Argyll had taken over the UK operation of Safeway in 1987, and quickly built up Safeway stores as the upmarket counterpart to the company's more utilitarian Lo-Cost and Presto operations.

By the early 1990s, Tesco, Sainsbury and Safeway were involved in a three-fold battle for market share, of which growth in store numbers was a key element.

Together Tesco and Sainsbury opened forty-three of the seventy grocery super-stores built in Britain in 1991 (Unit for Retail Planning Information, 1992b).

Land and development costs

In contrast with many other forms of retailing, grocery superstore development has taken the form largely of freehold land purchases and development by the retailers concerned. This is partly because the retailers are uninterested in occu-pying units in larger retail developments, and partly because property companies and financial institutions are uncertain about the potential for long-term rental growth (Kleinwort Benson, 1991). This latter point has implications for financing of superstore development.

Much of the attraction of suburban or semi-rural sites lay originally in their cheapness compared with the central area sites traditionally seen as necessary by most multiple retailers. However, this differential seems to have become eroded as suburban land prices rose during the 1980s. In addition, a differentiated market in suburban land arose, with retail uses fetching higher prices than industrial or residential. This situation arose partly through the intense competition between the major retailers, and partly because planning restrictions and the access requirements of retailers meant that many suburban sites were unsuitable for retail development.

The outcome in the late 1980s was that Tesco and Sainsbury were frequently paying between £2 million and £3 million per acre for superstore sites in the south-east of England. This would compare with figures of up to £1.5 million per acre for retail park sites, and £0.5 million for industrial or housing sites. Both firms occasionally paid what the market regarded as excessive prices for 'totem sites' that they felt to be of particular importance (Kleinwort Benson, 1991; Credit Lyonnais Laing, 1992). The latter source claims that 'currently opening sites are about 20–30 per cent overvalued and that disposal (via leaseback) for any site opened after 1986/7 would probably give rise to a capital loss' (cited in Wrigley, 1992). Argyll, although actively seeking new sites, was unable to compete at this level and has tended to purchase cheaper sites, which are unlikely to provide the level of sales sought by Tesco and Sainsbury. On average, Tesco is estimated to have paid £18.5 million for each store site in 1990/1991; Sainsbury £10 million; Argyll about £7 million and Asda about £10 million (Kleinwort Benson, 1991). Developing the store itself adds about £10 million to the total (ibid.). A. Brown (1991) draws similar conclusions, although his estimates are different in detail.

The implications of these high land prices for the major grocery retailers are serious. A company opening twenty new stores each year may be expected to pay hundreds of millions of pounds simply for the land required. Much of this expenditure will bear no immediate return as it goes towards the establishment of land banks: Tesco and Sainsbury attempt to have sufficient sites available for two to three years' future development (Credit Lyonnais Laing, 1991; Kleinwort

Benson, 1991). Following criticism in the press of apparently high prices paid in Britain by consumers for groceries, compared with other Western countries, Sainsbury claimed that a major factor in their pricing policies is the high cost of the land needed for developing new stores (Skeel, 1991).

Sources of finance

Major programmes of store development require substantial amounts of short-term finance, to pay for land and construction. The main sources available to retailers have been discussed in principle earlier in this chapter. The main grocery companies in Britain have used most of the available types of finance to enable their programmes of large-store development to take place.

In the early days of expansion, the grocery companies were able to use their own cash receipts to finance, wholly or partly, their own superstore development. This was partly because some firms relied on purchasing old industrial or warehouse properties that possessed little existing use value, and partly because the programmes of development were less ambitious.

An example of expansion through a combination of bank finance and cash resources is provided by the Greater Nottingham Co-operative Society:

> [The Society] still owns all the retail developments it carried out. The most difficult one to fund was the first, because ten years ago it had very few free assets to offer as security. However, eventually a suitable secured loan was raised to fund the first superstore. That superstore when completed was used as security to raise the funds for the second and so on, leapfrogging like that for a few years until, with rising profits, and a growing asset base, new units were actually being built without having to charge more assets. This happened around number five or six.
>
> (Doherty, 1990: 220)

However, the acceleration of development programmes in the 1980s meant that companies had to find extra sources of capital to finance their store development programmes. One source normally available to retail developers – long-term finance from a financial institution – was little used, largely because of reluctance of institutions to become involved in grocery store development. This, in turn, was for several reasons (Goldman Sachs, 1989b):

1 a lack of comparable transactions: superstores can be valued, but are rarely sold;
2 the market's perception that too high prices have been paid for certain sites, thus reducing the prospects of long-term growth;
3 lack of alternative types of occupier for superstore buildings should they be vacated;
4 the relatively short operational life of a superstore, possibly no more than fifteen years.

Companies were thus faced with a choice between taking out bank loans, raising money through share issues, or disposing of freehold ownerships through sale and leaseback arrangements. All of these methods have been used since 1980 by the major companies, but perhaps the most important has been the issuing of new shares. In 1991, Tesco, Sainsbury, Argyll and Asda all made rights issues (£572 million, £489 million, £387 million and £357 million respectively) to finance new store development or reduce debt (Asda). This method raises capital quickly but concentrates ownership more in the hands of institutional shareholders: in the case of Sainsbury's issue, the family's own shareholding declined from 47 per cent to 43 per cent of total equity, a fact that met with some criticism from the financial press (*Investors Chronicle*, 1991b; Wrigley, 1991).

The sale and leaseback method has been used by all the major companies, except Argyll, from the late 1980s onwards. For example, in 1989, Sainsbury sold about 1 million sq. ft. of freehold and long leasehold property (including six superstores) to the property company British Land. The portfolio also included two retail parks and some smaller 'high street' stores (Goldman Sachs, 1989b). Sainsbury then entered into lease for their stores at 'current market rents' (ibid: 4). Sainsbury then proceeded to sell a further eleven stores to British Land in late 1989, and fifteen more in 1991. Gateway also sold thirty-one stores to British Land in 1990. The total cost of these purchases amounted to £398 million, but the terms of the institutional leases that resulted from these deals allow substantial long-term growth prospects for British Land (Stanley, 1992).

More complex deals have occurred: for example, that made by Tesco and Slough Estates in 1988, setting up a joint venture 'Shopping Centres Ltd' to own and operate three of Tesco's district centres. This could be regarded as a form of long-term finance, although the stores involved had already been completed, using the company's own sources of capital. Tesco subsequently raised £70 million through the sale of four stores to Land and Property Trust.

The largest property disposal, apart from the sale of Gateway stores mentioned above, has been the setting up of a joint venture between Asda and Arlington Securities, the property subsidiary of British Aerospace. This, in effect, led to Asda receiving £375 million for thirty-four stores in 1989 (*Grocer*, 1989).

Prospects for the 1990s

There is a clear impression amongst financial commentators that the drive for increased profits and dividends, which has to be realised largely through new store openings, cannot be sustained indefinitely. The late 1980s saw two of the 'big five' – Asda and Gateway – taking on massive debts, losing the confidence of investors, and eventually virtually halting their store development programmes. These companies are now facing the task of updating or modifying their existing stores. There is critical appraisal also of the prospects for the so far successful 'big three' – Sainsbury, Tesco and Argyll. Three problems may be imminent. The first is the impact of a revived 'discount' sector in grocery retailing. The second fear is that the policy of increasing sales through developing new stores will become more and more difficult to maintain: 'saturation' may occur. Both these problems are discussed later in this chapter.

A final problem for the major grocery companies lies in the value of their property holdings. As explained above, competition between the companies led to inflation in land prices during the 1980s. Prices were paid for suburban land which would not in present circumstances be realised if the sites were sold for an alternative land use. The companies may need to allow for this problem by depreciating the freehold value of the sites they own, but this would lower their earnings (*Investors Chronicle*, 1992b; Wrigley, 1992).

Saturation

The problem of increasing difficulty in obtaining new grocery store sites has two causes. First, restriction upon new development may arise through increasingly strict planning control (see Chapter 5), and there is awareness among planners, politicians and civil servants that development of 'greenfield', edge-of-town stores appears to reinforce tendencies towards urban sprawl and the use of cars for routine trips. It is not clear whether sufficient numbers of inner urban ('brownfield') sites exist that would be acceptable to the grocery companies, or to institutional investors, should they become more involved in the development process.

The second aspect is the often discussed issue of 'saturation'. This is the notion that at some future date, the maximum possible number of profitable superstores will exist, such that new stores can only be developed if there are corresponding closures (of superstores) nearby. In the early 1980s, commentators suggested that about 800 grocery superstores could be built in Britain, after which saturation would occur. However, this total was reached in late 1992 or 1993, according to whether the Institute of Grocery Distribution or Unit for Retail Planning Information definition of 'superstore' is used. Yet both Sainsbury and Tesco identified in 1991 a further 150 target areas for new stores, and Argyll no less than 300 (*Investors Chronicle*, 1991a; Kleinwort Benson, 1991). Sainsbury have stated:

> Our long-term development plan identifies a requirement for over 150 new stores, about one-third of which would replace our oldest supermarkets. With about 30 per cent of the total population of Great Britain living outside the catchment areas of our stores, there remains, therefore, considerable scope for further expansion.
>
> (Sainsbury, 1992: 4)

Some further expansion should also be expected from Wm Morrison and some of the Co-operative societies.

Some commentators have observed differences between regions of Britain with respect to their coverage of superstores, as measured by population per superstore. In 1990 this varied from 73,300 in Yorkshire and Humberside, to 113,200 in Scotland (Kleinwort Benson, 1991). This might suggest that there is scope to continue building superstores until all regions are at the same level. However, Treadgold and Reynolds (1989) show that, if smaller modern supermarkets of between 10,000 and 25,000 sq. ft. sales area are taken into account, regional differences in grocery store provision per capita are small (see also Thorpe, 1991).

This finding indicates that saturation should be examined at a local level rather than a national or regional one. Some urban areas appear already to be saturated. Chesterton Consulting (1991) have suggested a four-stage 'food share market cycle', which attempts to describe the process of saturation of local markets with multiple grocery stores. Phase one, 'Introduction', involves the development of a single 'conforming' superstore, which captures a proportion of the local market for grocery products. Phase two, 'Expansion', involves development of further conforming stores, capturing further amounts of local expenditure while possibly taking some trade from the original store. Phase three, 'Characterisation', occurs after the area has become saturated with conforming superstores. The major operators try to tailor their stores to particular characteristics of the local catchment, and may consider refurbishment or even new development of town centre stores, to serve the town centre office worker and/or comparison shopper. Finally, phase four, 'rationalisation', involves closures or repositioning of food stores that appear surplus to the needs of the local catchment. No new development is likely except where old stores are replaced.

The city of Cardiff, with a convenience goods catchment population of probably less than 400,000, appears to exemplify the first three stages of this model. The city's first grocery superstore was opened in the early 1970s, as a conversion of a former biscuit factory, by Co-operative Retail Services. There followed a Tesco store in the city centre, opened in 1980. The first conforming superstore was opened by Tesco in 1982. By 1990, the city possessed six further superstores while the original CRS and Tesco stores had both closed. A further store was given planning permission for CRS in July 1991, but construction had not yet commenced at the end of 1993. At this time Tesco were said to be on the point of developing a 'Metro' style store (see the following section) in the city centre, while Kwik Save were developing a programme of replacement stores. This would seem to exemplify the 'characterisation' stage of the Chesterton (1991) model.

More generally, an analysis relating store numbers to travel-to-work area populations (as in Thorpe, 1991) would reveal other areas where new store development would seem feasible only at the expense of older stores.

Saturation would imply that further growth in market share cannot be achieved by developing new stores. The implications of such a situation for further growth in sales and profits for the major companies are serious (Duke, 1991; Wrigley, 1991). Store development would still occur, but would take mainly the form of improvements to, or relocations of, existing stores. It is not surprising that the major retailers, and some commentators, claim that saturation is a 'gradual concept' or a 'moving target'. One way in which the companies can expand their market is to provide an increasingly wide range of goods or services, but the North American experience is said to show that the scope for this is limited (Kleinwort Benson, 1991).

OTHER GROCERY STORE DEVELOPMENT PROGRAMMES

Large-store development by major grocery retailers, has been one of the most striking retail development programmes in Britain in recent years. However, development of other types of store by retailers has also been important. This section describes recent trends in the development of grocery stores of below superstore size, and also discusses repositioning of some of the older stock of superstores.

There is a vast stock of existing grocery stores of various sizes, ages and locations. Much of this stock is bought and sold on the open market, and it is possible for a grocery company to expand without needing to construct new stores. As shown in Figure 7.5, the tendency has been for the major companies to replace smaller with larger stores. However, programmes of development of new stores of below superstore size still remain important. These can be considered under three headings: neighbourhood stores, discount stores and convenience stores.

Neighbourhood stores

The 'neighbourhood food retailer' is a term coined by A. Brown (1991) to describe companies building stores in the 5,000–25,000 sq. ft. range, intended to serve smaller population catchments than are the superstores discussed above. All of the companies discussed in the previous section have built new stores in this size range, particularly Argyll and (to a lesser extent) Sainsbury. Tesco in 1992 announced its new 'Metro' chain of stores of around 10,000 sq. ft. sales area, to be opened in 'high street' or inner urban areas, although these may involve purchase of existing buildings rather than new development. Other companies, particularly Gateway, Waitrose, Wm Low and (recently) Marks & Spencer have concentrated on neighbourhood stores. Gateway's store development programme virtually ceased after the company's takeover by Isosceles in 1988 (*Investors Chronicle*, 1992d), but the other companies named are actively developing in the 1990s.

Figure 7.8 shows that the volume of store openings in the larger supermarket (10,000–25,000 sq. ft.) range was highest between 1982 and 1987. Prominent during this period were Safeway (120 stores opened) and Gateway (90). Many of these stores were close to the upper size limit in this category and would sell almost the entire food range associated with superstores. Their smaller size might have been related to site constraints, or the size of the catchment area involved. The falling-off in the number of stores of this size built after 1987 reflects the

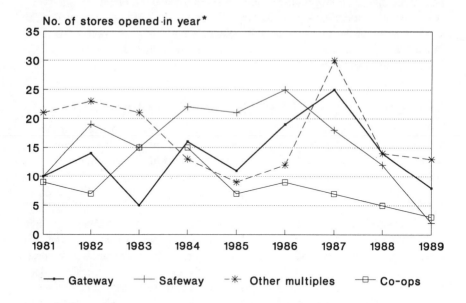

Figure 7.8 Supermarket openings in the 1980s

Source: Institute of Grocery Distribution, 1990b
Note: * Includes stores of 10,000–25,000 sq. ft. sales area

financial problems at Gateway, and the acquisition of Safeway by the Argyll Group, as much as changes in market demand. Waitrose (part of the John Lewis Partnership) and Wm Low still build all-purpose supermarkets and remain successful financially.

Recent development by Marks & Spencer and Tesco, however, involves a change of emphasis. Marks & Spencer describe their 'neighbourhood stores' as 'providing local communities with a range of everyday products such as food, basic clothing and seasonal lines' (Marks & Spencer, 1992: 19). Some of these stores are the company's first food-only stores, at around 15,000 sq. ft. sales area. The Tesco 'Metro' stores are likely to be in-town and targeted mainly at office workers requiring fresh foods and convenience foods.

Discount stores

Theories of retail evolution, such as the 'wheel of retailing' and 'polarisation' theories (S. Brown, 1987) suggest that new forms of retailing come into being when existing forms are established and successful: the new form is deliberately different, emphasising qualities that may be deficient in the successful model. A common method of entry to retailing is to emphasise cut prices, appealing to consumers who consider price to be more important than range of goods or quality of service, for example. Prices can be cut either through reducing the costs of a retail operation, or by increasing turnover of stock while accepting a reduced profit margin.

In several countries, grocery retailing is characterised by the majority of companies offering a wide selection of goods in pleasant, spacious stores, and a minority offering a more limited range of goods at lower prices and in more utilitarian surroundings. At the beginning of the 1990s the 'discount' grocery companies had captured between about 2 per cent (France) and 22 per cent (Germany) of the total grocery market, with Britain at 8 per cent (Institute of Grocery Distribution, 1991).

In Britain, the most successful discount grocery operator is clearly the Kwik Save company, which in 1991 took £1.3 billion food and grocery sales from 780 stores, making it the sixth largest grocery retailer in Britain. Kwik Save began in the 1960s as an out-and-out discount retailer, selling a limited range of standard branded items in utilitarian conditions from small stores (Sparks, 1990). Cost-cutting was founded in staff savings and the efficiencies that can result from selling a limited range of goods. The company's development programme has been based on a mixture of purchasing existing supermarkets in unplanned shopping centres, and developing purpose-built stores. Store size was originally in the range 2,000–7,000 sq. ft. sales area (Sparks, 1990), but has increased to around a 6,000–10,000 sq. ft. target for new stores (Kwik Save, 1991). Locations include existing unplanned centres, where Kwik Save may often be the only multiple grocer remaining, to free-standing stores which are less likely to be in the outer suburban locations than are the superstores discussed above. Kwik Save appears to prefer inner urban locations which are within easy reach by foot and public transport of their generally lower-income catchment population. The company also prefers to open several stores in the larger urban areas, rather than build just one or two on the outer periphery (Sparks, 1990).

Although Kwik Save's expansion has been based upon a steady programme of new store openings, it has been able to expand largely through its own cash resources. The company has been able to build new stores from cash reserves, although borrowing has been necessary to fund purchases of existing supermarkets from other operators (Kwik Save, 1991). Thus, the hazards involved in rights issues or sales and leasebacks have been avoided. The company's flexible require-ments have allowed a much greater choice of sites and/or existing buildings than has been the case with the superstore operators. Consequently, the company does not need to enter contests for prestigious 'totem sites' in the manner of Tesco or Sainsbury. As Graeme Seabrook, chief executive of Kwik Save, commented:

> We spend about £1 million on freehold stores and £450,000 on leasehold units. Those other guys spend about 20 times more than we do to open branches about five times larger. I know what I prefer!

> (*Grocer*, 1992g)

As well as developing new stores, the company has also bought 'bundles' of stores from other operators, as in the purchase of forty-two supermarkets from Gateway in 1991.

Kwik Save's early growth coincided with that of several other discount operators, some of whom no longer exist (Sparks, 1990). In the early 1980s, Tesco, Gateway and the Argyll Group all attempted to compete with Kwik Save through subsidiaries operating small, inner urban discount stores. The most prominent of these operations still in existence is Lo-Cost, part of the Argyll Group which also includes Safeway. Little separate information is available on Lo-Cost, but the impression is that most of this company's stores are in traditional supermarket buildings within unplanned centres. The discount stores have often become a way of using supermarket space abandoned by the more upmarket parts of the corporate body. For example, many Lo-Cost stores are in former Presto or Lipton's supermarket premises, both trading names associated with Argyll Stores. However, there is still a modest programme of development of new Lo-Cost stores.

Recent arrivals on the British discount grocery scene have been of two types. That which has caused most concern to commentators has been the entry of continental European grocery companies, of which the German company Aldi (sixty-five stores in Britain in September 1993) and the Danish company Netto (sixty stores) have been so far the main examples. These companies offer cut prices from very utilitarian settings, mainly through own brands or obscure 'exclusive' brands rather than the national brand leaders favoured by Kwik Save (Gascoigne, 1992; Wrigley, 1993). Aldi appears to be proceeding in a manner similar to Kwik Save, either developing its own stores or purchasing existing buildings, only some of which are supermarkets. Store sizes appear similar to those developed by Kwik Save a decade ago, in the range 2,000–7,000 sq. ft. sales area. Aldi declared at the start of their campaign that they would open 200 stores in Britain by 1993. This target has clearly not been achieved on schedule.

There appears to be no question of lack of finance for development – Aldi is privately owned and has plentiful cash resources available. The main reasons for this delay in the programme of store openings appear to lie in problems in acquiring suitable sites. First, the entry of Aldi has caused concern amongst British retailers, and there have been rumours that some of the leading companies have either blocked sale of their premises to Aldi, or put pressure on estate agents not to make available supermarket premises to the company (*Grocer*, 1990). Second, Aldi are reputedly attempting to purchase or develop freehold stores, thus ruling out the assignment of existing supermarkets which are on short leases. Third, the company's requirements for customer car parking rule out many existing supermarket premises in 'high street' locations.

Aldi and Netto are expanding within fairly narrowly defined geographical areas. Both firms are concentrating on major urban areas in the north and midlands of England, within easy reach of the warehouse storage facilities established so far (Gascoigne, 1992). Aldi intend, however, to enter the south-east of England once they have set up suitable warehouse facilities.

Two other German grocery firms – Norma and Lidl – may expand into the British market in the mid-1990s. In 1991 and 1992 respectively they withdrew their original plans, but subsequently renewed their interest (*Grocer*, 1993). One major reason quoted for their withdrawal was the difficulty of obtaining suitable premises, a problem also cited by the Isle of Man based discounter Shoprite, which is opening stores in Scotland (*Grocer*, 1992a). A further new entry is the French Carrefour group, which opened the first of its 'Ed' discount stores in Kent in early 1993.

The other major new development in discount grocery retailing has been a competitive response by some superstore retailers to Kwik Save and the continental firms. This has been the use of existing superstores for discount retailing, as practised by Gateway with their 'Food Giant' conversions, part of the Co-operative movement with 'Pioneer' stores, and Asda with 'Dales' stores. These stores are, of course, much larger than those operated by Kwik Save and the other discounters. Gateway's Food Giants, of which between forty and fifty are planned, typically sell about 10,000 food items, four times as many as a typical Kwik Save store and fifteen times as many as an Aldi store. Gateway are also converting some of their smaller supermarkets into 'Solo' limited line discounters. These plans represent attempts by the companies concerned to retain market share without having to build new stores.

A final comment on discount grocery retailing is that certain well-established principles of grocery store location appear not to hold in all circumstances. It was explained above that the major grocery retailers attempt to create local monopoly conditions through developing in sites isolated from other grocery retailers. Smiddy (1991) has observed, however, that Aldi tend to locate close to other grocery stores. Their limited number of lines means that the shopper may need to visit other stores as well in order to purchase a full range of groceries. The siting close to rival stores also allows the price advantages to be more apparent to shoppers. In 1992 Aldi began to co-operate with Gateway and Iceland Frozen Foods in joint developments (*Grocer*, 1992b). Kwik Save, however, have a wider variety of items on sale and sell national brands. They are more likely to fulfil shopping trip requirements. The company hence can trade from more isolated sites.

Convenience stores

The convenience store is a well-established North American concept (Kirby, 1976), which several operators have attempted to establish in Britain with only modest success. A convenience store has been defined as one that:

1 stays open seven days a week and has extended hours of trading;
2 sells a wide range of products in addition to 'core' grocery items;
3 is under 3,000 sq. ft. in sales area (*Grocer*, 1992e).

The convenience store is thus differentiated from the discount store by its wide range of items, which may include alcoholic drink, newspapers, medicines, toys, video hire, etc.; and from the supermarket by its small size. The distinction between the convenience store and the traditional 'corner shop' is less easy to draw: the convenience store is more likely to be owned by a multiple retailer; is likely to be larger; is probably more modern in appearance; and relies more upon non-foods than does the traditional store. The main role of the convenience store is to provide 'topping-up' goods that shoppers need to buy between their major grocery shopping trips to larger stores. This has led to two characteristic locations for such stores: within residential areas, serving a catchment population living mainly within walking distance of the store; and on main roads, serving the motorist who may wish to buy a few items while travelling for some other main purpose. Some convenience stores also become destinations for regular shopping trips (*Grocer*, 1992e).

The recent growth in convenience stores has taken place in three ways. First, there are the multiple retailers, of which the largest is Circle K, with 230 outlets in 1991. Altogether some thirteen multiple retailers operating convenience stores have been identified (*Grocer*, 1992c). Second, organisations to which independent grocers can affiliate have encouraged member grocers to develop a convenience store format, such as the Spar 'Eight till Late' and Mace 'Convenience Express'. In some cases these organisations have developed stores themselves rather than simply relying upon individual grocers. Third, the major oil companies are increasingly providing convenience stores within petrol filling stations. For example, Shell in mid-1992 operated 350 'Select' stores and planned to raise this total to 800 within five years (*Grocer*, 1992d). These stores, at around 800 sq. ft., are smaller than the typical multiple or affiliated convenience store of between 1,500 and 3,000 sq. ft. sales area.

Profit margins have been low in convenience retailing and the long-term growth prospects are uncertain. Nevertheless, there has been substantial development of new stores, mainly by the multiples and oil companies. Recourse to bank loans and rights issues seems unlikely to be necessary: these programmes should still be regarded as modest when compared with those of the 'big three' grocery retailers.

Conclusion: development in the grocery sector

This and the previous section have attempted to explain the complex patterns of change and development currently taking place in the British retail grocery sector. Despite the slow growth in overall demand for grocery products, much development of new grocery stores is occurring, most of it carried out by multiple retailers. Table 7.8 sums up their requirements as at the beginning of the 1990s. Most of the superstore, supermarket, discount and convenience operators are attempting to expand through new development: acquisition of existing redundant retail space appears to be generally a second-best solution. However,

Table 7.8 Grocery companies' size requirements gross area, in '000 sq. ft.

Company	Size	Location
Sainsbury	55–75	Edge-of-town
Tesco	55–75	Edge-of-town
Safeway	35–70	Edge-of-town
Budgen	20–35	In- or edge-of-town
M & S (food stores)	20–35	In- or edge-of-town
Waitrose	20–35	In- or edge-of-town
Kwik Save	10–15	In-town
Iceland	6–10	In-town or retail park

Sources: *Investors Chronicle* (1990) and company reports

development of new space is by no means straightforward. Superstore operators have been forced to pay inflated prices for the best sites, and discount operators seeking much smaller sites have reported a degree of obstruction from vested interests.

In the longer term, saturation of the market for grocery retailers seems likely to spread into many urban areas. Where this occurs, new development – which will still be favoured by sufficiently well-capitalised retailers – will replace older stores. Given the inflated prices paid for suburban sites, and the problems in 'recycling' older supermarket and superstore units, it is unlikely that the financial institutions will become any more involved in grocery store development than they have so far.

NON-FOOD LARGE-STORE DEVELOPMENT

Programmes involving the development of large stores, generally of the retail warehouse type, have been characteristic of several retail firms trading in non-food goods. Two phases may be discerned, which correspond broadly with Schiller's (1986) second and third 'waves' of retail decentralisation (the first wave having been of food retailing). The second wave was associated with firms selling household goods, including do-it-yourself (home improvement) goods, furniture, carpets, electrical goods, and motor accessories, and began in the 1970s in Britain. The third wave began in the mid-1980s and was associated with comparison goods such as clothing, footwear and toys.

'Second-wave' developments

The most important development programmes in sheer volume have been those of the *'do-it-yourself'* retailers. In early 1993 the largest six companies (B & Q,

Do It All, Texas Homecare, Great Mills, Homebase and Wickes) operated over 950 stores, almost all of 'retail warehouse' type. If some of the Jewson (builders' merchant) stores and also some independently owned stores are included, the total probably exceeds 1,100. This is larger than the total number of grocery superstores, and around half of the total number of retail warehouses in Britain.

Development of do-it-yourself stores was exceptionally rapid during the 1980s, a result mainly of substantial increases in consumer expenditure on the home maintenance and improvement goods sold in these stores (*Retail Business*, 1993a). Rapid expansion was facilitated by the ample financial resources available to the companies concerned. Five of the six major companies listed above are owned by larger retail or mixed enterprises: B & Q by Kingfisher; Do It All jointly by Boots and W.H. Smith; Texas by Ladbroke; Great Mills by RMC, and Homebase by Sainsbury.

In the early 1990s, the rate of development has been drastically reduced, because of much slower rates of growth in consumer expenditure. The opportunity has been taken to close some of the older stores. For example, in 1991 and 1992, Texas Homecare opened sixteen new stores and also closed sixteen, with a slight increase in floor area overall (*Retail Business*, 1993b).

Site requirements for do-it-yourself stores are also typified by Texas: 'a minimum selling area of 35,000 sq. ft. plus garden centre area, [with] car parking for 175 cars' (ibid.).

Other 'second-wave' stores of this type have been developed by companies specialising in *electrical goods, carpets* and *furniture*. Important firms include Comet, part of the Kingfisher Group (electrical goods), Curry's, part of the Dixon's Group (electrical goods), Allied Carpets, part of the Asda Group; Carpetright; Carpetland, a survivor from the Lowndes Queensway furniture and carpets group which collapsed in 1990; and MFI (self-assembly furniture). In total these six companies operated over 700 stores in early 1993, almost all of which were of the retail warehouse type. Taking other retailers into account, there were probably nearly as many electrical goods, carpets and furniture stores built off-centre in the 1970s and 1980s as there were do-it-yourself stores.

Locational criteria for these stores are slightly more flexible than those for grocery superstores. Highly visible sites close to major road junctions, similar to those favoured by grocery companies, are ideal, but sites in industrial estates or at almost any point adjacent to a major road appear to have been acceptable. The industrial estate location recalls the origins of the retail warehouse in the early 1970s, when standardised light industrial or warehouse units were often adapted by the companies concerned. Retail warehouses need less than half of the car parking spaces for an equivalent grocery store, and so can be built on smaller sites.

Broadly speaking, three types of retail area are available for the retail warehouse: the isolated or 'stand-alone' development, the retail warehouse cluster, and the retail park. There appears to be no published information on the relative importance of each of these types, or on retailers' preferences. The following account is thus brief.

Early growth of retail warehouses was mainly in stand-alone development, using either redundant industrial buildings or undeveloped sites close to major roads within urban areas. A few companies, notably the Swedish furniture retailer IKEA, still favour stand-alone development, in this case of around 150,000 sq. ft.

After the mid-1970s, some clusters of retail warehouses began to appear, as a result of unco-ordinated development on adjacent sites, for example in the Swansea Enterprise Zone (Thomas and Bromley, 1987). Experience showed some trading advantages, particularly where adjacent stores sold different products. Finally, the retail park, a co-ordinated group of retail warehouses under one ownership, appeared first in 1982 and became the norm for retail warehouse development during the mid- and late 1980s. Further discussion of retail parks may be found in Chapter 8.

As in the case of grocery retailing, there has been debate on the likelihood of *saturation* of Britain by do-it-yourself stores or other retail warehouses. Treadgold and Reynolds (1989) show that some do-it-yourself stores exist with catchment populations of under 30,000, but that the average population served by each store in 1988 was 60,000. This implied that many more stores could be developed and would still trade successfully. However, it should be noted that the catchment population for a Texas Homecare store is still said to be at least 50,000 (*Retail Business*, 1993b).

It is arguable that signs of impending saturation may be detected. Many of the first generation of do-it-yourself and other stores were poorly located or too small for modern requirements, and future developments are intended to replace these obsolete stores as much as extend geographical coverage:

> A cornerstone of the Texas strategy has been the belief that the DIY superstore sector will reach saturation by the mid-1990s and that expansion thereafter will have to be at the expense of other superstore operators. The rapid store opening programme has thus been intended to ensure that the company has a comprehensive network of stores in place while latterly the focus has shifted to enhancing the quality of the portfolio by store replacement.
>
> (*Retail Business*, 1993b: 52)

'Third-wave' developments

The 'third wave' of off-centre development (Schiller, 1986) has been typified by companies such as Toys 'R' Us, Children's World (a subsidiary of Boots), and Marks & Spencer. These stores sell comparison goods more often found in the town centre. Some commentators would add specialist furniture retailers such as Habitat (now owned by IKEA) and World of Leather to this list. Marks & Spencer form a special case and are discussed below. The other companies in this group have, along with many of those in the first group discussed above, tended to take up premises within retail parks. Firms selling comparison goods can clearly derive advantage from locating alongside other retailers.

Marks & Spencer had by the end of 1992 developed twelve large, single-level stores in off-centre locations. These stores, of up to 100,000 sq. ft. sales area, sell the whole range of goods associated with the firm's town centre stores. Unlike other non-food superstores, they have avoided the retail park, but are usually located next to a grocery superstore. For this purpose, the company has undertaken several joint developments with Tesco, and more recently with Sainsbury and Asda. These developments should not be confused with the large, sometimes two-level stores which the company has opened in some of the enclosed regional centres discussed in Chapter 8.

Warehouse clubs

The 'warehouse club' is the most recent retail innovation to reach Britain from the USA: at the time of writing, a handful of such schemes have obtained planning permission with none yet built. These warehouses sell some 4,000 items, food and non-food, at very low prices in 'no-frills' surroundings. Admission is restricted to club members who pay an annual fee. Despite this condition, central government guidance indicates that such developments are, in fact, retail in nature and subject to the context of retail planning policies (Department of Education, 1993: para. 26).

The warehouse club is said to be the fastest-growing retail format in the USA, with between fifty and one hundred outlets opening every year (Buckley, 1993). In Britain, the pioneer developers are Costco (the third largest American operator) and Nurdin and Peacock (a British wholesale grocery operator). Outlets may reach 150,000 sq. ft. in size and would presumably be in stand-alone sites. It seems unlikely that land use planners will prove sympathetic to applications for this type of retailing.

Sources of development finance

As most of the companies involved in non-food superstore development are subsidiaries of very large retail or mixed function companies, it is difficult to establish how their superstore developments are financed. The normal mode of development appears to have been similar to that used by the major grocery firms: development of freehold stores by the firm itself, financed by cash resources. This has certainly been the case for Marks & Spencer (Hallsworth and McClatchey, 1993: 11–12). Premises in retail parks are, however, usually leased on standard institutional terms from the company owning the retail park.

There is no evidence of non-food superstore programmes having had to be funded by rights issues or sales and leaseback, in the manner of the major grocery companies (see above).

SHOPPING CENTRE AND MIXED DEVELOPMENT BY RETAILERS

Retail firms have also been involved in the development of retail space which is partly owner-occupied and partly let to other tenants. This section discusses two main forms of such development: the 'district centre' developed by grocery retailers, and town centre development by 'property' subsidiaries of major comparison retailers.

District centres

The 'new district centre' emerged in the 1970s (Unit for Retail Planning Information, 1977). It took the form essentially of a grocery superstore plus a small number of small retail units, selling everyday goods not available in the superstore. In some centres, community facilities such as clinics were also provided. The retail component, including the small shop units, was built by the grocery retailer, who would let the small units to other multiples or independents. Centres were located within residential areas, and were intended to act as local shopping for the residents of these often new suburbs. Two such centres are depicted in Figure 2.6.

The 'centres intercommunaux' common in French cities are similar in nature to the British 'district centre', but they tend to be anchored by hypermarkets and are probably much larger on average than their British counterparts (Dawson, 1983: Chapter 6; Reynolds, 1992).

The processes of negotiation typically involved in the development of district centres are not generally recorded in print. In two cases known to the author in South Wales, district centre development formed part of a co-ordinated programme of suburban expansion which was planned in the late 1970s and carried out in the early 1980s. The local authority purchased substantial areas of land which it deemed to be ready for urban development. Parcels of land were then sold to residential developers to build housing estates, mainly for owner occupation. At the same time, sites were designated for district centre development in approved local plans prepared by the same local authority. These sites were offered for sale by tender. Although the local authority had originally preferred development of smaller supermarkets, the highest bids were offered by superstore retailers and thus development of the district centres was carried out by these companies.

It seems unlikely that the grocery companies, left to their own devices, would have wanted to build shopping centres of this type. They would have little desire to build small shop units to let, and would have preferred free-standing locations visible from major roads, rather than locations within residential areas. However, compliance with a district centre policy allowed the companies to provide superstores in accordance with local authority policy, hence avoiding the delay and uncertainty of planning 'by appeal'. It may also have been the case that the companies were able to buy or lease land from local authorities, at favourable rates.

Limited survey evidence suggests that these centres do not really function as local shopping, as intended by planners. Instead, superstore customers tend to be drawn by car from a wide surrounding area, just as they would be for a free-standing development. Furthermore, they make little use of the other shops in the centre, which do perhaps have a more local function. Thus, the place of the centre within the sub-regional retail hierarchy was more apparent than real.

In retrospect, development of these district centres appears to have peaked around 1980. In the late 1980s, few grocery superstores were built in this manner, operators preferring free-standing developments (see Figure 7.6). It is also likely that expenditure restrictions on local government, which became more and more severe during the 1980s, prevented local authorities from purchasing land in advance of organising a phased programme of residential and retail development.

Development by retailer subsidiaries

Several retailers have been involved in shopping centre developments in a rather different way. This occurs where the retailer possesses a subsidiary company that is a property developer in its own right. Formation of such subsidiary companies appears to take place for two reasons. The first is to place the management of the parent company's freehold assets on a sound financial basis. The second is to attempt to add to the parent group's profitability through property transactions. These two purposes may be difficult to disentangle in practice.

An example of the first purpose was the formation of Kingfisher's subsidiary Chartwell Land in 1988. This company formally owns Kingfisher's retail property assets, and lets them at market rents to the trading companies – Woolworth, Comet, Superdrug and B & Q. The company is also likely to become a developer in its own right when conditions improve (Goldman Sachs, 1989a: 50).

Two 'high street' retailers whose property assets were more likely to be scattered across many small stores in unplanned retail areas also set up property development subsidiaries in the 1980s. These were the Burton Group (Burton Property Trust) and Dixon Group (Dixon's Commercial Properties). Burton, which already owned freehold several Debenhams department stores, embarked upon a massive shopping centre development programme which at one time would, if completed, have built over three million sq. ft. of town centre floorspace (Goldman Sachs, 1989a: 44). Subsequently, following considerable criticism of what was seen by commentators as an ill-advised venture, most of the schemes have been cancelled. Dixon's ventures into property development have been much more modest, but in July 1992 the company announced that it was withdrawing from property development in Britain, although continuing to develop in continental Europe.

Another venture into property development has been by the Boots company, which owns freehold most of its trading properties. The Boots Properties subsidiary, set up in 1989, had spent £125 million by mid-1992 on property investments, but unlike Kingfisher's subsidiary, does not own most of the Boots stores. Thus, this venture corresponds more to the second purpose noted above – property development with a view to increasing the profitability of the company as a whole. Similarly, both Tesco (Spen Hill Properties) and Asda (Gazeley

Properties) possess subsidiaries that carry out largely non-retail development projects.

Retailer participation in enclosed shopping centres

Finally, the participation of some retailers in the development of large enclosed centres should be mentioned. These centres, which are discussed in more detail in Chapter 8, are usually developed principally by property companies and/or financial institutions. However, of crucial importance to the developer is the incorporation in the centre of one or more 'anchor stores': department and/or variety stores operated by the major multiples.

In some cases, the anchor store retailer may be persuaded to finance its own part of the shopping centre, in order to maximise certainty for the lead developer and to reduce his up-front costs. This reflects a long history in North America of involvement of department store chains in shopping centre development. A typical method in Britain is for the retailer to pay a premium for a 125-year lease, at a low ground rent (Thompson and Wythe, 1988: 154). In effect, the retailer becomes part of the development team and can presumably set conditions as to siting and size of its part of the development.

CONCLUSIONS

This chapter has discussed the involvement of retail firms in shopping development. Two models have emerged: the development by retailers of new, free-standing stores for their own use, and participation in larger and more complex developments because of pre-existing land ownership or through the setting up of property companies. The free-standing store development programme has been the more important in recent years, although retailers' town and city centre property holdings are still significant.

A common feature of both programmes has been the increased attention paid to retailers' store and property development programmes by financial commentators. The much-criticised 'short-termism' of financial interests has arguably exacerbated competition for growth in market share among the grocery multiples. This has led to escalation in store development programmes, and in turn to some unwise financial ventures and inflation in land prices. The involvement of 'high street' retailers in property development has not been particularly successful, and has probably harmed the image of the firms involved.

Another common feature of most retailer development programmes has been the lack of involvement of the financial institutions, even though these have played such an important role in what they would see as more 'mainstream' retail development. The institutions generally believe that free-standing large stores have been built on over-valued land, and that they are not suited to alternative uses. Absence of long-term financial participation by the institutions has been another reason for retailers' reliance on rights issues or debt finance. There are no convincing signs that the institutions are likely to become more involved in retailer-led developments in the near future.

Land and property holdings of retail firms play a major part in the commercial land market, but remain an under-researched topic. Two contrary trends have characterised the 1980s: (a) new land purchases and development; and (b) disinvestment, or at least formal separation of land ownership from purely retail operations. In the near future, retail profitability will be constrained by low increases in consumer expenditure, by the high shop rents which resulted from the expansion of the 1980s, and possibly by saturation in many local markets. The signs are thus that disinvestment may continue but that retail-led developments will be less significant than in recent years.

Chapter 8

Shopping centre development

INTRODUCTION

This chapter examines the most complex type of retail development: the construction and operation of shopping centres involving several retail units. Characteristics of such centres were described briefly in Chapter 2. This chapter discusses the process of development for shopping centres of various types, giving particular attention to British examples.

The emphasis is on planned shopping centres that have been developed by 'third parties' rather than retail firms: property companies, financial institutions, local authorities or some combination of these three. Such centres are usually developed on a part purpose-built and part speculative basis, as explained in Chapter 3. Most centres are 'anchored' by one or more large retail outlets or 'major space users', whose size, layout and access requirements are determined at an early stage of construction. Other retail units are designed in a more standardised fashion before being let to 'minor space user' retailers. The development of such centres is a complex affair requiring considerable experience and skill in organisation and negotiation.

For these reasons, attention in this chapter is confined to shopping developments of at least 50,000 sq. ft. gross retail area that include at least three retail units. 'District centres' developed by grocery retailers, some of which would conform to this definition, are dealt with in Chapter 7.

In this chapter a progression is made from relatively simple situations to very complex ones. After an examination of the main characteristics of shopping centre development and finance in Britain, sections explore the recent development history of two main types of centre. These are the retail park and the shopping mall. The latter, comprising one or more anchor stores and several small retail units, is discussed under two headings. First, the 'regional' or 'out-of-town' centre, and second, the shopping centre developed within existing (unplanned) town or city centres. This order is adopted because the second type present more complex issues of planning and design. Within all these discussions, attention is given to issues such as the types of developer typically involved, sources of short- and long-term finance, choice of anchor stores, locational criteria for the centres concerned, land use planning issues, and design and layout of the centre itself. Changes in these aspects during the 1970s and 1980s are discussed, together with some comments on possible events during the 1990s. Following the discussion of shopping malls, two further sections deal with refurbishment of shopping centres, and the development of speciality and festival retailing.

SHOPPING CENTRE DEVELOPMENT AND FINANCE IN BRITAIN

This section presents a general overview of shopping centre development in Britain, to set the scene for detailed discussion of the different types of shopping centre in later sections.

The record of shopping centre development

Between 1965 and 1990 (inclusive), some 706 shopping centres of over 50,000 sq. ft. (gross area), plus 214 retail parks, were built in Great Britain (Hillier Parker, 1991a, 1991b). Their total floor area amounted to 140 million sq. ft. (ibid). Table 8.1 lists the twenty companies that developed the largest amounts of retail floorspace in shopping centres between 1965 and 1987, according to Hillier Parker (1987). Of these, sixteen may be classed as property companies, most of which specialise in shopping centre development; and three as financial institutions. The remaining company in this list is the retailer Asda, which has been responsible for several district centres. These 'top twenty' developers accounted for 47 per cent of all shopping centres built during the period 1965–1987, and 55 per cent of the total retail space.

In addition, if all of the New Town Development Corporations (public bodies with special statutory powers to buy land and carry out development) are taken together, they would be in second place with 8.4 million sq. ft. of shopping centre space developed during this period. The combined local authorities that have built shopping centres would not be far behind with 5.6 million sq. ft. in total.

The table shows which companies have been the most important 'lead' developers, but does not give a fair representation of the other contributions made towards shopping centre development. Both financial institutions and local authorities have contributed to many schemes as partners in the development process.

Shopping centres in Britain: the development process

Sources of finance for development have undergone substantial changes since the early stages of enclosed shopping developments in Britain. The late 1950s and early 1960s saw development mainly by specialist developers, using short-term finance mainly from banks (Marriott, 1967). A few major developers were able to retain ownership of centres once these were developed, becoming in effect

Table 8.1 Leading shopping centre developers[1] 1965–1986

Developer	Type[2]	Total floorspace ('000 sq. ft.)	No. of schemes
Town and City	P	10,706	45
(All New Town Development Corps	L	8,383	26)
Land Securities/Ravenseft	P	7,545	43
(All Local Authorities	L	5,620	31)
MEPC	P	4,406	30
Hammerson	P	3,838	16
Norwich Union	F	2,882	17
Laing Properties	P	2,786	15
Asda	R	2,749	35
Grosvenor Developments	P	2,506	10
Capital and Counties	P	1,949	5
Neale House	P	1,628	6
Samuel	P	1,464	10
Taylor Woodrow	P	1,435	10
St Martins	P	1,339	8
Cameron Hall	P	1,300	1
Crudens	P	1,119	6
Costain	P	1,111	7
Coal Industry Nominees	F	1,030	5
Prudential	F	997	5
Land and House	P	932	6
Heron	P	815	4

Source: Based upon Hillier Parker (1987: Table A)

Notes: 1 Companies shown are the original sole or leading developers of shopping
           centres of over 50,000 sq. ft. gross retail area
       2 P   Property company
          L   Local authority or New Town Development Corporation
          F   Financial institution
          R   Retailer

property investment companies rather than simple developers. These included
Town & City, which developed several Arndale Centres during this period. In the
late 1960s and early 1970s, financial institutions began to be involved in the
development process. Initially they took a largely passive role as ultimate purchasers of completed developments, but soon some institutions pursued more
active policies of shopping centre development. This occurred first through
attempts to appropriate some of the developers' profits from development, in
return for providing favourable terms of finance. Soon, however, institutions

became involved as joint or sole developers of large retail schemes. Prominent among these were the Norwich Union and Prudential insurance companies.

Shopping centre developments gathered pace during the late 1960s, reflecting the growing property boom generally and the successful experience of the early schemes. These were almost entirely located within existing town centres, and involved the participation of local authorities as assemblers of central area land for development (see Chapter 5). This phase came to an end in 1973–1974, with the so-called 'property collapse'. The property market had overstretched itself, building increasingly speculative schemes which were only viable if increasing streams of rent incomes would return to investors in the indefinite future. Once it became clear that this would not happen, the burst bubble of confidence led to sharp declines in values of completed schemes. This, in turn, reduced the assets of major property companies and hence their share values. Several companies went into receivership or were rescued by institutions, banks and even foreign, government-owned investment companies. A further problem lay in the very high interest rates charged during the mid-1970s by sources of capital. This meant that most major property schemes became unprofitable: the stagnating rents meant that returns on investment could not overcome the cost of short-term finance. The result was a sharp decline in the number of shopping centre schemes commenced during the mid- and late 1970s, compared with the early 1970s (see Figure 8.1). This figure shows shopping centre completions, which normally occur some four or five years after the scheme is first planned.

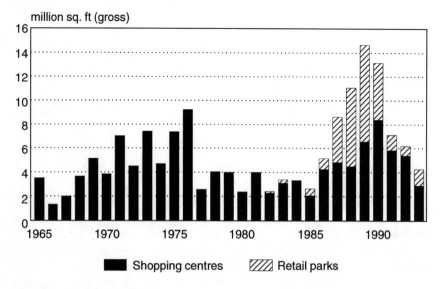

Figure 8.1 British shopping centre development: total floorspace opened in year
Source: Hillier Parker Research

The mid-1980s saw a revival of interest in shopping centre development. This appears to have occurred for three reasons. First, the slow progress made during the preceding few years meant that many town centres were ready for growth or modernisation of their prime retail space. Second, consumer expenditure on comparison goods (upon which enclosed shopping centres depend for most of their sales) was beginning to rise more rapidly in real terms, after several years of virtual stagnation. This, in turn, led to demands from major retailers for more space in major centres. Finally, the property market 'took off' again, fuelled by easier availability of finance. The effects, particularly on proposals for schemes rather than schemes actually built, can be seen in Figures 8.1 and 8.2.

While property development in general in the 1980s was financed mainly by banks rather than financial institutions, the financial institutions continued to be involved in shopping centre development. The great majority of shopping centres developed during the 1980s appear to have been funded by the institutions, who also were lead or joint developers for a much smaller number of schemes. The only major exceptions to this rule have been the 'district' centres discussed in Chapter 7, which were usually funded by the grocery retailers concerned.

During the 1980s, new property development companies became established. Some of these were associated with the out-of-town 'regional' schemes described later in this chapter. New companies also came into being as developers of retail parks. These new developers were already established in local property markets and saw opportunities to build new types of shopping centre. They were able to

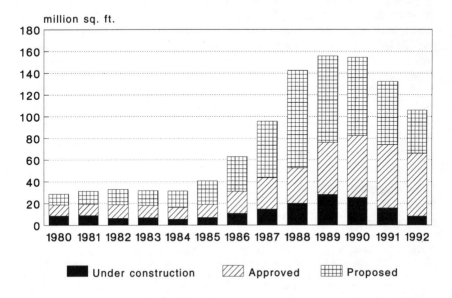

Figure 8.2 Shopping schemes in the pipeline 1980–1992

Source: Hillier Parker Research (1991b; 1992a)

obtain short-term finance from the banks, which were eager to lend to property interests during a period of increasing land and property values. At this time, the financial institutions continued to invest mainly in 'safe' schemes in prime retail locations; that is, town and city centres. Hence, they showed little interest initially in becoming actively involved in novel types of shopping centre development. However, towards the end of the 1980s the institutions became more interested in purchasing some of these new centres from the original developers.

The overall situation over the period 1965–1985 is summarised in Table 8.2, which provides information for a sample of fifty shopping centres taken from the list in URPI (1987). Of these, the majority show local authority involvement as ground landlord; financial institutional involvement in funding; and ultimate development by a property company rather than local authority or institution. However, the 'classic' model of local authority landownership, institutional funding and development by a property company applied only to fourteen out of the forty cases for which full information is available.

The extent of overall institutional ownership of shopping centres is not clear. Funds that reported to the Investment Property Databank (IPD) owned 186 shopping centres in 1991 (Investment Property Databank, 1992: 131). The IPD definition of 'shopping centre' is the same as that used by Hillier Parker. Since the funds which report to IPD own about 70 per cent of institutional assets in Britain, the true total is probably between about 250 and 275 centres. This amounts to about one-third of the 706 centres reported in Hillier Parker (1991a). The number of centres reported in the IPD data has decreased slightly from a maximum of 198 in 1988, during a period in which over one hundred new shopping centres were built. The data quoted in Callender (1991), based upon a looser definition of 'shopping centre', show a sharper net decline in institutional ownership. The main reason for this decline appears to be that the institutions

Table 8.2 Landowners, funders and developers of fifty shopping centres[1]

Actor	Type of Organisation					
	Local authority[2]	Financial institution	Property company	Other[3]	Mixed	Not known
Ground landlord	33	6	2	5	–	4
Funder	3	29	10	1	–	7
Main developer	6	3	37	1	3	–

Notes: [1] The centres, all of at least 100,000 sq. ft. gross retail area built between 1965 and 1985 inclusive and located in Great Britain, were chosen at random from the Register of Managed Shopping Schemes (URPI, 1987)
[2] Including New Town Development Corporations (3 cases) and Land Authority for Wales (1)
[3] Including private landowners (3 cases), British Rail Property Board (1) and a grocery retailer (1)

have sold to property companies some of the older centres which are in need of refurbishment or replacement. The implications of this are discussed in a later section.

Shopping centres generally appear to form acceptable investments for the institutions, with a preference for well-designed schemes in prime locations. Nevertheless, because of the extra management and marketing responsibilities involved in shopping centre ownership, and because of possible future obsolescence, shopping centres generally carry yields of around 2 per cent higher than those for individual shop units in prime locations (Morgan, 1992).

Recent trends

During 1989, with the onset of another economic recession, consumer expenditure for comparison goods suddenly ceased to rise in real terms. Together with the effects of increased rates of interest, this change of trend had drastic effects on the shopping centre development industry. At the end of 1988, the volume of floorspace in shopping centre schemes proposed but not yet granted planning permission amounted to 93 million sq. ft. (Hillier Parker, 1991c). Much of this vast amount of floorspace was given planning permission, and some of it has actually been constructed, but many of the 1988 schemes were subsequently withdrawn by prospective developers. The perception grew over the next four years that rents, which were now declining, would not increase in the near future; nor was the demand from major retailers likely to be maintained at the level found in the late 1980s. As a result, the amount of proposed floorspace shrank to 40 million sq. ft. in March 1992 (Hillier Parker, 1992a: see also Figure 8.2). The volume of space under construction fell even more rapidly, from 27 million sq. ft. in 1988 to 8 million in 1992 (ibid.); moreover a very small total by historic standards (about 4 million sq. ft.) is likely to be opened in 1993 (Hillier Parker, 1993a).

Developers who have commenced schemes in recent years have found difficulty in letting the retail units when they were completed. Hillier Parker (1992b) show that centres opened after 1985 showed on average a 20 per cent vacancy rate in 1992, compared with less than 6 per cent for centres opened between 1965 and 1985. Thus, the 'slump' part of the 'boom and slump' cycle has returned, in fairly similar vein to the mid-1970s. However, as in the 1970s, retail development experienced a less drastic loss of confidence (and probably, far fewer bankruptcies) than the office development sector. In particular, the retail sector did not have the vast glut of space experienced in London's office market in the early 1990s. Prime retail space continued to be in demand by investors.

The following four sections explore in more detail the recent development histories of various types of shopping centres in Britain. The first, on retail parks, describes a type of centre which became significant in the mid-1980s. The next three sections discuss the shopping mall: first, in general, and then in its 'regional' format located outside existing town and city centres. Lastly, shopping malls built within an existing town or city centre are discussed.

RETAIL PARKS

The 'retail park' is a type of shopping centre that appears to be common only in Britain. It is generally defined as comprising three or more large, single-level stores, of either the 'superstore' or 'retail warehouse' types, as defined in Chapter 2. The stores within retail parks usually share common car parking areas, and benefit from co-ordinated access arrangements and landscaping. The centre as a whole will have a name and will probably be marketed as an entity. Some examples of retail parks in Britain are shown in Figure 2.7. It will be noted that in some cases the stores are joined together, while in others they are separate. However, in either case, each store will have its own access arrangements for customers and for delivery purposes. Retail parks do not generally include small retail units of the type found within conventional shopping centres (planned or unplanned); nor do they include covered walkways.

The retail park is based upon the notion that the superstore or retail warehouse can benefit from external economies of scale, without sacrificing its individual features of size, internal layout and access. Prototype retail parks occurred in the early 1980s, almost by accident, when pairs or groups of retail warehouses, were developed in a piecemeal manner on industrial estates or in other areas where land use planning control allowed. A good example of this is in the Swansea Enterprise Zone, where some twenty-seven separate retail units, mainly super-stores and retail warehouses, were constructed in an unco-ordinated manner during the late 1970s and early to mid-1980s, within an area of about 1 square kilometre (Thomas and Bromley, 1987; Sparks, 1987). Surveys of shoppers at these stores established that some shoppers were visiting several stores in one trip (Bromley and Thomas, 1989). Strong links existed between stores selling similar items, for example DIY goods; weaker links existed between stores selling different products, for example DIY and groceries.

It became clear that a group of large stores might together attract more trade than the sum total of the individual stores were they located in separate areas. In addition, a co-ordinated development would be more efficient, and attractive to shoppers, than an unco-ordinated cluster of stores in different architectural styles and with different access arrangements. Planning approval might more easily be gained for a co-ordinated development. Such schemes would also possess greater 'respectability' in property circles and might interest sources of long-term finance. Parallels with the fast-growing 'business park' and 'office park' markets could be established in the minds of major investors in property.

Thus, the planned retail warehouse park or retail park became an important new addition to the retail scene in suburban Britain.

Retail park developers

The first specialist retail warehouse park built in Britain appears to have been the Cambridge Close development in Aylesbury, opened in 1982. Retail park development became significant from 1985 onwards, and some 235 developments had been completed up to the beginning of 1993 (Hillier Parker, 1991b, 1993a). Retail parks became, in both number and total floorspace, the largest component of retail development in the late 1980s, with seventy-one schemes totalling over 8 million sq. ft. opened in 1989 alone. However, totals after 1989 have been much smaller (Figure 8.3), and only thirteen schemes totalling some 1.4 million sq. ft. are likely to open in 1993 (Hillier Parker, 1992a, 1993a).

Retail park development has so far been much more fragmented among development agencies than has been the case for shopping centres generally. The leading developers have been Citygrove (nineteen schemes completed up to the end of 1990), Ravenside (seventeen), Peel Holdings (fourteen), and CCL (thirteen) (Hillier Parker, 1991b). These and several other companies were retail park specialists, who appear to have started in a small way using bank loans as short-term finance. Several of the specialists encountered financial problems at the beginning of the 1990s when the demand for space in retail parks faded as a result of the slowdown in consumer spending.

The main retailers involved in retail warehouse development have taken a relatively small part in retail park development, with Ladbroke Retail Parks (nine schemes) and Portswood (a subsidiary of Kingfisher plc: nine schemes) taking the most important role in this respect. Only fourteen schemes were developed by other retailers or their subsidiaries up to the end of 1990 (Hillier Parker, 1991b).

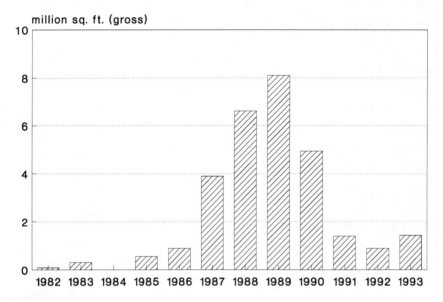

Figure 8.3 Retail park development: total floorspace opened in year

Source: Hillier Parker Research

The financial institutions have played little direct part in retail park development, opening only four schemes in total. Many schemes have been carried out by smaller development companies: these may have been formed specifically for the retail park concerned or may be local to the area where the development itself has been carried out. This is unusual in British retail development, but matches the situation found in the United States, where much shopping centre development is carried out by local development companies (Guy and Lord, 1991).

Finance for development

Sources of short-term finance are not known in detail, but it seems likely that banks have been the main source. So far as is known, some developers are retaining ownership of their schemes, but offers of long-term finance have been made by the institutions, who in the late 1980s regarded a well-conceived retail park as a good, long-term investment (Thompson and Wythe, 1988). This contrasts with the generally indifferent attitude of the institutions towards grocery superstores (see Chapter 7). The retail park is seen as an adaptable form of development in which vacated units can easily be let to new occupiers. Where units are physically joined together, greater flexibility is possible, allowing merging of adjacent units, or subdivision of single units. The institutions also feel that prices paid for retail park sites have been reasonable, and that a long-term appreciation in land values is likely.

Around 1990 there appears to have been a temporary reluctance to continue investing in retail parks, and yields rose sharply from around 7 per cent in 1989 to as much as 12 per cent (Wicks, 1990; Eade, 1992). The institutions have more recently begun to show renewed interest in retail parks, but prefer small schemes in which there is a greater certainty that all of the units will be let to reputable retailers (ibid).

Agreements with retailers

The retail park differs from the conventional planned centre in that there is no distinction to be made between major and minor space users. Only a small number of retailers need to be persuaded to take up units in the scheme. Early involvement can mean that the retailer can obtain a unit that exactly suits its requirements.

Units within a retail park are generally taken on conventional 'institutional leases' (see Chapter 4). There is now some doubt whether this is the most appropriate arrangement in the retail park situation. Obsolescence of the stores' product mix and image might occur much more rapidly than in the typical town centre retail unit, and retail parks are subject to competition from other, perhaps better located developments. Whether this will lead to more flexible arrangements remains to be seen.

Location and planning issues

A retail park will inevitably require several acres of land for the stores, access roads and car parking. It should also be located adjacent to a main road and within, or on the edge of, an urban area. The catchment population will reflect that of the constituent stores. A retail park including a furniture store may require around 50,000 population living within twenty minutes' drive time.

These requirements indicate that retail parks cannot generally be fitted into existing unplanned centres. The most common type of site has probably been the industrial area, either existing or proposed.

Despite the often large amounts of floorspace included in retail parks, they have generally suffered less obstruction from local authority planners than either free-standing grocery superstores or out-of-town 'regional' centres. Indeed, some commentators have credited planners with encouraging the growth of the retail park, which appears to be a peculiarly British phenomenon (Schiller, 1987). This is because planners would oppose the inclusion of small unit stores within off-centre shopping developments, on the grounds that these might be occupied by comparison retailers who would thus take trade away from town centres. The retail warehouses normally found in retail parks are considered to be less of a competitive threat to conventional shopping centres. This is particularly true of do-it-yourself retailing and garden centres, which have no real equivalent in older shopping areas. Thus, it is difficult to make out a case for opposing retail parks on the grounds of their competitive impact, unless they include comparison goods stores that are similar to those found in older centres.

Another argument is that the co-ordinated and landscaped retail park is seen as preferable to piecemeal development of the same amount of retailing on different sites: its physical appearance is somewhat better, and it allows the often heavy volumes of traffic to be accommodated in a more organised way.

Some retail park proposals, however, have met opposition from local authority planners. The main reason is probably their supposed impact upon existing shopping centres. This is more likely to be the case where the proposed park includes 'high street' retailers such as Habitat (furniture) or an Electricity Board showroom, or stores that sell comparison goods such as children's clothing or toys. Several retail parks have thus been prevented from being developed, or have been built only after a successful appeal to the relevant Secretary of State. In other cases, planning permission may have been granted, but with conditions that prohibit the sale of certain 'high street' comparison goods. A second reason for refusal can be that the land concerned is required for industrial development. This argument is common, because many retail park proposals are for land within or close to existing industrial estates.

Prospects for retail parks in the 1990s

The late 1980s were notable for a spate of retail park developments and proposals.

However, a combination of factors at the start of the 1990s led to a sudden downturn in the number of proposed schemes (Figure 8.3). The most important of these was probably the ending of the upward trend in consumer expenditure during the 1980s, which was particularly strong in do-it-yourself and electrical goods, two areas very strongly represented in retail parks. The main retailers cut back their expansion programmes, and hence developers of potential retail parks would have found difficulty in securing occupiers. A second reason for the slowdown in development may have been the general slump in the property market. Developers would have found both short- and long-term finance difficult to obtain.

At present (late 1993) there is some evidence that consumer expenditure is rising again. Retail parks depend for much of their business on purchases directly related to people's homes: their furnishings, repairs and elec- trical goods, for example. Thus, their success is related to rates of house removal and purchase. When this market picks up again, the retailers involved should be expected to resume the process of geographical expansion undergone in the 1980s. Expansion may, however, be met for the time being through the taking-up of recently built retail parks, or the revival of postponed schemes, rather than through completely new developments. As mentioned above, and anticipated by S. Brown (1989), retail park schemes seem likely in the future to be modest in size compared with some of the parks of 300,000 sq. ft. or more which were built in the late 1980s.

In the longer term, the question of possible saturation needs to be faced. Ultimately, the further expansion of retail parks may involve the abandonment by retailers of the first generation of *ad hoc* retail warehouses, some of which are on cramped sites or in poor locations.

Finally, a possible new type of shopping centre, which has some similarities with the retail park in terms of size and location at least, should be mentioned. This is the *factory outlet centre*, of which there are nearly 300 in the US, but only one so far in Britain, at Hornsea in Humberside (Buckley, 1993). These centres sell cut-price merchandise direct from manufacturers, but in a purpose-built centre rather than from the factory itself. Although there is said to be develop- ment interest in Britain, prospects for this type of centre are uncertain.

THE SHOPPING MALL

The shopping mall was defined in Chapter 2 as a planned centre incorporating one or more anchor stores and many smaller stores. Most malls are, in effect, a single building with fully enclosed internal pedestrian ways. This section examines the recent history of such centres in Britain, as a prelude to more detailed discussion of 'out-of-town' and 'in-town' developments, in the following sections. While it is more common in the British literature to consider in-town and out-of-town centres as entirely different animals, they are similar in design and purpose and have a common ancestry in the North American shopping mall.

The North American experience and its application in Europe

In North America, enclosed shopping malls were first developed in the 1950s, following three decades of development of planned centres. The largest malls, generally defined as being over 400,000 sq. ft. gross retail area, are known as 'regional centres' and have been almost entirely built in suburban or edge-of-town locations. The first such centre appears to have been built near Seattle in 1950, and the Southdale development near Minneapolis, opened in 1956, was the first fully enclosed, climate-controlled shopping mall (Frieden and Sagalyn, 1989: 65).

The regional centre, and its big brother the 'super-regional' centre (of over 800,000 sq ft), has spread to all parts of the United States. By 1991, there were almost 1,800 centres of over 400,000 sq. ft. (Table 8.3). Most, but not all of these are fully enclosed centres.

The regional and fully enclosed centres have spread to many other parts of the world (Dawson, 1983). In Britain, such centres began to appear from 1963 onwards, with the Merrion Centre, Leeds (290,000 sq. ft. gross area), and the Bull Ring, Birmingham (300,000 sq. ft.), being prominent early examples. In France, the Parly II centre (592,000 sq. ft.), which opened in 1969, was the first of several fully enclosed centres to be built within the Paris region (Delobez, 1985).

The locational pattern of such centres in Britain has differed from the American precedent. Most enclosed centres of 'regional' size (usually defined in British circumstances as being at least 500,000 sq. ft.) have been built either in existing town and city centres, or as the main shopping areas of government- sponsored new towns (Table 8.4). This reflects the British desire to protect town and city centres from competition from off-centre developments. The regional centre, with its concentration on comparison goods retailing, was seen on the one hand as the means of modernising the unplanned town centre, and on the other hand as a major threat to the town centre if allowed to go ahead in suburban locations. Hence, strenuous efforts have been made to accommodate regional-sized malls within town centres; until the late 1980s, efforts to prevent regional centres being built in suburban or edge-of-town areas were almost entirely successful. The implications of each of these policies are discussed in the following sections of this chapter.

Table 8.3 Regional shopping centres in USA developed up to 1991

Size (sq. ft. gross)	Number
Over 1,000,000	364
800,000–1,000,000	294
400,000–800,000	1,141
Total	1,799

Source: Unit for Retail Planning Information

Table 8.4 Location and size of enclosed centres of over 500,000 sq. ft. in Britain

Town	Centre	Year opened	Size ('000 sq. ft.)
In-town			
Manchester	Arndale	1976	1,189
Newcastle	Eldon Square	1976	830
Luton	Arndale	1972	700
Poole	Arndale	1969	631
Nottingham	Victoria	1972	622
Cardiff	St Davids	1981	581
Maidstone	Stoneborough	1976	542
New towns			
Milton Keynes	Central Milton Keynes	1979	1,065
Redditch	Kingfisher	1973	676
Peterborough	Queensgate	1982	650
Telford	Telford S.C.	1973	650
Runcorn	Shopping City	1971	600
Washington	The Galleries	1977	543
Basildon	Eastgate	1980	517
Out-of-town			
Gateshead	Metro Centre	1986	1,630
Dudley	Merry Hill	1989	1,410
Thurrock	Lakeside	1990	1,150
Sheffield	Meadowhall	1990	1,100
Hendon	Brent Cross	1976	760

Source: Hillier Parker, *British Shopping Centre Developments*, various years.

Note: For centres developed in several phases, 'Size' includes all phases of development. 'Year' is that of the opening of the largest phase

Another characteristic of British shopping centre development is that fully enclosed centres are often much smaller than the typical American regional centre. Within British central areas, enclosed centres of as little as 100,000 sq. ft. can be found (Hillier Parker, 1987). They may include one major anchor store instead of the two, three or four department stores typical of American enclosed centres. An American suburban centre of equivalent size would normally be of open layout, although some small enclosed developments exist within American central areas.

Major and minor space users

It will be recalled from Chapter 3 that the developer's task at an early stage in the development of a centre is to secure one or more major space users ('anchor stores') for the centre. These users may then be able to negotiate favourable financial terms, and some influence over the design and layout of the centre itself. Major space users are usually a supermarket, a variety store or a department store. The former is perhaps appropriate to a smallish centre whilst the latter two are necessary for larger centres. Marcus (1978, 1983) has shown that supermarkets tend to make unsatisfactory major space users for enclosed shopping centres. From a study of forty planned shopping centres in Britain, he found that centres with supermarkets as anchors had higher vacancy rates than those with variety or department stores as anchors. This appeared to be because the supermarket did not attract shoppers who wanted to spend time and money on comparison shopping; rather, grocery shopping is generally carried out as a single-purpose trip.

Since the Marcus study was carried out, the situation has changed in any case. The 'big five' grocery companies are unlikely to be interested in becoming anchors to enclosed shopping centres. They prefer to develop their own stores in free-standing locations (see Chapter 7). However, some other grocery companies might still see advantage in anchoring a small centre, perhaps of 50,000–100,000 sq. ft. gross retail area. This is particularly likely in small towns that cannot support a larger new shopping centre.

Variety and department stores form more appropriate anchors for a shopping centre. Of the variety stores, Marks & Spencer are undoubtedly seen as the most desirable. Other multiples such as Boots, C & A, BHS and W. H. Smith commonly act as major space users but not necessarily as the main anchor store.

The process of negotiation between shopping centre developers and major space users is shrouded in secrecy: there appear to be no published case studies of British practice. Generally it appears that the anchor store(s) in a development obtain very favourable terms, either amounting to a share in the development financing and centre ownership, or very low rents per unit area, compared with the minor space units. When the market is slack, anchor stores may also be able to extract a 'reverse premium' from the developer. It appears that the most desirable anchor tenants can extract payments of up to £3 million for agreeing to enter a new shopping centre, and one payment of £8 million has been alleged (*Guardian*, 1993).

It also appears that major space users generally pay less rent per square foot than do minor space users. This may be initially part of the developer's inducements to the company concerned to enter the scheme, but following rent review there may still be disparities, as shown in a study of rent reviews in Brent Cross and the Metro Centre (Hillier Parker, 1993b: 11).

The second stage in letting a centre – negotiation with minor space users – is also discussed little in the literature on shopping centre development. Major national retailers are routinely targeted by developers or shopping centre owners attempting to entice them into proposed or completed schemes. In most cases, developers prefer national multiple firms because local retailers are not felt to be sufficiently well established or reliable to become ideal tenants. Thus, the tenant mix of shopping malls is dominated by multiples (Centre for Advanced Land Use Studies, 1975). However, in a few of the larger 1980s developments, attempts have been made to incorporate independent retailers, usually by offering specialised areas of small units, or 'barrows' situated in the main pedestrian ways. The Metro Centre demonstrates both of these features (Howard, 1989).

Tenant mix in a successful enclosed centre is not simply a matter of fitting in any retailer that can offer the rent demanded and fulfil the usual financial security requirements. It is designed to cover as wide a selection of retail goods as possible. Even where an enclosed centre is part of a larger central shopping area, the enclosed centre is expected to fulfil this function. Also, tenants are discouraged from competing with each other through covenants attached to their leases (Savitt, 1985).

Layout of enclosed centres

The main design principles for an enclosed shopping centre are to impose a presence and authority for the centre through its external appearance; to encourage visits through the quality and convenience of the internal circulation areas; and to attempt to maximise levels of trade throughout the centre by suitable arrangement of the pedestrian circulation areas and retail units.

The external appearance of shopping centres is one of the issues discussed in texts written by and for architects, such as Gosling and Maitland (1976), Scott (1989), Beddington (1991) and Maitland (1985, 1990). As developed in the suburban context of North America, the shopping mall needs to be highly visible from nearby major roads. Use of appropriate signage and exterior cladding materials helps convey messages about the status of the centre and the type of shopper it attempts to attract. In the European city centre context, problems occurred in relating the large scale of the shopping mall to the more intimate and varied scale of the traditional shopping street. These problems are discussed in a later section.

Modern shopping malls are generally fully enclosed, and in many instances climate controlled. In Britain, full enclosure became common during the late 1960s; previously, centres had been fully pedestrianised, but the circulation areas were often left open to the elements or partially covered. The enclosed centre provides increased protection from bad weather, and better security, since pedestrian entrances to the centre can be locked when the centre is not in use. This means, however, that the shops within enclosed centres tend to look inwards towards the pedestrian malls: a problem when integration into the wider shopping environment of a town centre is expected. Air conditioning is unusual in British centres, but common in the United States and the Far East.

The internal arrangement of pedestrian malls and retail units has been recognised as an important matter for many years. A traditional layout in North American centres has been the 'dumbbell', with one of the main anchor stores at each end of the pedestrian mall. The anchor stores are the main attractions to shoppers, and while walking from one to the other, all the other shops are passed. This illustrates the main principle, which is to ensure a high level of pedestrian movement throughout the centre. Other principles of tenant placement within shopping centres, which include clustering of similar retailers, separation of incompatible tenants, and relegation of service units to less frequented parts of the centre, are discussed by S. Brown (1992: 176–187).

The location of retail and service units within the shopping mall thus reflects deliberate manipulation by the shopping centre owner, rather than the competitive bid-rent process which occurs in unplanned shopping areas (see Chapter 3).

A second major question is the number of floor levels to be adopted for retail sales. In Britain, the majority of shopping centres have been developed on one level only so far as retail sales are concerned, with storage and delivery access either above or below the sales area. Table 8.5 demonstrates this for a sample of fifty centres, and also shows that the fully enclosed centres are more likely to have been built on more than one level. This probably reflects their greater size and more recent construction, compared with the partially enclosed and open centres. Construction on one level might seem rather wasteful of land, given that land values in town and city centres are so high, but British developers have often claimed that shoppers are reluctant to use 'upper floor' shopping levels. Some centres have been developed on two or more levels to take advantage of uneven sites. However, until the 1980s it was fairly unusual for a two-level shopping mall to be built on an even town centre site.

Centres conceived and developed during the 1980s have more frequently involved two or even three shopping levels. This appears to have had several causes. First, the use of escalators and lifts in recent developments has made it much easier for shoppers to change levels within a centre. Indeed, the glass-walled lift has become a prominent design feature in some centres, encouraging shoppers to change levels. Second, land values have escalated so much in town centres that it has become necessary to include as much retail floorspace as

Table 8.5 Number of shopping levels in fifty shopping centres

Centre type	Number of Levels			
	1	*2*	*3*	*Total*
Open	5	1	–	6
Partially enclosed or covered	14	7	–	21
Fully enclosed	12	9	2	23
Total	31	17	2	

Source: Unit for Retail Planning Information (1987)

Note: Sample of centres is the same as used in Table 8.2

possible to provide sufficient return on investment. Third, the four very large 'regional' centres opened after 1985 contain so much retail space that placing it all on one level would oblige shoppers to carry out excessive walking in order to visit all the shops. Use of two levels makes both the centre, and some of the stores within it, more compact. Anchor stores are thus usually built on two levels, while minor space users are usually single level.

One way to minimise the 'upper level' problem is to make positive use of variations in level around the perimeter of the centre. Thus, one access from car parking can be at the upper level, another at the lower level.

In some centres of three or more levels in North America and the Far East, the different levels may specialise in types of retailing. For example, the Parkway Parade centre in Singapore has five specialist retail levels (Sim and Way, 1989).

The final question concerning internal layout is whether to provide non-retail attractions. In shopping centres developed in the 1970s and earlier in Britain, the space was used simply for shopping and associated service uses such as banking and restaurants. However, the largest North American centres had already for many years included one or more cinemas. It became common to use the spaces where pedestrian malls meet, for purposes which could attract shoppers or other visitors to the centre. Two common examples are the ice skating rink and the 'food court'. The latter comprises several kiosks serving cooked dishes, snacks or drinks, sited around a communal area for eating and drinking. Food courts became established in British shopping centres during the mid-1980s, with fifty-four courts in existence by 1992 (Hillier Parker, 1992c). The question of including 'leisure' uses within or adjacent to shopping malls is considered in a later section.

Location of shopping malls

In the United States the shopping mall was, until the 1980s at least, what we would call in Britain an 'out-of-town' development. They were typically built in or at the outer edge of fast-growing suburban areas, with good access to major highways. They fulfilled the needs of department store companies to access the fast-growing and wealthy suburban consumer markets. They also reduced development costs by taking up cheap suburban land, a factor which has kept typical American shop rents at a much lower level than is the case in Britain. The shopping mall in North America is often well isolated from other retail development, and it is intended to provide a complete shopping experience in itself.

In Britain, planners, politicians and most of the retail and property development industries have consistently supported the notion that major new retail developments should be confined to existing town and city centres. Thus, the shopping mall in Britain has been developed typically in existing central shopping areas, despite its suburban origins. This has brought problems in establishing the role of in-town enclosed centres, and in integrating them into the shopping area as a whole.

The following two sections discuss enclosed shopping centre development, in 'out-of-town' and 'in-town' locations, respectively, referring mainly to British examples.

'OUT-OF-TOWN' OR 'REGIONAL' CENTRES

The North American idea that large new shopping centres should be built in areas of rapid suburban growth first reached Western Europe in the early 1960s. It took root in a climate of retail expansion and rapidly growing car ownership. The movement coincided with the growth of demand for new large stores in edge-of-town and suburban locations. Since this time, the out-of-town regional shopping centre has been perhaps the major focus of argument and concern in retail planning and development circles. This section reviews the growth in pressure for such centres, especially during the 1980s in Britain, and discusses the characteristics of those centres so far built. The term 'regional centre' is used in this section to denote an enclosed, free-standing shopping centre of at least 500,000 sq. ft. gross retail area, built away from existing (unplanned) town or city centre retail areas.

The American background

In the United States, regional centres form the top level of a vast structure of planned centres located almost entirely in suburban areas and accessible to major road networks. Large cities may have several such centres. For example, in Metropolitan Atlanta (population around 2 million in 1980), twelve regional and super-regional centres were built between 1955 and 1983 (Dent, 1985). Three super-regional enclosed malls have been built in the suburbs of Charlotte (population 400,000), completely overshadowing the central business district's retail trade (Lord and Guy, 1991). Many regional centres have been built in the USA by large specialist property development companies, including the Edward DeBartolo Corporation, Melvin Simon and Associates, and the Rouse Company (Carlson, 1990).

In most of the States, there are no systematic land use planning restrictions on retail development as such. This means that in deciding whether to build a new regional centre, the economic impact on town and city centres (or, for that matter, on existing out-of-town centres) is not a matter which the developer need consider. The developer will base the decision to develop simply on his judgement of catchment population, ease of access by road to the site, and will possibly make heroic assumptions about the ability of the new centre to attract custom away from existing centres. The key to success, as in any major retail development, lies in attracting variety and department store companies (mainly the latter) into the new scheme. Thus, the viability of a regional centre proposal will depend largely upon the location of existing department store branches, and whether there is sufficient consumer demand for a new branch at the centre concerned.

The major department store companies in turn possess their own store location appraisal units, which will consider carefully any offers from regional shopping centre developers. In some cases, the store company will join forces with the developer to carry out a regional centre scheme.

As in Britain, many of the centres originally developed by specialist property companies or retail firms are now under the ownership of financial institutions (Carlson, 1991).

Since the 1970s the rate of construction of regional centres has declined substantially. During the period 1971–1975, thirty regional centres were started each year; in 1981–1987, the average had fallen to eighteen centres each year (Carlson, 1990). The main reason for this decline appears to be that local markets were in many areas saturated with retail space. Developers and investors have increasingly turned their attention to renovating the centres first developed in the 1950s and 1960s (Lord, 1985).

In Canada a similar change has arisen. Hallsworth (1988) draws a distinction between western Canada, where the free-market situation still obtains, and eastern Canada, where state and city governments have attempted to restrict the growth of out-of-town shopping in recent years. In Toronto, the city government has encouraged investment in the city centre and restricted growth in the suburbs (Shaw, 1985).

Regional shopping centre development in Western Europe

Out-of-town regional centres appeared first in Europe, in Germany, Sweden and France, during the 1960s. Several such centres were built around major conurbations in the period up to the mid-1970s. During the same period large numbers of hypermarkets and superstores were also built in these two countries. These developments together caused considerable concern, and following pressure from local politicians and chambers of commerce, restrictive legislation was put into effect in France, Belgium, the Netherlands and Germany (Dawson, 1982; TEST, 1989; Sljivic, 1990; François and Leunis, 1991). The essence of these restrictions was that retail development of more than a certain size and lying outside existing town or city centres could only take place if approved by local commercial and political interests, and (in Belgium and the Netherlands) following an impact study carried out by civil servants.

Development of regional centres has proceeded much more slowly since then, owing to a combination of restrictive legislation, high land values and, locally, market saturation (Healey & Baker, 1988; Reynolds, 1992).

Regional shopping centres in Britain: early events

In Britain, pressure for regional centres emerged in the early 1960s, with an application for a centre of around 1 million sq. ft. at Haydock, situated midway between Manchester and Liverpool. This application was refused in 1964 by the then Ministry of Housing and Local Government, following an appeal by the prospective developer. The main grounds for dismissal were the projected impact upon existing town centres in the region (Manchester University, 1964). Thus, the general opposition to major new off-centre development was made clear by local and central government interests at an early stage. Regulation was, however, to be carried out through the normal operation of the land use planning system, rather than through special legislation, as in continental Europe. Thus, the planning system's response to applications for major off-centre developments could potentially be changed at short notice and without the need for legislation, simply through the relaxing of constraints by central government ministries. This, in fact, threatened to take place during the 1980s, as explained below.

During the 1970s very few serious proposals for regional shopping centres in Britain were made. The cautious central and local government reaction to the early proposals for grocery superstore and retail warehouse developments made it seem unlikely that much larger schemes would be approved. In any case, the mid-1970s saw the 'property slump' which included the termination of several property companies, and a lack of available capital for new shopping centres. The only regional centre built in Britain in the 1970s was Brent Cross, developed in suburban north-west London. Being built in an area without major existing shopping facilities, the centre gained the approval of local authorities, since it appeared that its impact on other centres would be widespread over a large area. This centre of 760,000 sq. ft. was developed by the Hammerson Group and opened in 1977. It was anchored by two large department stores (John Lewis and Fenwicks), was built on two levels, and had car parking facilities for over 5,000 vehicles. Most, although not all, commentators would class this centre as the first 'out-of-town' regional shopping mall to be built in Britain. Brent Cross has been enormously successful commercially, and retailers there are now faced with some of the highest rents payable in Britain (Debenham Tewson Research, 1992a; Hillier Parker, 1993b).

As shown in Table 8.4, several regional-sized centres were built in government-financed new towns during the 1970s. Of these, the centres in Runcorn, Telford and Washington were built well away from existing town centres and thus could be regarded as the first free-standing regional centres to be built in Britain. The first free-standing super-regional centre to be built in Britain was Central Milton Keynes, opened in 1979. Although intended as the central shopping area for the new town of Milton Keynes, its floor area of 1,065,000 sq. ft. was well in excess of the size required for the town's population at that time, some 90,000. Long-term plans (since modified) were for the town to expand to a population of 250,000. However, the centre was intended to 'offer . . . an ease of car access which no other town centre in this country can rival – comparable with . . . out-of-town regional shopping centres' (Milton Keynes Development Corporation, 1987). The centre was developed by the Milton Keynes Development Corporation (a government-appointed body set up to develop and administer the new town) with long-term finance from the Post

Office Staff Superannuation Fund. It is in the form of a large rectangular building with enclosed open spaces used for exhibitions and entertainments. It is built on one level and is anchored by a John Lewis department store.

The 1980s: the boom that never was

Up to the early 1980s, a handful of regional centres had been built outside established shopping locations in Britain, and a small number of regional-sized centres had also been built within existing central areas (Table 8.4). The focus of concern amongst retail planners was still the superstore and the retail warehouse. No centre had been built – and very few proposed – that would threaten major existing town or city centres, as had been the case in North America, and (to a lesser extent) France and Germany.

This was to change. The mid-1980s saw a spate of proposals for new regional shopping centres, most of them apparently threatening established major town centres. In December 1987, no less than forty-two separate 'proposed out-of-town regional shopping centres' were shown on a map issued by Hillier Parker (reproduced in Figure 8.4). These were firm proposals, although most of them were yet to be submitted for planning approval. Altogether, fifty proposals of 500,000 sq. ft. or above were made between 1982 and 1991 (BDP Planning, 1992: 27–28).

Two main factors accounted for this sudden surge in interest in regional centre development in Britain. The first was the expansion in demand for premises by comparison goods multiples, particularly the growth and diversification of multiples in clothing, footwear, leisure, electronic and luxury goods (see Chapter 2). This demand for good quality retail premises in prime town centre areas led to a rapid rise in rents. Some developers saw an opportunity to build completely new centres to absorb this demand, assuming that expansion of existing centres would be insufficient. The retail parks that were beginning to be developed at this time would not meet the requirements of the comparison retailers concerned, most of whom wanted to rent smaller premises in large shopping centres.

It should be noted, however, that most of these retailers were lukewarm in their support for completely new regional centres, preferring to expand within the existing network of central shopping areas (Henley Centre, 1988).

The second factor to encourage the spate of regional centre proposals was an apparent change in attitude by central government to the land use planning issues concerned. This has been described in detail in Chapter 5. A general presumption in favour of development, 'enterprise' and generation of employment was augmented by specific comments on the desirability of encouraging competition between retailers and between methods of retailing (Department of the Environment, 1988). Developers appear to have taken this as an encouragement to propose large, new, enclosed centres, and were no doubt further encouraged when Nicholas Ridley, then Secretary of State for the Environment, said of the out-of-town shopping movement:

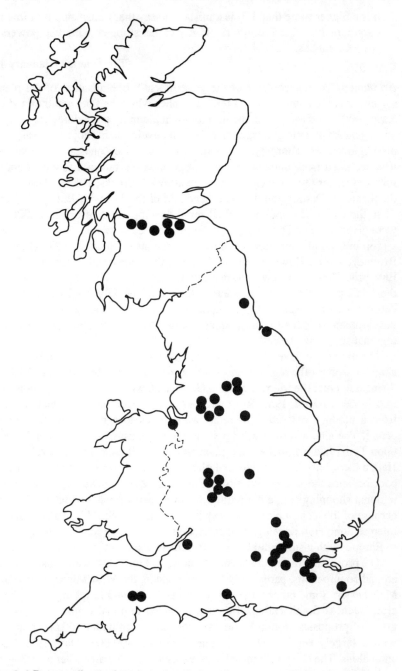

Figure 8.4 Proposed out-of-town regional shopping centres, December 1987
Source: Hillier Parker Research

It is a bigger force than I. It is a mistake to say that I must stop it or that it can be stopped . . . . I don't think it can be stopped with the powers that government has.

(The Times, 17 January 1987)

An unintended consequence of the government's liberalisation of the planning system arose in some of the Enterprise Zones which had been authorised in the early 1980s. In these zones, the normal town planning procedures are suspended and a general planning permission exists for development subject to prespecified, broad guidelines (Thornley, 1991). In most Enterprise Zones, retail development was excluded from automatic planning permission, but in a few of them some forms of major retail development were allowed (Sparks, 1987). These included the Swansea, Dudley and the Gateshead part of the Tyneside Enterprise Zones.

In the Swansea zone, individual retail developments of under 45,000 sq. ft. were given a general permission but larger centres were not. The result has been a proliferation of superstores and retail warehouses (Sparks, 1987; Thomas and Bromley, 1987). However, in Dudley, and the Gateshead part of the Tyneside Enterprise Zones, there was no restriction except on food retailing. It seems that the retail prospects of these areas, which were heavily blighted by industrial dereliction, were thought to be so poor that no control was necessary over retail development. Ironically, these areas became the sites for Europe's two largest regional shopping centres.

The event that several commentators have claimed to be the most important single reason for the regional shopping centre boom was the decision of Marks & Spencer to enter the Metro Centre in Gateshead, when it was being planned in the mid-1980s (Howard, 1989; Reynolds, 1993). This decision transformed the Centre from a planned collection of retail warehouses to a major enclosed regional centre. The site, a former ash-tip some 5 miles west of the centre of Newcastle upon Tyne, had originally been planned as a retail park by the developer, John Hall, a local businessman. Normal planning control was not required for a retail park because the site lay within an Enterprise Zone. However, the change to a regional shopping centre did require planning permission – which was granted – because of the inclusion of a food hypermarket. Encouraged by Marks & Spencer's interest, John Hall developed what became the largest enclosed shopping centre in Europe, with a substantial 'leisure' element also.

The proposals for regional centres, shown in Figure 8.4, were clustered mainly around conurbations, particularly Greater London, the West Midlands and Greater Manchester. Some other large cities such as Leeds and Edinburgh, or urbanised areas such as South Hampshire, also attracted regional centre proposals. The group of proposals around Exeter, an isolated city of under 100,000 population, with a largely rural catchment area of around 400,000 (Day, 1992), seems anomalous. The reason for this cluster appears to be that an earlier planning study had found that the central area of Exeter could not easily expand in retail floorspace and hence there was scope for a modest amount of edge-of-town development. This became interpreted as justification for a full regional centre of up to 650,000 sq. ft., by no less than five separate developers. This suggests that here, as elsewhere, a 'bandwagon' effect occurred with several developers competing over proposals which were probably barely viable economically.

The sudden emergence of up to fifty separate proposals for regional centres caused a certain amount of panic in retail planning circles. An example of this attitude can be found in an article by Latham (1988), who identified no fewer than seventy-two out-of-town schemes. On closer inspection, his list is found to contain duplication of single proposals and a scattering of retail parks and district centres. Nevertheless, the total floorspace in these proposals was added together, to total some 56 million sq. ft. This scale of development would clearly have had major competitive effects upon existing centres, both in taking away existing shopping trade and in diverting expansion schemes already proposed in these centres. However, it should have been clear already that only a small proportion of the proposed centres was likely to be built in the foreseeable future, even if central government planning attitudes were substantially relaxed. This was because, as in the Exeter case, several competing proposals tended to be made where only one might be viable. In contrast to the difficulties of assembling central area land for retail development, it was relatively easy to arrange first refusal to purchase a suburban or out-of-town site, and announce a massive shopping scheme. At this stage there was no need to arrange finance or to agree terms with major space users.

In the event, central government policy was reformulated and turned out to be less liberal than many expected, although the element of encouragement of competition was retained. The Planning Policy Guidelines (Department of the Environment, 1988) ruled out any major retail development in official Green Belts or (in general) in the open countryside. Other locations for new centres might be permissible, especially if they contributed to the reclamation of derelict land. However, the need to maintain the 'vitality and viability' of town and city centres was to be a major consideration.

Between 1986 and 1990 several of the proposals shown in Figure 8.4 were worked up in detail and applications were made for planning permission. Those cases in which there was a successful outcome for the developer are listed in Table 8.6, and their locations are shown in Figure 8.5. Of these, centres in Sheffield (Meadowhall Centre), Dudley (Merry Hill), and Thurrock, Essex (Lakeside) were given permission by the local authorities concerned, were built, and are now trading successfully. In none of these cases did the Secretary of State for the Environment use his powers to 'call in' the application for his own determination.

Several other proposals were given planning permission between 1987 and 1992, either by local authorities or by the Secretary of State for the Environment, following an appeal by the developer or a 'call-in' by the Secretary of State (Table 8.6). Of these, none was even under construction at the end of 1992, and two had been definitely abandoned by the developers. One of these abandonments

Figure 8.5 Location of enclosed centres of over 500,000 sq. ft. in Britain

Table 8.6 Regional shopping centre proposals in Britain

Name	Location	Size ('000 sq. ft.)	Planning status	Current status (end 1992)
Metro Centre	Gateshead	1,630	App (E)	Open
Merry Hill	Dudley	1,410	App (E)	Open
Lakeside	Thurrock	1,150	App	Open
Meadowhall	Sheffield	1,100	App	Open
Blue Water Park	Dartford	1,500	App	
Sandwell Mall	Sandwell	1,400	App	Abandoned
Royal Albert Dock	London	872	App	Abandoned
Cribb's Causeway	Bristol	700	All	
White Rose	Leeds	650	All	
Cheshire Oaks	Chester	623	App	
Barton Dock	Manchester	667	Pending	
n.k.	Cambridge	500–624	Pending	
= 3 schemes			Refused	
= 20 schemes			Dismissed	
= 18 schemes			Withdrawn	

Source: BDP (1992: Table 2.3); Hillier Parker (various); Unit for Retail Planning Information (1991)

Note: App – Approved
All – Allowed on appeal by Secretary of State
(E) – Within enterprise zone

(Royal Docks, in London) took place in 1990 when it appeared that it would not prove economically viable. The other, Sandwell Mall in the West Midlands, ran into problems, over the excessive costs needed to reclaim a derelict industrial site, and over the agreement of terms between the local authority and a series of prospective developers. The centre was eventually deemed to be inviable, following the successful completion of the Merry Hill centre some six miles away. The retail proposals for the site have now been replaced by a business park scheme.

Several other regional centre proposals were refused by local authorities and were taken to appeal by the developers. Most of these were refused permission by the Secretary of State (Table 8.6; a full list is provided in BDP (1992): Table 2.3). The main reasons for refusal have been the precedence given to Green Belt and other open countryside, and the impact upon existing town centres. Traffic issues were important determinants in only two of the eighteen cases examined by the Unit for Retail Planning Information (1990).

Most of the remaining proposals listed in BDP (1992) have been withdrawn by the prospective developers. Stated reasons for withdrawing schemes are difficult to obtain. It appears, however, that several schemes were withdrawn following the approval of other centres in the area. These would include Fort Dunlop, Birmingham (830,000 sq. ft.), and Parkgate, Rotherham (1,500,000 sq. ft.). Some 'Green Belt' schemes may have been withdrawn when it became obvious that they would not be supported by the Secretary of State on appeal.

Thus, the anticipated boom in regional shopping centre development has not taken place. Since 1985, only four centres have been opened, and a further six have planning approval and appear likely to be built (see Table 8.6). The centres opened and likely to open are all within or close to major conurbations, and have mainly been built in areas of industrial or mining dereliction. Thus, few 'out-of-town' regional centres in Britain are in the American mould of true edge-of-town developments related to the major road system. Rather, the schemes that are most likely to gain planning approval (or indeed, to be promoted by local authorities, as in the cases of Sheffield and Sandwell) involve reclamation of large and heavily despoiled former industrial areas. Such reclamation for shopping purposes is also encouraged in government advice to local planning authorities (Department of the Environment, 1988).

The development process for regional centres

The regional centres built in Britain correspond closely to the conventional model of an enclosed shopping centre, with variety and department stores as major space users, and comparison shops run by major multiple retailers forming the great majority of the smaller units. There is perhaps more emphasis on leisure uses within the centre than is characteristic of enclosed schemes within unplanned centres. Car parking provision is on a scale comparable with food superstores, at between about 6.5 and 10 spaces per 1,000 sq. ft. of gross retail area (based upon Howard, 1992: Table 3). This is a more generous provision than that typical in North American centres (4–5 spaces per 1,000 sq. ft.), and much more generous than typically found in town centres (Burt and Sparks, 1991; Howard, 1992).

A major contrast with in-town centres lies in patterns of shopping centre finance and ownership. In-town development has since the 1960s been the focus of investment and development by established financial interests. Out-of-town development has, on the contrary, been viewed as less 'respectable' by the financial institutions: it does not conform with the rather conservative definitions of 'prime' retail opportunity typical of the institutions (see Chapter 4). Generally, proposals for regional centres have arisen from locally based property development firms rather than the national property companies and financial institutions. Three of the four super-regional centres built since 1985 were developed by local businessmen who saw an opportunity to develop on derelict industrial land (Metro Centre – John Hall; Merry Hill – Roy and Don Richardson; Meadowhall – Paul Sykes and Eddie Healey). Several other out-of-town proposals that proved abortive were put forward by locally based property developers.

This phenomenon represents a combination of local knowledge and opportunism, reminiscent of much of the early development of in-town shopping centres in the 1950s and early 1960s (Marriott, 1967). The developers concerned were able to buy large areas of derelict land at low prices, and had the vision to see their potential for large-scale retail development. There was also a degree of encouragement from local planning authorities, despite the general opposition to out-of-town shopping which is characteristic of British planning practice (see Chapter 5).

Towards the end of the 1980s, the major financial and development interests began to realise the opportunities in regional shopping centres. The first centre developed by a major property company was the Lakeside Centre at Thurrock in Essex, opened in 1990 by Capital & Counties plc, a company that had already developed several major shopping malls within town centres. Property companies and financial institutions also proposed some of the centres that have now been abandoned, refused permission, or delayed. For example, the Prudential Insurance Company proposed a regional centre at Cribb's Causeway, near Bristol. Institutions have also taken an interest in two regional centres through the purchase of completed developments, including the Metro Centre (purchased by the Church Commissioners) and Merry Hill (purchased by Mountleigh Securities). The latter company has since gone into receivership and, after a long delay, the centre was sold to the Chelsfield property company in 1993. These moves suggest that regional centres are becoming more 'respectable', but institutions are more likely for the time being to purchase completed centres than to initiate the development process itself.

Prospects for the 1990s

At present (late 1993) there are only six proposed out-of-town regional shopping centres that appear likely to be built in the next few years (see Table 8.6). This would represent almost a doubling of the floorspace built in the 1980s. The question can be asked whether other proposals will emerge in the 1990s, putting pressure again on central and local government and arousing controversy on the scale of the mid-1980s?

A major issue concerns the financial prospects of regional centres as property investments. While the major new out-of-town centres are all virtually fully let to retailers, and are said to be performing well, there are longer-term doubts. First, the exemption from payment of business rates (property taxes) which has applied in Enterprise Zones is being phased out. This will increase retailers' costs, along with the inevitable increase in rent demands at the five-year rent review points (Hillier Parker, 1993b). Second, regional centres are so large and so valuable that few institutions are willing to buy them from developers or other institutions. For example, the Lakeside Centre was valued in 1992 at over £300 million. Using the normal rules for acceptable levels of risk in property investment (see Chapter 4), few if any of the institutions would be prepared to buy a single property of such high value. The answer to this problem would appear to lie in unitisation (Thompson and Wythe, 1988: 160).

There are also more general arguments concerning future development of regional centres. In their favour, Howard (1992) argues that for the shopper, the regional centres fulfil a somewhat different function to that of conventional city centres. They cater more for the 'family day out', with their provision of fast food and entertainment outlets; and attract the motorist with their abundant free car parking. These views are supported by a comparison of shoppers' images of the Metro Centre with the in-town Eldon Square centre (McGoldrick and Thompson, 1992). This means that the regional centres do not simply act to take trade away from nearby town centres. Retailers may wish to expand into new regional centres provided they have large catchment populations and are accessible from the national motorway network. It should be stated though that this opinion is at odds with the view of several retailers that their stores in out-of-town centres are taking trade from their in-town stores rather than adding much to total sales volume.

On the supply side, large derelict sites in urban areas still exist. Potential developers may soon again begin to see retailing as the 'highest and best' use for these sites. And, given the largely successful performance of the early regional centres (Howard, 1992), institutions may see greater reason to become involved in the early stages of development.

The arguments against further regional shopping centres rest on planning and environmental issues. The case against such centres on grounds of economic impact on town centres will continue to be made. With the increased status of approved local plans in the planning system (see Chapter 5), regional centre applications which are contrary to local planning policy seem unlikely to win through on appeal. Thus, promoters of such centres will need to gain the support of the local planning authority, which is likely only if very substantial 'planning gain' in the form of environmental improvements is forthcoming. The other opportunity open to developers is to target areas under the control of Urban Development Corporations, which have been set up in several areas of urban decay to promote new development (Thornley, 1991). These corporations, which possess substantial land use planning powers, are likely to take a more liberal attitude to retail schemes. The clearest example of this was the proposed Royal Docks regional shopping centre in east London, which was approved by the London Docklands Development Corporation but was later withdrawn by the developers. However, there are only twelve such corporations in England and Wales, and in most of their areas the scope for regional centres appears small.

Added to the established planning case against regional centres is a more recent concern to reduce the demand for private car travel, in order to conserve energy and inhibit global warming. The British government's statement of environmental policy (Department of the Environment, 1990) hints that out-of-town shopping proposals will be viewed critically for these reasons. The European Commission's 'Green Paper' (Commission of the European Communities,

1990) supports strongly the notion of the compact, high-density city as a way of reducing energy consumption. Campaigners have strongly attacked out-of-town shopping of all kinds, claiming that European governments are now firmly in support of retaining major shopping provision in city centres. In England and Wales, the revised Planning Policy Guidance Note Six (Department of the Environment, 1993) mentions these concerns and gives stronger support to central city retail development and weaker support to off-centre development, than the original Guidance Note (Department of the Environment, 1988).

Thus, there appears to be less likelihood of further approvals of regional centres than there was in the 1980s, in Britain and in most European countries.

IN-TOWN SHOPPING MALLS

The shopping mall was then originally developed as a free-standing, suburban shopping facility. It was a major feature in the decentralisation of shopping in North America, leading eventually to the virtual elimination of central area shopping in many American cities (Lord, 1988). In Western Europe, however, the shopping mall has been transformed into a vehicle for enlarging and modernising central area shopping. Nearly all large enclosed centres exist within older and largely unplanned shopping areas.

This section first discusses some of the problems which this location can create for the shopping centre developer. This is followed by a progress review *vis-à-vis* development in Britain since the 1950s of design and layout issues, and of developers and sources of finance. The section ends with a discussion of future prospects for the in-town shopping mall.

Adapting the shopping mall to the in-town environment

The large enclosed centre is intended to have a distinctive identity and to provide a wide and balanced variety of retail goods and shopping experiences to the consumer. The aim of the American regional centre is to provide 'one-stop shopping', so that the shopper can obtain all necessary items by visiting the centre in question. 'Convenience' is also important; the shopper should be able to reach the centre easily, park without fuss, and have refreshments and services available in the centre if desired.

Providing an identifiable, balanced and convenient centre is more difficult when the centre has to be fitted into an existing shopping area. Several problems may arise. First, there is the problem of assembling a sufficiently large site, of a shape which allows a conventional mall layout and adequate arrangements for goods delivery and pedestrian access. This may take several years to achieve in older and densely built-up town centres, with or without the assistance of compulsory purchase powers of the local authority. In this context, the experienced shopping centre architect Keith Scott commented in 1980:

Without question, central area schemes are the toughest nuts to crack. To me it is a continuing miracle that any get built at all ... firstly there is never a fixed site . . . . You can put money on the probability of its being changed – often, and sometimes radically. . . . Then there is never a fixed brief for the designer to assimilate. The brief evolves from the subtle commercial pressures that shift constantly with time and fashion.

(quoted in Maitland, 1990: 20)

Second, attracting an appropriate major space user can be difficult if all the likely retailers are already represented in the town centre. Their stores may be owned freehold, or in what appear to be good locations, in which case they are unlikely to wish to move to the new centre. In this situation the developer will try to bring a new major multiple into the town centre.

A third problem concerns the range of shopping and other facilities available in the new centre. It is more difficult to enable a full range of shopping types and experiences when the new centre is but a small part of the town centre as a whole. Shoppers cannot be expected to visit the new centre in isolation. The solution may be to give the new centre some competitive edge over the remainder of the town centre, perhaps by encouraging 'up-market' or specialist retailers. The recent emphasis on food courts is also designed for this purpose.

A further problem concerns car parking. The generous provision of ground-level, free parking characteristic of American centres and European out-of-town centres is not feasible in town centres: space is too scarce and land values too high. Howard (1992: Table 3) shows that regional scale centres within central shopping areas have far lower levels of parking provision than the major out-of-town schemes discussed in the previous section. On this point, see also Burt and Sparks (1991).

Car parking provided as part of the centre is likely to be multi-storey, because of the high cost of land. This raises costs to the developer and also deters the shopper if free parking is available elsewhere. Some enclosed centre developers have failed to provide any car parking at all for customers, leaving it to the local authority concerned to provide parking on adjacent sites at public expense. An example of this is the very successful St David's Centre in Cardiff, opened at a difficult time for developers (1981) when interest charges were high and consumer demand sluggish. Under these economic circumstances, the developer was presumably not prepared to pay the costs of the car parking which the centre's own shoppers would require. Similar results occurred in the case of several North American in-town shopping centres (Frieden and Sagalyn, 1989).

A final set of problems concerns the physical integration of the new centre into the town centre as a whole. In a sense these are problems that concern local authority planners rather than developers, but the developer may need to pay attention to them in order to gain approval for the scheme. One aspect of this is the relationship between the appearance, height, bulk and building materials used for the new centre and those used in the adjoining parts of the older shopping area

(Scott, 1989). Many centres built during the 1960s and 1970s have been widely criticised not only for sweeping away older buildings, but also for their insensitivity in relation to their surroundings.

A separate but related problem is the arrangements for pedestrian access and internal security in the new centre. The developer will prefer the centre to be a self-contained unit which can be made secure from unauthorised entry at times when the shops are closed. This means locking the pedestrian entrances, and in effect denying the public any right of way through the centre. The planners and local public may prefer to maintain access, especially where the centre is built across former rights of way. More generally, it is seen as unfortunate that the intensive pedestrian movement within a centre is cut off visually and functionally from other areas of pedestrian activity within the town centre, often by blank walls and traffic routes (Maitland, 1990: 63). In most cases it appears nevertheless that the developer's views have prevailed.

Rates of development of enclosed centres

The development of planned shopping centres on the American model began in British town centres in the late 1950s, as discussed in an earlier section. The early centres used mainly sites bombed in the Second World War, and were unsophisticated groups of shops around an open space or uncovered walkway (Marriott, 1967). As the early centres proved successful, larger centres were proposed, with the often enthusiastic support of local councils (see Chapter 5). The development of the first fully enclosed centres in the early 1960s has been described in an earlier section of this chapter.

During the late 1960s and early 1970s, many towns and cities gained their first, and in some cases, second, shopping mall within the central area. The number of centres opened each year increased substantially during this period (Figure 8.6). Altogether some 300 town centre shopping schemes of 50,000 sq. ft. and over were completed between 1965 and 1975, although not all of these were fully enclosed shopping malls (Hillier Parker, 1991a). This surge in development resulted from the need to expand and modernise central area shopping, from the co-operation of local authorities, and from the ready availability of finance for property development.

This period was followed by one in which relatively little development took place, lasting until about 1985 (Figure 8.6). This lull reflected, first, the low rate of growth of the retail sector generally and, second, inhibitions on property development brought about by the financial crisis of 1974–1975 and by continuing high interest rates.

The mid- and late 1980s saw a resurgence in interest in in-town shopping schemes, despite the concurrent increase in out-of-town development. In 1989 and 1990, in-town shopping developments reached a total of around 5 million sq. ft., a total exceeded only in the years 1971–1976 (Hillier Parker, 1991a). This development was in response to the expansion of multiple retailing in clothing,

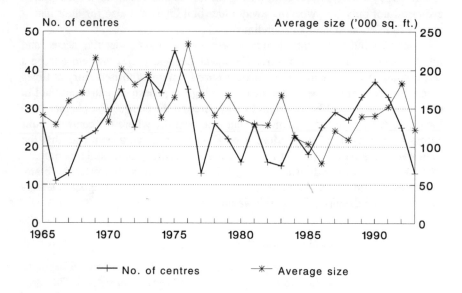

Figure 8.6 Town centre shopping developments, 1965–1993
Source: Hillier Parker Research

fashion and other areas of comparison shopping (discussed in Chapter 2), although the new space often arrived too late to prevent excessive pressures on existing space, resulting in large increases in town and city centre rents for prime locations.

Changes in layout and character

The 1980s town centre developments were, however, rather different in character to those of the 1960s and early 1970s. The 1980s schemes have been somewhat smaller on average (Figure 8.6) and more specialist in nature. Some of these schemes are deliberately 'up-market' in nature, or linked with leisure and entertainment provision. This change has occurred for two reasons. First, the conventional 'one-stop' centre with department stores as major space users and a complete range of other retail goods is difficult to provide if this type of centre has already been built in a previous generation of developments within the same town. Second, the increasing sophistication of comparison shopping and the growing association of shopping and leisure – following American practice – has encouraged the new generation of centres. An example may clarify these points. The Guardian Royal Exchange company first proposed an enclosed shopping mall within the city centre of Cardiff in 1984. This scheme included 198,000 sq. ft. of gross retail area and included a department store as the major space user.

Following rejection of the planning application by the local authority and (on appeal) by the Secretary of State for Wales, an amended scheme (Capitol Exchange centre) was produced. This included a smaller volume of retailing (117,000 sq. ft.), and replacement of the department store by a five-screen cinema. The centre was also intended to attract specialist and up-market comparison retailers to Cardiff (Guy and Lord, 1993). In this way it would complement, rather than compete with, the adjacent mass-market St David's Centre. The retail element in Capitol Exchange (opened in 1990) comprises a two-level arcade running be- tween two relatively small major space users (Virgin Megastore and Reject Shop: both examples of retailers who expanded rapidly at the end of the 1980s).

Noticeable changes have also occurred in the design of in-town centres, again following trends in North America and the Far East. The 1970s centres were often monolithic concrete structures, paying little heed to their setting within the town centre. The 1980s centres usually fit in better with their surroundings, and are faced in brick or local stone (Scott, 1989). Inside, as in modern office blocks, the 'atrium' (a high open space with natural lighting and plentiful greenery) is a common feature. Paving materials are better quality, and retail tenants are en- couraged to be individualistic in their shop front design and window displays.

Trends in development and funding

The first generation of in-town shopping centres was developed in the 1960s, largely by specialist retail developers who sought short-term finance from banks or financial institutions. Funding was provided in the manner of a mortgage, with repayments at a fixed rate irrespective of the rental income following completion of the centre. Major developers included Ravenseft, Town & City, Hammersons, Laing and Murrayfields (Marriott, 1967; Thompson and Wythe, 1988).

Many of these early developments turned out to be highly profitable, not least because the developers were able to purchase properties at existing rather than development value (see Chapter 3). The financial institutions recognised an opportunity to make greater profits from town centre development, so became involved as active partners with the property companies listed above.

Financial institutions tightened their grip on central area schemes in the mid-1970s, when several property companies went into liquidation and jointly developed schemes became the sole responsibility of the institutions (Thompson and Wythe, 1988). The scene would appear to have been set for almost complete domination of central area development by the financial institutions in the 1980s. However, this did not occur. Although some institutions, such as Norwich Union Insurance, continued to be involved in town centre schemes, the bulk of new developments was by property companies. This reflects the resurgence of the property developer as such, and the increasing preference of institutions for non-property investments during the 1980s.

The role of local authorities in town centre shopping development has already been discussed in Chapter 5. Although in some cases the local authority was the lead developer, more often it purchased the freehold of the land required, and the lead developer then took out a long lease at very low rent. The local authority sometimes went into a 'partnership' arrangement, taking a share of the profits. These arrangements characterised the 1970s rather than later periods, because from 1980 onwards local authorities would have found difficulty in obtaining loan sanction from central government for these purposes.

Prospects for the 1990s

At the end of the 1980s the town centre retail market was affected, as were all other sectors of the commercial property market, by the economic recession and its associated high interest rates, by lack of demand, and by the collapse of some property companies. A number of schemes were completed in the early 1990s but have tended to suffer from lack of demand for new premises. Other schemes were abandoned or postponed. Shopping centres generally offer yields well above those of individual prime 'high street' units, indicating the greater risk attached to 'lumpy' investments (Morgan, 1992).

In the early stages of the current recession, it appeared that retail development in town centres was affected less by the property slump than were most other forms of investment. In 1991 and 1992, town centre schemes constituted the majority of retail development (Hillier Parker, 1993a). However, this may simply have reflected the longer lead times for town centre schemes (typically 4 years or more) compared with retail parks (1–2 years). Schemes that were planned and funded when rents were rising fast have been completed at a time of falling rents. This phase has now almost ended: less than 2 million sq. ft. of town centre space was likely to be opened in 1993, possibly the lowest total since 1966 (Hillier Parker, 1993a).

In the meantime, town centre schemes planned in the late 1980s are still opening and in some cases are suffering high vacancy rates (Hillier Parker, 1992b). One short-term answer to this problem is the letting of excess shopping space to independent retailers on short leases. The 'In-Shops' Group has become prominent in this respect, owning sixty-three such 'centres' in early 1993.

Future trends in retail development in central shopping areas are difficult to assess at present. The institutional investors appear to have retained much of their faith in town centre shops, continuing to regard them as sound investments and being prepared to purchase good-quality properties in prime locations. A great deal of institutional money is invested in 'high streets', and this money is spread over a large number of complete shopping centres as well as individual shop premises. It is not clear at present whether the institutions are likely to encourage new development of additional shopping space in town centres. In the short term, it also seems unlikely that smaller developers will easily raise short-term finance from other sources: the major banks are still attempting to reclaim money owed by 1980s 'boom' developers (see Chapter 4).

The longer-term prospects for town centre schemes appear brighter, however. Such schemes generally have support from local and central government interests and are unlikely to encounter the opposition now being levied against off-centre shopping malls. Development may be spurred on in the late 1990s if a steady rise in consumer expenditure gives retailers the confidence to expand into the currently large amounts of vacant floorspace in many shopping centres. Such development may, however, take the form largely of refurbishment and enlargement of the first generation of in-town shopping centres, built up to the mid-1970s. The next section discusses this topic in more detail.

OBSOLETE DEVELOPMENTS: DISINVESTMENT OR REFURBISHMENT?

Shopping centres can lose their attraction for a number of reasons. These can include physical wear and tear, changing requirements and preferences of retailers and consumers, or external changes in the environment such as alterations to transport networks, or removal of complementary land uses on neighbouring sites. This section explores these issues and reviews current practice.

Much unplanned shopping exists, in Western Europe, in buildings which may be tens or even hundreds of years old. The shops themselves though may need to rearrange and update their display and storage arrangements on a regular short-term basis. From time to time, shop fronts need to be replaced and modernised. The development of modern shopping centres has brought with it the view that the whole centre needs to be 'renewed' from time to time: either demolished to make way for new development, or substantially modernised. The term 'refurbishment' is often used for the latter process. It can include anything from replacement of parts of the structure (for example, flooring) to extensive rebuilding and reorientation of the centre's 'offer' to the shopper.

Commentators speak of the 'lifespan' of a shopping centre: the period of time after which extensive refurbishment is likely to be necessary. A typical lifespan might be between 10 and 20 years, although circumstances vary considerably. The main reasons for refurbishment are, first, physical deterioration of the building fabric and surrounds; second, obsolescence of the type of retailing offered in the centre; and third, obsolescence of the centre as a whole (Morgan and Walker, 1988: Chapter 14; Scott, 1989: Chapter 9; Beddington, 1991: Chapter 11). The second case may involve, for example, splitting up a department store. The third case may involve covering or enclosing an open centre.

In some cases, centres become abandoned by their original tenants before physical decay sets in (although abandonment can accelerate the decay). This is usually because of initial design or location faults, which mean that the centre is not able to sustain the role envisaged by the developer; or because external changes have made the centre's location less attractive. Examples of the latter abound in the United States, where movement of population outwards from the inner city has led to some of the early planned shopping centres losing much of their original catchment population. Lord (1985: 227) draws a distinction between 'renovation' (which means 'physical changes which alter the centre but do not change its type') and 'recycling' (which means 'a re-tenanting and re-marketing of a centre which does result in a change in the type of centre'). Recycling of a centre is problematic in the British context, because tenants are usually offered 25-year full repairing leases.

Commentators (e.g. Morgan, 1992) have suggested that refurbishment of shopping centres will be a major task in Britain in the 1990s and beyond. Indeed, a substantial amount of refurbishment is already occurring. Some fifty-five centres will have been refurbished during the three years 1991–1993 (*Chartered Surveyor Weekly*, 1993). As an example, the recent refurbishment of the 300,000 sq. ft. Camberley Precinct, originally opened by Town & City properties in 1969, cost over £25 million. It involved replacing the flat roof with a 'Victorian' steel and glass structure; replacing stepped changes in floor level with gradual slopes; improving access for the disabled; increasing the trading area of existing shops by narrowing the pedestrian ways; creating thirty new retail units; and renaming the centre as 'Main Square' (*Chartered Surveyor Weekly*, 1992; 1993).

There are many other 'tired' town centre developments dating from the late 1960s and early 1970s that now appear outdated and have lost trade to newer schemes. A good example is the Overgate Centre in Dundee (Braithwaite, 1989). There are signs that the institutions have been disposing of old centres to property developers, who may be contemplating refurbishment when funds become available. As there are very few central shopping areas without at least one shopping centre already in existence, refurbishing old centres would seem less expensive and less risky to the investor than building entirely new centres, even if land and finance is available for the new development.

SPECIALITY AND FESTIVAL RETAILING

As explained in Chapter 2, speciality retail centres, including 'festival market-places', fulfil a rather different function from the conventional shopping mall. The speciality centre, strictly speaking, comprises one particular type of retailing and derives its trade from a specialised clientele. Thus, a street market selling cheap or second-hand goods to people on restricted incomes could form an example. The term has recently though come to be used to describe centres developed for a particular type of shopping activity rather than a particular segment of the market. This shopping activity is related to enjoyment of shopping, often combined with tourist interests. Thus, Maitland (1990) describes the pioneering speciality centres built in San Francisco in the 1960s:

> Against the bland and predictable character of the new regional malls set in their featureless car parks, they offered characterful old buildings on attractive urban sites, and they filled them with small and intriguing shops designed to cater to increasing affluence for leisure, tourism and eating out .... Specialty centres, in the sense of groups of small, specialised traders operating in a

specially-designed setting peripheral to the mainstream of retailing functions, were not new, but had been catering to specialised areas of the market, especially in novelty and luxury goods, since at least the seventeenth century. What was new was the types of market being served and the physical forms being adopted.

(Maitland, 1990: 25)

Festival marketplaces in North America

The 'festival marketplace' became a feature of several of North America's largest cities during the 1970s and 1980s. The most quoted example is probably Faneuil Hall Marketplace, opened in Boston in 1976. This involved use of early-nineteenth-century wholesale market buildings close to the waterfront, to provide some 219,000 sq. ft. of retail space. The project was developed by the Rouse Company, up to that time one of North America's leading shopping mall developers. The Faneuil Hall scheme was very much a leap into the unknown, and involved substantial financial support from the Boston City administration. It turned out to be profitable for the developer as well as a major tourist attraction for the city (Frieden and Sagalyn, 1989: 178).

The Rouse Company and the architect Benjamin Thompson went on to develop several other festival marketplaces in cities such as Baltimore, New York and Miami. In some cases, new buildings were constructed rather than old ones adapted. In each case, the outcome has been very different from the conventional shopping mall: shop units are small and leased mainly to local businessmen rather than multiple retailers, on short leases. The tenant mix is tightly controlled, to provide variety and interest to shoppers. Restaurants and fast-food outlets should take up at least 40 per cent of the floor area (English Tourist Board, 1989: 93). These marketplaces tend to be open or partly covered rather than fully enclosed: pedestrian areas may be narrow and congested, and open spaces given over to various forms of informal entertainment.

Following the success of the schemes in San Francisco, Boston, Seattle and other cities in the 1970s, festival marketplaces were attempted in many other cities. Invariably this involved substantial financial assistance from local government, the true extent of which was often concealed from electors (Frieden and Sagalyn, 1989; Sawicki, 1989). Several such schemes, mainly in smaller cities, have not proved viable economically, and some have closed down altogether for lack of support from shoppers and retailers (Guskind and Pierce, 1988; Guy and Lord, 1993). It appears that in North America, successful festival retailing requires a very large support population, probably of at least 1 million (English Tourist Board, 1989: 93). This should ideally include office workers as well as local residents. Alternatively, an important tourist attraction in close proximity may provide sufficient support. The festival marketplace does not appear in itself to be a strong enough attraction to bring tourists to a city.

Festival retailing in North America has become important largely through the efforts of city administrations. They have been prepared to assist developers with land purchase, and offer various types of tax rebate and other subsidies. The developers feel that central city areas are basically unattractive to shoppers, and that the normal attributes of shopping malls – especially the free, ground-level car parking – cannot be provided economically in the city centre. Financial institutions can be persuaded to support city centre schemes, but only provided that the local administration provides subsidies and takes on much of the financial risk. Given that the conventional mall is usually inappropriate and infeasible within the city centre, the festival marketplace has become an acceptable alternative. Typically, both costs of operation and revenues are much higher per square foot than in conventional shopping malls. However, the most successful examples date from the late 1970s and early 1980s: whether there is scope for further development in the future is uncertain.

Speciality and festival retailing in the UK

In Britain, speciality shopping development has taken place within a context quite different from that of North America. As we have seen, retail development in city centres can be profitable without state subsidies and is normally supported by long-term finance from the institutions. Hence there is no need to create an unusual form of retailing – the festival marketplace – to compensate for the deficiencies of the city centre location. However, some speciality and festival development has taken place in Britain.

There appears to be no directory of speciality centres in Britain, and one can only proceed through discussion of a few examples. The nearest approach to Faneuil Hall and other American examples is probably Covent Garden Market in central London, where former wholesale market buildings have been adapted for retail use. Other successful conversions of nineteenth-century buildings which outlasted their initial use have occurred in Glasgow (Princes Square), Leeds (Corn Exchange) and London (Whiteleys: a former department store). However, the Tobacco Dock conversion in London's Docklands has been unsuccessful commercially. This appears to be owing largely to its location, which is remote from other tourist attractions. A rare example in a smaller city has been the successful Canute's Pavilion in Southampton, which is part of the Ocean Village waterfront marina and residential development. All of these centres display to a greater or lesser extent the typical features noted above: the largely independent retailer tenants, the small retail units, and the mixture of retail with restaurants and entertainment uses.

Generally speaking, speciality retailing is unlikely to attract investment from the financial institutions. This is owing to its reliance upon independent retailers and short leases, and deliberate avoidance of reputable anchor tenants.

Retail and leisure

The development of such centres has taken place within a wider debate on the appropriateness of mixing retail and 'leisure' uses within the same development. Following the example of North American shopping malls, which for many years have tended to include cinemas and ice rinks, British developers began to include these attractions in both off-centre and town centre developments. The huge West Edmonton Mall in Canada (Johnson, 1987; Hallsworth, 1988), which includes substantial 'funfair' type attractions, became a model for British developers such as John Hall, who was responsible for the Metro Centre. It was assumed that: 'there is a synergy between [retail and leisure], one benefiting the operation of the other, so that the overall attraction is greater than the sum of the two halves' (Howard, 1989: 25).

This argument was enthusiastically promoted during the mid- and late 1980s, for example in the review of successful schemes published by the English Tourist Board (1989). However, experience of combining retail and leisure uses has not been entirely successful, and more cautious views are now common (Howard, 1990). Research at the Metro Centre has not entirely supported the 'synergy' argument expressed above, although both retail and leisure elements appear to be successful commercially. Leisure facilities (other than the ubiquitous food court) have been provided at Merry Hill and Lakeside super-regional centres, but outside the shopping mall itself. Meadowhall Centre was planned to include leisure facilities but they have not yet been provided.

Integrating shopping and leisure presents some problems for the development industry. First, different development companies would normally be involved for the two uses. A leisure developer might consider first a free-standing suburban site, or a retail park scheme, when developing a multi-cinema complex or indoor bowling arena, for example. The retail park location allows sharing of car parking areas with the retail units. Siting within a shopping mall involves some loss of identity, problems of access, and a more complex development procedure subject to various causes of uncertainty.

The rents obtainable, and hence site values, are much lower for leisure uses than for comparison retailing (Jaffa, 1989). This presents difficulties in funding a joint retail and leisure scheme. In addition, prospects for refurbishment in the long term are more difficult for joint schemes, because the allocation of space between the two types of use cannot readily be altered, and leases for leisure operators may be different in length from those for retail tenants (Harrison, 1990).

CONCLUSIONS

This final section draws together several themes in order to make a critical review of the process of shopping centre development.

Major influences on shopping centre development

Three sets of influences appear to have affected both the characteristics of shopping centres and the rates of development over time. The first of these has been growth and change in consumer expenditure and shopping preferences. Consumer expenditure increases have led in an indirect way to booms in shopping centre development, although this process suffers from time lags and has led to various problems which are discussed later in this section. Shoppers have also shown preferences for high-quality shopping environments protected from extremes of weather and easily accessible by car. This has encouraged increasingly higher standards of construction of shopping malls, and appears likely to encourage substantial refurbishment of older covered shopping centres during the 1990s.

The second general influence has been that of the funding institutions. Shopping centre developers have generally been dependent upon the institutions to underwrite such large and expensive schemes. The institutions are naturally cautious, hence it has been difficult to secure funding for any scheme that is either novel in character or located outside conventional shopping areas. This may help explain the slow rates of development of retail parks (until the mid-1980s) and also of regional centres. Once that it was demonstrated that such schemes were successful, then institutions were prepared to buy completed developments. There is still some reluctance amongst the institutions to initiate any type of shopping centre development, outside central shopping areas.

The third general influence has been that of land use planning control. Many, though not all, of the differences between North America and Western Europe in their urban retail structures are due to contrasts in planning control over new development. The much looser degree of control in North America has led not only to much greater volumes of retail floorspace overall, and a much higher prevalence of suburban and edge-of-town schemes than in Western Europe, but also to more innovation and faster rates of change in the retail environment. In Britain, the shopping mall concept was translated into the in-town shopping centre, with the enthusiastic participation of local government as well as the financial institutions. More recently, retail parks and regional shopping centres were encouraged in 'brownfield' sites of past industrial use rather than the 'greenfield' sites typical of American development. In other parts of Western Europe, there appears to have been less enthusiasm and funding available for in-town centres, and many central shopping areas have altered little in physical appearance for many years. At the same time, off-centre shopping malls have been restricted just as strongly as in Britain.

Boom and slump in shopping centre development

The shopping centre has been a major focus of attention in the property development industry since the 1950s. Rates of development respond generally to fluctuations in the property market, and at local level to perceptions of and opportunities for development. However, the perceived demand from both major and minor space users is of great importance. In a general sense, fluctuations in rates of shopping centre development have followed fluctuations in consumer expenditure. Nevertheless, shopping centre development has fluctuated much more than consumer expenditure (Figure 8.7).

This process has led to considerable inefficiency and even waste in the retail property market, characterised by alternate shortages and gluts of floorspace in prime areas, and alarming fluctuations in property values. Figure 8.7 shows a tendency for a time lag in development, with the most recent peak in shopping centre development (1988–1990) occurring after the most rapid increases in expenditure (1985–1988). The mechanism concerned is for demand from consumers to increase: this leads to expansion attempts by multiple retailers, which leads to new shopping centre developments. One would expect there to be a gap of several years between increased demand from retailers and new supply of floorspace, because of the four years or more needed to complete a city centre scheme. This time lag should be characterised by sharply increasing rents. However, the experience of the 1980s was that the sharp increases in rents and in the volume of new floorspace (including retail parks) occurred at almost exactly the same time (Figure 8.8). However, there was a lag of 1–2 years between rent increases and completions of shopping centre floorspace when retail parks are excluded (Figure 8.9).

It appears that during the 1980s, the expansionary activities of the 'space bandits' had two almost simultaneous effects: pushing shopping centre rents up,

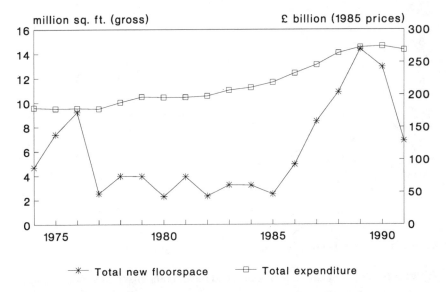

Figure 8.7 Retail floorspace and expenditure: comparison of trends

Source: Hillier Parker Research; Central Statistical Office

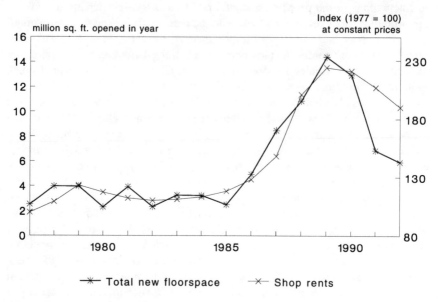

Figure 8.8 Retail floorspace and rents: comparison of trends
Source: Hillier Parker Research

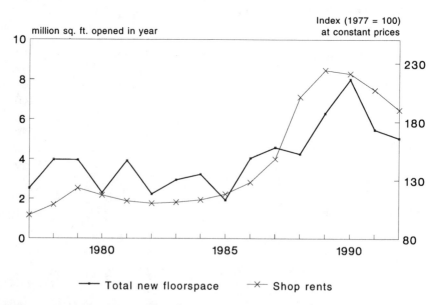

Figure 8.9 Shopping centre floorspace and rents: comparison of trends
Source: Hillier Parker Research

and encouraging new development. At the end of the decade, the space bandits ran into financial difficulties, rents fell, and the volume of shopping centre development also fell, but much more sharply.

Now that the new developments are completed, demand from retailers for new space has dropped, space cannot easily be let, and rents fall and land values drop. Consequently, the property companies also run into trouble. Alternatively, companies maintain rents at high levels, in order to stabilise land values, and hope that demand from retailers will return. This carries the risk that new retail premises will remain vacant for considerable periods of time. Expensive and unlet new shopping centres are a powerful deterrent to development of further schemes, and it is likely that at present, despite reduced land prices, few proposals for new shopping centres are being formulated. The inevitable future rise in demand by retailers for new space in prime locations may be met in the first instance by these empty premises.

Nevertheless, there may again occur in the late 1990s a lag between demand and supply of retail space, with the resulting increases in shop rents. Whether this gap can be met through the redevelopment or refurbishment of older shopping centres remains to be seen. If not, then pressure for new off-centre development may return, despite the hardening of opposition to such development from central and local government.

Chapter 9

The retail development process
Comparisons and conclusions

This chapter summarises the essential features of retail development and identifies some particular characteristics of the situation in Britain. This is followed by a critical review of certain aspects of the development process. Finally, some current and future influences upon rates of retail development are examined.

RETAIL DEVELOPMENT

Shops and shopping centres are very visible and familiar parts of the urban built environment. Their development is often a matter of controversy: since nearly everyone goes shopping, many people feel they are entitled to express views on the desirability of any proposal for retail development. New shops are often seen as a sign of municipal progress and achievement; but at the same time vested commercial interests decry new retailing as 'unfair' and unnecessary competition. Hence, retail development in most developed societies has been regulated by central and local governments, through land use planning systems (as in Britain) or by general legal restriction (as in several other European countries). The various battles and dialogues between the development industry and local opposition, with governments taking either side or attempting to mediate, have raised the profile of retail development to that of a continuously controversial issue. Indeed, one of the main purposes of this book has been to offer explanations of the various points of view, and analyses of the interactions of private and public sector attitudes.

Another important feature of retail development is its scale in relation to most of the property industry. Shopping centres often occupy very expensive land and are complex and expensive structures in their own right. Development within existing retail areas brings extra costs and delays associated with land acquisition, planning negotiations and site preparation. The vast sums of money necessary for retail development programmes involve the world of finance capital to an extent rarely seen in other types of development, outside central London at any rate. This capital is either directed towards retail firms that carry out their own development, or injected into the shopping centre development process in the form of long-term finance or participation in the development itself.

Peculiar features of British retail development

Most of the literature consulted in the writing of this book is based upon British experience, and a reader might assume that the practices described in this literature are typical of retail development generally. It is important nevertheless to recognise the extent to which the UK differs from other developed countries in its retail development processes and outcomes. This could be the subject of a book in its own right: the following tentative suggestions might form a basis for future research.

There is, of course, much in common between certain types of development outcome, such as the hypermarket in various countries in Western Europe, or the regional shopping mall in North America, Britain, Australia and elsewhere. However, some other physical outcomes appear to be specialist products, such as the retail park in Britain, the factory outlet centre in North America, and so on.

Equally important differences exist in the scale and costs of retail development overall. Although international comparisons are hard to make because of differing definitions, the United States would appear to lead the world in the volume of free-standing shopping mall development, not to say retail development in total (Teale, 1989). Reasons for this are worth investigating.

It is, of course, the case that the one major country where public sector planning has been of relatively little importance in affecting retail development has been the United States. Europeans tend to view North American retail patterns as essentially wasteful of land and anti-urban: the supposed effects upon city centre retailing of suburban development are particularly decried. North American shopping is held to be a horrible example of what would happen in a deregulated local economy.

However, differences between the United States and Britain in the volume and location of retail provision do not simply reflect differences in planning control. In many parts of the United States, retail development involves a profusion of low-cost, speculative schemes built on cheap land by local and regional development companies operating in a favourable or neutral planning environment. Considerable risks can be taken by developers in this low-cost environment: unsuccessful shopping centres can be 'recycled' or redeveloped for some other use. In Britain, retail development involves high costs of land acquisition and is funded mainly by large retail, development or financial companies operating in a highly regulated planning environment. Most schemes are completed only if there is substantial evidence that there will be a satisfactory return to investors, and completed schemes have a degree of permanence and cannot easily be recycled.

Figure 9.1 summarises these relationships. Influences on the retail development process – land costs, planning control and perceived risk – are interrelated.

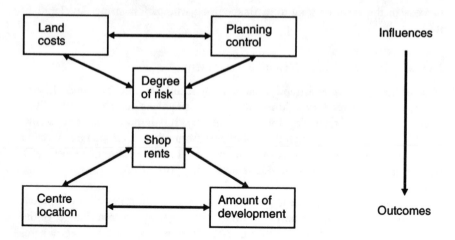

Figure 9.1 The retail development process: influences and outcomes

So are the physical outcomes of these influences: shopping centre location, shop rents and the total amount of development. Figure 9.2 summarises the contrasts in these influences and outcomes, between the UK and USA.

A second source of contrasts lies between Britain and its continental European neighbours. This contrast does not lie so much in off-centre retailing: this has been roughly on a par with developments in France and Germany, although there is more off-centre development in these countries than in southern Europe (Reynolds, 1992).

Britain is probably though the international leader in shopping mall development within existing town and city centres. British town centres appear to have been physically redeveloped for shopping centres much more than has been the

	UK	US
Influences:		
Planning control	Strict	Lax
Land costs	High	Low
Degree of risk	Low	High
Outcomes:		
Shop rents	High	Low
Centre location	CBD + Suburbs	Suburbs
Amount of devt.	Low	High

Figure 9.2 Retail development in the UK and US

case in France, Germany or the Netherlands, for example. Here, town centres have usually retained their physical form over the centuries without the wholesale redesign common in Britain. As a result, retailing in Britain has probably involved much greater injections of finance capital than in other countries. It could be argued that the presence of abundant finance capital flowing into pension schemes and the like has encouraged shopping centre development which may not have been strictly necessary. One also gains a strong impression that British town centres are dominated by a smallish number of major multiple retailers, to a much greater extent than in other parts of Western Europe. Thus, an alliance of retail demand, financial capital and local government ambition appears to have created the typical British central retail area.

CRITICAL COMMENTS ON THE RETAIL DEVELOPMENT PROCESS

Actors involved in the retail development process in Britain would no doubt claim that it has on the whole been successful in producing attractive and efficient shopping environments for the shopper to enjoy. But many criticisms of modern shopping conditions are evident in the academic literature as well as the technical press and newspapers. This section summarises these criticisms and attempts to derive some positive guidelines for future retail planning.

Institutional funding and management practices

Ownership of retail property by funding institutions appears to be exceptionally high in Britain, by international standards. This means that the character of many shopping centres and other retail areas reflects the priorities of the institutions, as well as local retail and consumer preferences. Some critics allege that institutional objectives, which are concerned with long-term capital appreciation and minimisation of risk, are detrimental to the attractiveness and environmental quality of retail areas, as well as violating principles of natural justice (Burton, 1992). Three particular problems are often discussed.

The first area of controversy concerns the 'institutional lease'. It is argued that landlords who impose this type of arrangement on retail tenants have an unfair advantage. The tenant is responsible not only for insuring and repairing the premises, but also for finding a replacement tenant if the business turns out to be not viable. Furthermore, tenants can be held responsible for debts incurred by previous tenants who have defaulted on rent payments. In today's rapidly changing retail climate, the full period of such leases (typically 25 years) may be much longer than the life of even a successful retail company or its mode of retailing.

The second problem concerns rent reviews and in particular, the 'upwards only' condition in typical institutional leases. The imposition of substantially increased rents at a time when the property market is declining generally, as in the years since 1989, indicates a monopoly position for the landlord and raises severe problems for retailers (Burton, 1992; Hillier Parker, 1993b). Several commentators have urged the adoption of turnover-based rents, typical of North American planned centres. These are not only more acceptable to retailers, but also provide incentives for shopping centre managers to attempt to increase turnover through good management and promotion measures.

Third, funding institutions may be unwilling to support retail developments that are seen as unconventional, although they may have environmental or economic advantages. For example, festival retailing is seen as problematic by most institutions, although it can bring substantial external gains in the form of environmental improvement and tourist attraction. Another result of this attitude appears to be the preponderance of multiple retail stores in planned shopping centres and 'prime' areas of town and city centres. These appeal to the institutions as 'safe' tenants, but can detract from the vitality and variety of centres.

These effects of increased institutional ownership of shopping centres and town centre properties have frequently been criticised, as in the following extract:

> The success of the multiples has been at the expense of local retailing, service industries and even production. Only the multiples have been able to afford the rent in the new malls and high street locations and local firms have been driven out of business . . . . The owners of the shopping malls often have no direct interest in retailing, and certainly not in the life of the towns they are located in, for the majority of owners are pension funds and insurance companies which have invested in retail property as part of a wider portfolio . . . . Their interest in the towns their money is invested in is remote if not non-existent; it is a financial relationship only, and only questions of the long-term economic viability of town-centre retailing will bring these companies to the local civic table.
>
> (Worpole, 1992: 18–20)

Criticisms have also been raised concerning the unsympathetic appearance of many of the shopping malls built in town centres during the 1960s and 1970s. There now appears to be more awareness of these issues amongst shopping centre developers and town planners.

Planning policies and control

Town planners in Britain have also been the target of considerable criticism for their attitudes towards retail development. Much of this criticism has been from pro-development interests, and can be interpreted simply as hostility to the principle of strategic planning control over retail development. However, there has been more general frustration with the caution and lack of understanding that planners and local authority councillors have typically shown when faced with proposals for new types of property development, or for off-centre development generally (e.g. Gayler, 1984).

The debates over off-centre development have perhaps obscured some more general issues concerning planning intervention in the retail system. Changes in planners' control over retailing have reflected wider changes in government attitudes towards property development. In the 1970s, government interests supported the view that planners should determine the broad location and type of development, in the interests of protecting existing (generally unplanned) facilities and providing good quality shopping for the local population. In the 1980s the government moved to a position of leaving the impetus for retail growth and change to the private sector developers and retailers. Local authorities were no longer expected to specify the location and type of new development. However, leaving these decisions to the market led to intense pressures for off-centre retailing, leading to the boom in regional centre proposals in the mid-1980s. Faced with this pressure, and the possible consequences for established town centres, the government has now offered more support for town centres and has attempted to set more strict conditions for off-centre development, in the revised version of Planning Policy Guidance Note Six.

The outcome has been that government guidelines are seen on the one hand as vague or even ambiguous (Davies, 1986), and on the other hand are implemented only reluctantly by local authorities, which generally would prefer to adopt stricter control over new development in the interests of protecting local traders from adverse competition. This latter stance is characteristic of several European countries, but there it has legal backing involving locally organised impact studies and regulatory committees. In Britain, the extent of control over new retail development remains the province of inexact government advice and variable local policies. The price of this uncertainty has been not only geographical disparities in rates of off-centre development, but also long delays in decision-making and the expensive spectacle of lengthy and costly planning inquiries into new retail schemes (Couper and Barker, 1981; Stocks, 1989).

The results of 'planning by appeal' have, in turn, been unfortunate. Developments have been allowed that may be satisfactorily located from the point of view of maximising retail sales or developer's profit, but which may prove unsatisfactory in the wider interest. Many off-centre developments are easily accessible only by private car, or have occupied sites that might have provided opportunities for much-needed industrial or housing development.

There also seems little doubt that planning control over retailing has inflated land prices for retail development, to an extent where developers need to provide standardised, cost-minimising schemes which are intended solely to maximise sales densities. This criticism applies equally to town centre developments and off-centre large stores and retail parks.

If central government were to accept the validity of public sector strategic planning of retail development, and local government were better equipped to anticipate and provide for the legitimate development needs of new types of retailing, then these schemes could be built in places that were more accessible and more acceptable in the general public interest. It is to be hoped that these principles can inform the policies for retail development, which should become an important feature of the new generation of local plans.

SOME INFLUENCES ON RETAIL DEVELOPMENT IN THE MEDIUM-TERM FUTURE

A final section which presented firm forecasts about retail development within the next few years would be a hostage to fortune. Instead, this section discusses some of the outside influences that bear upon retail development, and how these might change in the medium term.

In normal times, the two main factors that help determine the volume and type of retail development are, first, trends in consumer expenditure, which lead to retailers' decisions to seek new space, sit tight or even abandon existing space; and, second, trends in funding for development. Future trends in consumer expenditure are extremely hard to predict at the time of writing: there appear to be contradictory signals suggesting either continuing stagnation or the resumption of steady growth. In any case, many multiple retailers are likely to want to seek to use their existing store portfolios more efficiently before committing themselves to further growth in store numbers.

Trends in finance for development are perhaps easier to discern. The 1980s were to some extent exceptional in that property development companies were able to borrow large sums from banks to finance development schemes that the institutions would not readily accept. The major banks are still experiencing problems in reclaiming some of these debts, and are not likely to support retail schemes of innovative types or in unusual locations for several years to come. The major funding institutions may become more willing to finance 'safe' schemes than in recent years, but this will depend as much on the profits to be made from other forms of investment as on prospects for the retail market itself. The most likely directions for investment in the near future appear to be, first, suburban retail parks and, second, refurbishment of the first generation of in-town shopping malls.

Changes in land use planning principles are well under way in the early 1990s, and these may turn out to have the most important effects upon the medium-term future of retail development, although not always as intended. Concern arose in the 1980s over increasing consumption of natural resources and pollution of the natural environment. As a result, official British government policy is, as elsewhere in the European Community, to stabilise the emissions of carbon dioxide and other 'greenhouse gases' (Department of the Environment, 1990). This has led to a concern for 'sustainable development', generally defined as 'development that meets the needs of the present without compromising the ability of future generations to meet their own needs' (World Commission on Economic Development, 1987: 8). Related to these concerns is the idea that urban development should be designed so as to reduce the need for car travel (Commission of the European Communities, 1990; Breheny, 1992). It follows that the revised version of the British government's Planning Policy Guidance Note Six, on major retail development, refers specifically to these issues. New shops or shopping centres that are accessible only by car, or that are likely to stimulate more or longer car journeys, are much less likely to be approved by land use planners than would have been the case in the 1980s.

This does not mean that there will a major change of government attitude in favour of protecting existing town centres against competition from off-centre development. Rather, the proponents of new developments will have to demonstrate that shoppers can reach them by foot, cycle or public transport; and/or that they can reduce car travel overall by substituting a close destination for a more distant one. Thus, new grocery stores, retail warehouses and retail parks will still receive planning approval, but are more and more likely to be located within the urban fabric. Ironically, this is likely to lead to more severe competitive effects upon established town centres than occurred in the 1980s, when new off-centre development was often located at substantial distances from town centres.

However, the overall effect of this concern for sustainable development may well be a tightening of restrictions on new shopping development. This is likely to lead to increases in land prices, perhaps in inner urban as well as outer suburban locations. As a result of these factors, and the understandable caution of investors and developers, it seems unlikely that the next major boom in retail development will occur for several years.

A deeper issue is whether the processes of retail development and the underlying financial, economic and political structures discussed in this book will continue in their present form. A variety of future paths could be suggested, ranging from almost complete domination by multinational and national financial interests, to a much more decentralised system of financial support for new development; or from a heavily regulated planning environment dominated by existing local retail interests, to a virtually deregulated planning environment along the North American model. Time alone will tell to what extent the relationships and trends examined in this book will continue to apply.

References

Aldous, T. (1990) *New Shopping in Historic Towns: The Chesterfield Story*, London: English Heritage.

Alonso, W. (1960) 'A theory of the urban land market', *Papers and Proceedings of the Regional Science Association* 6: 149–157.

Alonso, W. (1964) *Location and Land Use*, Cambridge, Mass.: Harvard University Press.

Ambrose, P. (1986) *Whatever Happened to Planning?*, Andover: Methuen.

Ambrose, P. and Colenutt, R. (1975) *The Property Machine*, Harmondsworth: Penguin Books.

Amery, C. and Cruickshank, D. (1975) *The Rape of Britain*, London: Paul Elek.

Ashworth, W. (1954) *The Genesis of Modern British Town Planning*, London: Routledge and Kegan Paul.

Association of Town Centre Management (1992) *Starting Town Centre Management in Your Area*, London: PTRC Education and Research Services.

Baldock, J. (1989) 'Town centre management: its importance and nature', in Civic Trust, *Creating the Living Town Centre*, London: Civic Trust.

Barras, R. and Broadbent, T.A. (1982) 'A review of operational methods in structure planning', *Progress in Planning* 17: 55–268.

BDP Planning and Oxford Institute of Retail Management (1992) *The Effects of Major Out of Town Retail Development: A Literature Review for the Department of the Environment*, London: HMSO.

Beaujeu-Garnier, J. and Delobez, A. (1979) *Geography of Marketing*, London: Longman.

Beaumont, J.R. and Inglis, K. (1989) 'Geodemographics in practice: developments in Britain and Europe', *Environment and Planning A* 21: 587–604.

Beavon, K.S.O. (1977) *Central Place Theory: A Reinterpretation*, London: Longman.

Beddington, N. (1991) *Shopping Centres: Retail Development, Design and Management* (second revised edition), Oxford: Butterworth Architecture.

Begg, H.M. and Pollock, S.H.A. (1991) 'Development plans in Scotland since 1975', *Scottish Geographical Magazine* 107: 4–11.

Benwell Community Project (1979) *From Blacksmiths to White Elephants: Benwell's Changing Shops*, Newcastle: Benwell Community Project, Final Report Series No. 7.

Bernard Thorpe & Partners and Oxford Institute of Retail Management (1990) *Who Runs Britain's High Streets?*, London: Bernard Thorpe.

Berry, B.J.L. (1963) *Commercial Structure and Commercial Blight*, University of Chicago, Department of Geography, Research Paper 85.

Berry, B.J.L. and Parr, J.B. (1988) *Market Centers and Retail Location: Theory and Applications*, Englewood Cliffs: Prentice–Hall.

Boddy, M. (1981) 'The property sector in late capitalism: the case of Britain', in M. Dear and A.J. Scott (eds) *Urbanisation and Urban Planning in Capitalist Society*, Andover: Methuen.

Bowlby, S. (1987) 'Planning town centres for women', *Town and Country Planning* 56, 9: 261–264.

Braithwaite, J. (1989) 'The Overgate, Dundee: 80 years of plans and planning', *Scottish Geographical Magazine* 105: 85–93.

Breheny, M. (ed.) (1992) *Sustainable Development and Urban Form*, London: Pion.

Brett, M. (1991) 'Act two', *Investors Chronicle* 15 November (Survey of Industrial and Commercial Property): 3–4.

Brett, M. (1992) 'The new property crisis', *Investors Chronicle* 10 April: 16–17.

Brewer, P. (1990) 'Turnover rents now more acceptable', *Investors Chronicle* 6 July: 74.

Bromley, R.D.F. and Thomas, C.J. (1989a) 'Clustering advantages for out-of-town stores', *International Journal of Retailing* 4, 3: 41–59.

Bromley, R. and Thomas, C. (1989b) 'Shopping linkages in retail parks', *Town Planning Review*, 60, 1.

Brown, A. (1988) 'Superstore saturation in perspective: reasons to be cheerful', in *Retail Perspectives I*, London: Morgan Stanley.

Brown, A. (1991) 'Food retailing in the UK', in A. Treadgold (ed.) *The City View of Retailing*, London: Longman.

Brown, G.R. (1991) *Property Investment and the Capital Markets*, London: E. & F.N. Spon.

Brown, S. (1987) 'Institutional change in retailing: a review and synthesis', *European Journal of Marketing* 21, 6: 3–36.

Brown, S. (1989) 'Innovation and evolution in UK retailing: the retail warehouse', *European Journal of Marketing* 24, 9: 39–54.

Brown, S. (1990) 'Innovation and evolution in United Kingdom retailing: the retail warehouse', *European Journal of Marketing*, 24, 9.

Brown, S. (1991) 'Retail location: the post hierarchical challenge', *International Review of Retail, Distribution and Consumer Research* 1: 367–381.

Brown, S. (1992) *Retail Location: A Micro-Scale Perspective*, Aldershot: Avebury.

Brownill, S. (1990) *Developing London's Docklands: Another Great Planning Disaster?*, London: Paul Chapman.

Buchanan, C.D. (1963) *Traffic in Towns*, London: HMSO.

Buckley, N. (1993) 'US takes the cut-price lead', *Financial Times* 15 June: 33.

Building Design Partnership (1992) 'Local Planning Authority Case Studies' (unpublished report), London: Building Design Partnership.

Burns, W. (1959) *British Shopping Centres*, London: Leonard Hill.

Burt, S. and Sparks, L. (1991) 'Setting standards for car parking provision: the case of retailing', *Traffic Engineering and Control* 32: 253–258.

Burton (1988) *Burton plc: Annual Report and Accounts 1988*, London.

Burton, J. (1992) *Retail Rents: Fair and Free Market?*, Adam Smith Research Trust.

Business Statistics Office (1992) *Retailing 1989: Business Monitor SDA25*, London: HMSO.

Cadman, D. (1984) 'Property finance in the UK in the post-war period', *Land Development Studies* 1: 61–82.

Cadman, D. and Austin-Crowe, L. (1978) *Property Development*, London: E. & F.N. Spon.

Cadman, D. and Austin-Crowe, L. (1991) *Property Development, Third Edition*, London: E. & F.N. Spon.

Callender, M. (1991) 'Shopping centres as an institutional asset', *Shopping Centre Horizons* 23: 2–4.

Carlson, H.J. (1990) 'How shopping centers reshape retailing: past, present, future', in *International Trends in Retailing*, 7, 1, Chicago: Arthur Andersen.

Carlson, H.J. (1991) 'The role of the shopping centre in US retailing', *International Journal of Retail and Distribution Management* 19, 6: 13–20.

Carter, H. (1981) *The Study of Urban Geography*, London: Edward Arnold.

Carter, H. and Lewis, C.R. (1990) *An Urban Geography of England and Wales in the Nineteenth Century*, London: Edward Arnold.

Central Statistical Office (1992a) *Financial Statistics*, London: HMSO.

Central Statistical Office (1992b) *Business Monitor MQ5: Insurance Companies' and Pension Funds' Investment*, London: HMSO.

Centre for Advanced Land Use Studies (1975) *Rent Assessment and Tenant Mix in Planned Shopping Centres*, Reading: College of Estate Management.

Chartered Surveyor Weekly (1992) 'The architects of a dramatic facelift', 14 May: 52–53.

Chartered Surveyor Weekly (1993) 'Refurbishment', 21 January: 33–39.

Cherry, G. (1988) *Cities and Plans*, London: Edward Arnold.

Chesterton Consulting (1991) *Food Stores: A Taste of the Future*, London: Chesterton.

Christaller, W. (1966) *Central Places in Southern Germany* (trans. C.W. Baskin), Englewood Cliffs: Prentice–Hall.

Civic Trust (1989) *Creating the Living Town Centre*, London: Civic Trust.

Clayform (1989) *Report and Financial Statements*, London: Clayform Properties plc.

Commission of the European Communities (1990) *Green Paper on the Urban Environment*, Luxembourg: Office for Official Publications of the European Communities.

Conzen, M.R.G. (1960) *Alnwick, Northumberland: A Study in Town-Plan Analysis*, London: Institute of British Geographers, Publication no. 27.

Couper, M. and Barker, A. (1981) 'Joint and linked inquiries: the superstore experience', *Journal of Planning and Environmental Law*, 631–655.

Credit Lyonnais Laing (1991) *Tesco PLC: A Company Capitalising Too Much Interest?*, London: Credit Lyonnais Securities.

Credit Lyonnais Laing (1992) *How Much Hot Air Do You Like in Your Accounts? Food Retailer Property Valuations and their Effect on the P & L*, London: Credit Lyonnais Securities.

Cross, D.T. and Bristow, H.R. (eds) (1983) *English Structure Planning: a Commentary on Procedure and Practice in the Seventies*, London: Pion.

Cullingworth, J.B. (1988) *Town and Country Planning in Britain* (tenth edition), London: Allen & Unwin.

Darlow, C. (1989) 'Property development and funding', in R. Grover (ed.) *Land and Property Development: New Directions*, London: E. & F.N. Spon.

Davies, B.K. and Sparks, L. (1989) 'The development of superstore retailing in Great Britain 1960–1986: results from a new database', *Transactions of the Institute of British Geographers* 14: 74–89.

Davies, H.W.E., Edwards, D. and Rowley, A.R. (1986) *The Relationships between Development Plans, Development Control and Appeals*, Reading: University of Reading, Department of Land Management and Development.

Davies, R.L. (1974) 'Nucleated and ribbon components of the urban retail system in Britain', *Town Planning Review* 45: 91–111.

Davies, R.L. (1977a) *Marketing Geography: With Special Reference to Retailing*, London: Methuen.

Davies, R.L. (1977b) 'A framework for commercial planning policies', *Town Planning Review* 48: 42–58.

Davies, R.L. (1984) *Retail and Commercial Planning*, Beckenham: Croom Helm.

Davies, R.L. (1986) 'Retail planning in disarray', *The Planner* 72, 7: 20–22.

Davies, R.L. and Rogers, D.S. (1984) *Store Location and Store Assessment Research*, Chichester: Wiley.

Dawson, J.A. (1979) *The Marketing Environment*, London: Croom Helm.

Dawson, J.A. (1982) *Commercial Distribution in Europe*, London: Croom Helm.

Dawson, J.A. (1983) *Shopping Centre Development*, London: Longman.

Dawson, J.A. and Lord, J.D. (1985) 'Federal and state intervention in shopping centre development in the USA', in J.A. Dawson and J.D. Lord (eds) *Shopping Centre Development: Policies and Prospects*, London: Croom Helm.

Day, C. (1992) 'Exeter: traffic congestion and the survival of an historic city', *The Planner* 78, 21: 52–54.

Debenham Tewson (1988) *Planning Gain: Community Benefit or Commercial Bribe*, London: Debenham Tewson & Chinnocks.

Debenham Tewson Research (1992a) *Index of Retail Trading Locations, July 1992*, London: Debenham Tewson & Chinnocks.

Debenham Tewson Research (1992b) *Money into Property*, London: Debenham Tewson & Chinnocks.

Delobez, A. (1985) 'The development of shopping centres in the Paris region', in J.A. Dawson and J.D. Lord (eds) *Shopping Centre Development: Policies and Prospects*, London: Croom Helm.

Dent, B.D. (1985) 'Atlanta and the regional mall: the absence of public policy', in J.A. Dawson and J.D. Lord (eds) *Shopping Centre Development: Policies and Prospects*, London: Croom Helm.

Department of the Environment (1972) *Development Control Policy Note 13: Out of Town Shops and Shopping Centres*, London: HMSO.

Department of the Environment (1975) *Commercial Property Development: First Report of the Advisory Group on Commercial Property Development*, London: HMSO.

Department of the Environment (1977) *Development Control Policy Note 13: Large New Stores*, London: HMSO.

Department of the Environment (1988) *Planning Policy Guidance 6: Major Retail Development*, London: HMSO.

Department of the Environment (1989a) *Planning Control in Western Europe*, London: HMSO.

Department of the Environment (1989b) *Improving Inner City Shopping Centres*, London: HMSO.

Department of the Environment (1990) *This Common Inheritance*, London: HMSO.

Department of the Environment (1991) *Planning Obligations, Circular 16/91*, London: HMSO.

Department of the Environment (1992a) *Planning Policy Guidance 1: General Policy and Principles*, London: HMSO.

Department of the Environment (1992b) *Planning Policy Guidance 12: Development Plans and Regional Planning Guidance*, London: HMSO.

Department of the Environment (1992c) *Development Plans: A Good Practice Guide*, London: HMSO.

Department of the Environment (1992d) *Town and Country Planning Development Plans (England) Direction 1992*, London: HMSO.

Department of the Environment (1993) *Planning Policy Guidance 6: Town Centres and Retail Developments*, London: HMSO.

Department of Transport (1992) *Developers' Contributions to Highway Works*, London: Department of Transport.

Distributive Trades Economic Development Council (1988) *The Future of the High Street*, London: National Economic Development Office.

Doherty, F. (1990) 'Developments in retailing', in S. Trench and T. Oc (eds) *Current Issues in Planning*, Aldershot: Gower.

Dubben, N. and Sayce, S. (1991) *Property Portfolio Management: An Introduction*, London: Routledge.

Duke, R. (1991) 'Post-saturation competition in UK grocery retailing', *Journal of Marketing Management* 7: 63–75.

Dyos, H.J. (1966) *Victorian Suburb: A Study of the Growth of Camberwell*, Leicester University Press.

Eade, C. (1992) 'Reviving the spirit of a bygone era', *Chartered Surveyor Weekly* 14 May: 47.

Economist Intelligence Unit (1991) 'Company profiles: Gateway', *EIU Retail Business Quarterly Trade Reviews* 20: 57–63.

English Tourist Board and Jones Lang Wootton (1989) *Retail, Leisure and Tourism*, London: the authors.

François, P. and Leunis, J. (1991) 'Public policy in the establishment of large stores in Belgium', *International Review of Retail, Distribution and Consumer Research* 1: 469–486.

Fraser, W.D. (1985) 'The risk of property to the institutional investor', *Journal of Valuation* 4: 45–59.

Fraser, W.H. (1981) *The Coming of the Mass Market 1850–1914*, London: Macmillan.

Frieden, B.J. and Sagalyn, L.B. (1989) *Downtown, Inc.: How America Rebuilds Cities*, Cambridge, Mass.: MIT Press.

Gascoigne, R. (1992) 'The entry of European limited line discounters into the United Kingdom', paper presented at the Institute of British Geographers' Annual Conference.

Gayler, H.J. (1984) *Retail Innovation in Britain: The Problems of Out-of-Town Shopping Centre Development*, Norwich: Geo Books.

Ghosh, A. and McLafferty, S. (1987) *Location Strategies for Retail and Service Firms*, Lexington: Lexington Books.

Gibbs, A. (1981) 'An analysis of retail warehouse planning inquiries', *URPI Report U22*, Reading: Unit for Retail Planning Information.

Gibbs, A. (1986) 'Retail warehouse planning inquiries 1981–1985', *URPI Report U28*, Reading: Unit for Retail Planning Information.

Gibbs, A. (1987) 'Retail innovation and planning', *Progress in Planning* 27: 1–67.

Goldman Sachs (1989a) *Retail Property: Unlocking the Value*, London: Goldman Sachs International.

Goldman Sachs (1989b) *Funding Food Superstores: An Emerging Option*, London: Goldman Sachs International.

Gore, T. and Nicholson, D. (1991) 'Models of the land development process: a critical review', *Environment and Planning A* 23: 705–730.

Gosling, D. and Maitland, B. (1976) *Design and Planning of Retail Systems*, London: Architectural Press.

Grocer, The (1989) 'Asda's £375m lease-back deal on 34 superstores to reduce £1bn debt', 9 December: 4.

Grocer, The (1990) 'Aldi sites race turns into obstacle course', 4 August: 4.

Grocer, The (1992a) 'Shoprite is going for partnership deals', 8 February: 9.

Grocer, The (1992b) 'More joint ventures by Iceland', 7 March: 4.

Grocer, The (1992c) 'C-store multiple margins "universally low" ', 28 March: 11.

Grocer, The (1992d) 'Shell C-store plans to win a bigger SHARE', 13 June: 4.

Grocer, The (1992e) 'C-stores are for regular shoppers says Mintel', 11 July: 5.

Grocer, The (1992f) '"Give us three years to get it right" – ASDA', 11 July: 11.

Grocer, The (1992g) 'Kwik Save prove discounting pays', 28 November: 9.

Grocer, The (1992h) 'Market shares', 5 December: 14.

Grocer, The (1993) 'Two more German discounters are coming to the UK', 23 January: 4.

Guardian (1993) 'Size matters for success of shopping centres', 23 January: 35.

Guskind, R. and Pierce, N.R. (1988) 'Faltering festivals', *National Journal* 20: 2307–2311.

Guy, C.M. (1976) *The Location of Shops in the Reading Area*, University of Reading, Department of Geography, Working Paper no. 46.

Guy, C.M. (1980a) *Retail Location and Retail Planning in Britain*, Farnborough: Gower.

Guy, C.M. (1980b) 'Policies for the location of large new stores – a case study', *Area* 12: 279–284.

Guy, C.M. (1984) 'The urban pattern of retailing: B. within the UK', in R.L. Davies and D.S. Rogers (eds) *Store Location and Store Assessment Research*, Chichester: Wiley.

Guy, C.M. (1987) 'Accessibility to multiple-owned grocery stores in Cardiff: a description and evaluation of recent changes', *Planning Practice and Research* 1, 2: 9–15.

Guy, C.M. (1988) 'Retail planning policy and large grocery store development', *Land Development Studies* 5: 31–45.

Guy, C.M. (1991a) 'Urban and rural contrasts in food prices and availability – a case study in Wales', *Journal of Rural Studies* 7: 311–325.

Guy, C.M. (1991b) 'Spatial interaction modelling in retail planning practice: the need for robust statistical methods', *Environment and Planning B: Planning and Design* 18: 191–203.

Guy, C.M. (1992) 'Estimating shopping centre turnover: a review of survey methods', *International Journal of Retail and Distribution Management* 20, 4: 18–23.

Guy, C.M. and Lord, J.D. (1991) 'An international comparison of urban retail development', in G. Heinritz (ed.), *The attraction of retail locations, IGU Symposium August 1991*, Munich: Department of Geography, Technical University of Munich.

Guy, C.M. and Lord, J.D. (1993) 'Transformation and the city centre', in R.D.F. Bromley and C.J. Thomas (eds), *Retail Change: Contemporary Issues*, London: UCL Press.

Guy, C.M. and O'Brien, L.J. (1983) 'Measurement of grocery prices: Some methodological considerations and empirical results', *Journal of Consumer Studies and Home Economics* 7: 213–227.

Guy, C.M. and Wrigley, N. (1987) 'Walking trips to shops in British cities: An empirical review and policy re-examination', *Town Planning Review* 58: 63–79.

Haggett, P., Cliff, A.D. and Frey, A. (1977) *Locational Models*, London: Edward Arnold.

Hall, P. (1988) *Cities of Tomorrow*, Oxford: Basil Blackwell.

Hall, P., Gracey, H., Drewett, R. and Thomas, R. (1973) *The Containment of Urban England*, London: Allen & Unwin.

Hallsworth, A. (1988) *Regional Shopping Centres: Some Lessons from Canada*, London: TEST.

Hallsworth, A.G. (1991) *Financial Pressures and Retail Change*, Service Industries Research Centre, Portsmouth Polytechnic, Working Paper no. 8.

Hallsworth, A.G. and McClatchey, J. (1993) *Funding Retail Restructuring*, Service Industries Research Centre, University of Portsmouth, Working Paper no. 12.

Harrison, J. (1990) 'Leisure facilities in shopping centres', *Shopping Centre Horizons* Autumn: 13–21.

Harvey, D. (1985) *The Urbanisation of Capital*, Oxford: Basil Blackwell.

Harvey, J. (1992) *Urban Land Economics, Third Edition*, Basingstoke: Macmillan.

Hass-Klau, C. (ed.) (1988) *New Life for City Centres: Planning, Transport and Conservation in British and German Cities*, London: Anglo-German Foundation.

Hass-Klau, C. (1990) *The Pedestrian and City Traffic*, London: Belhaven.

Healey, P. (1983) *Local Plans in British Land Use Planning*, Oxford: Pergamon.

Healey, P. (1991) 'Models of the development process: a review', *Journal of Property Research* 8: 219–238.

Healey, P. (1992) 'An institutional model of the development process', *Journal of Property Research* 9: 33–44.

Healey, P. and Nabarro, R. (1990) *Land and Property Development in a Changing Context*, Aldershot: Gower.

Healey, P., McNamara, P., Elson, M. and Doak, A. (1988) *Land Use Planning and the Mediation of Urban Change*, Cambridge: Cambridge University Press.

Healey, P., Davoudi, S., O'Toole, M., Tavsanoglu, S. and Usher, D. (1992) *Rebuilding the City: Property-led Urban Regeneration*, London: E. & F.N. Spon.

Healey & Baker (1988) *French Shopping Centres: A Decade of Performance*, London: Healey & Baker.

Healey & Baker (1992) *Retail Issue No. 1*, London: Healey & Baker.

Henley Centre (1988) *The Demand for Retail Space*, Henley: Henley Centre.

Herbert, D.T. and Thomas, C.J. (1990) *Cities in Space: City as Place*, London: David Fulton.

Hillier Parker (1987) *British Shopping Developments Master List*, London: Hillier Parker.

Hillier Parker (1988) *Commercial and Industrial Floorspace Statistics, England 1983–86*, London: Hillier Parker.

Hillier Parker (1989) *Retail Parks Spring 1989*, London: Hillier Parker.

Hillier Parker (1991a) *British Shopping Centre Developments 1990 Supplement*, London: Hillier Parker.

Hillier Parker (1991b) *Retail Warehouse Park Development Master List*, London: Hillier Parker.

Hillier Parker (1991c) *Shopping Schemes in the Pipeline, February 1991*, London: Hillier Parker.

Hillier Parker (1992a) *Shopping Schemes in the Pipeline, June 1992*, London: Hillier Parker.

Hillier Parker (1992b) *Shopping Centre Vacancies, November 1992*, London: Hillier Parker.

Hillier Parker (1992c) *Shopping Centre Food Courts, December 1992*, London: Hillier Parker.

Hillier Parker (1993a) *Scheduled Shopping Centre Openings, January 1993*, London: Hillier Parker.

Hillier Parker and Price Waterhouse (1993b) *Brent Cross and Metrocentre: Reviewing Rent Reviews by Audit*, London: the authors.

Holliday, J.C. (1983) 'City centre plans in the 1980s', in R.L. Davies and A.G. Champion (eds) *The Future for the City Centre*, London: Academic Press.

Hollins, C. (1993) 'Town centre management – the private sector view', in C.M. Guy (ed.) *Town Centre Investment and Management*, University of Wales College of Cardiff, Papers in Planning Research no. 143, Cardiff.

Howard, E. (1989) *Prospects for Out-of-Town Retailing: The Metro Experience*, Harlow: Longman.

Howard, E. (ed.) (1990) *Leisure and Retailing*, Harlow: Longman.

Howard, E. (1992) 'Evaluating the success of out-of-town regional shopping centres', *International Review of Retail, Distribution and Consumer Research* 2: 59–80.

Howells, P.G.A. and Rydin, Y.J. (1990) 'The case for property investment and the implications of a unitized property market', *Land Development Studies* 7: 15–30.

Institute of Grocery Distribution (1989) *Food Retailing: A Review of Food Retailing Structure and Trends*, Watford: The Institute of Grocery Distribution.

Institute of Grocery Distribution (1990a) *Grocery Stores '90 Volume One: 25,000 sq. ft. and above*, Watford: The Institute of Grocery Distribution.

Institute of Grocery Distribution (1990b) *Grocery Stores '90 Volume Two: 10,000–25,000 sq. ft. and above*, Watford: The Institute of Grocery Distribution.

Institute of Grocery Distribution (1991) *Discount Grocery Retailing in Europe*, Watford: The Institute of Grocery Distribution.

Investment Property Databank (1986) *The IPD Annual Review 1986*, London: Investment Property Databank.

Investment Property Databank (1992) *The IPD Property Investors' Digest 1992*, London: Investment Property Databank.

Investors Chronicle (1991a) 'Tesco sets its sights even higher', 1 February: 38–39.

Investors Chronicle (1991b) 'Surprise rights from Sainsbury', 21 June: 34–35.

Investors Chronicle (1991c) 'New strategies in asset allocation', 18 November (Survey on Pension Fund Management): 11.

Investors Chronicle (1992a) 'Banks come to the rescue', 10 April: 52.

Investors Chronicle (1992b) 'Putting a value on high-price superstores', 29 May: 32–33.

Investors Chronicle (1992c) 'Investors need to return to basics', 5 June: 8–9.

Investors Chronicle (1992d) 'Caveat emptor', 24 July: 12–13.

Jaffa, G. (1989) 'Fun needs funding', *Accountancy*, September: 107–108.

Jeffreys, J.B. (1954) *Retail Trading in Britain 1850–1950*, Cambridge: Cambridge University Press.

Johnson, D.B. (1987) 'The West Edmonton Mall – from super-regional to mega-regional shopping centre', *International Journal of Retailing*, 2, 2: 53–69.

Johnson, M. (1989) 'The application of geodemographics to retailing – meeting the needs of the catchment', *Journal of the Market Research Society* 31: 7–36.

Jones, K. and Simmons, J. (1990) *The Retail Environment*, London: Routledge.

Jones, P. (1981) 'Retail innovation and diffusion – the spread of Asda stores', *Area* 13: 197–201.

Kaye, C. (1990) 'Turnover rents: the developer's view', *Shopping Centre Horizons* 19: 11–13.

Key, T., Espinet, M. and Wright, C. (1990) 'Prospects for the property industry: an overview', in P. Healey and R. Nabarro (eds) *Land and Property Development in a Changing Context*, Aldershot: Gower.

King, W. (1987) 'The future roles of town centres', *The Planner* 73, 4: 18–22.

Kirby, D.A. (1976) 'The convenience store phenomenon: the rebirth of America's small shop', *Retail and Distribution Management* 4, 3: 31–33.

Kleinwort Benson (1989) *Retailers and Property: Risk or Reward?*, London: Kleinwort Benson Securities.

Kleinwort Benson (1991) *Food Retailing: Survival of the Fittest*, London: Kleinwort Benson Securities.

Kwik Save (1991) *Annual Report and Accounts*, Prestatyn: Kwik Save plc.

Latham, D. (1988) 'The need for balanced development', in A. West (ed.) *Handbook of Retailing*, Aldershot: Gower.

Lee Donaldson (1986) *Shopping Centre Appeals Review*, London: Lee Donaldson Associates.

Lee Donaldson (1987) *Retail Warehouse Appeals Review*, London: Lee Donaldson Associates.

Lee Donaldson (1991) *Superstore Appeals Review Three*, London: Lee Donaldson Associates.

Lichfield, N. and Darin-Drabkin, H. (1980) *Land Policy in Planning*, London: Allen & Unwin.

Lord, J.D. (1985) 'Revitalization of shopping centres', in J.A. Dawson and J.D. Lord (eds) *Shopping Centre Development: Policies and Prospects*, London: Croom Helm.

Lord, J.D. (1988) *Retail Decentralisation and CBD Decline in American Cities*, University of Stirling: Institute for Retail Studies, Working Paper 8802.

Lord, J.D. and Guy, C.M. (1991) 'Comparative retail structure of British and American cities: Cardiff (U.K.) and Charlotte (U.S.A.)', *International Review of Retail, Distribution and Consumer Research*, 1: 391–436.

McClelland, W.G. (1966) *Costs and Competition in Retailing*, London: Macmillan.

McClelland, W.G. (1990) 'Economies of scale in British food retailing', in C. Moir and J.A. Dawson (eds) *Competition and Markets: Essays in Honour of Margaret Hall*, London: Macmillan.

McGoldrick, P.J. (1987) 'A multi-dimensional framework for retail pricing', *International Journal of Retailing* 2, 2: 3–26.

McGoldrick, P.J. (1988) 'Spatial price differentiation by chain store retailers', in E. Kaynak (ed.) *Transnational Retailing*, Berlin: Walter de Gruyter.

McGoldrick, P.J. and Thompson, M.G. (1992) *Regional Shopping Centres: Out-of-town versus In-town*, Aldershot: Avebury.

MacKeith, M. (1985) *Shopping Arcades*, London: Mansell.

Mackenzie, A. (1989) 'The Scottish planning system', *The Planner* 75, 2: 8–11.

McKinnon, A.C. (1989) *Physical Distribution Systems*, London: Routledge.

McLoughlin, J.B. (1973) *Control and Urban Planning*, London: Faber & Faber.

McNamara, P. (1990) 'The changing role of research in investment decision making', in P. Healey and R. Nabarro (eds) *Land and Property Development in a Changing Context*, Aldershot: Gower.

Maitland, B. (1985) *Shopping Malls: Planning and Design*, London: Construction Press.

Maitland, B. (1990) *The New Architecture of the Retail Mall*, London: Architectural Design and Technology Press.

Manchester University (1964) *Regional Shopping Centres in North West England*, Manchester: Department of Town and Country Planning.

Marcus, M. (1978) 'Retail blight and planned shopping precincts in England and Wales', PhD dissertation, University of Reading.

Marcus, M. (1983) 'A behavioural approach to retail blight', *Environment and Planning A* 15: 739–750.

Marks & Spencer plc (1992) *Annual Report and Accounts*, London: Marks & Spencer.

Marriott, O. (1967) *The Property Boom*, London: Hamish Hamilton.

Massey, D. and Catalano, A. (1978) *Capital and Land: Landownership by Capital in Great Britain*, London: Edward Arnold.

Mathias, P. (1967) *Retailing Revolution*, London: Longman.

Millington, A.F. (1988) *An Introduction to Property Valuation* (third edition), London: Estates Gazette.

Milton Keynes Development Corporation (1987) *Shopping in Milton Keynes*, Milton Keynes: Milton Keynes Development Corporation.

Ministry of Housing and Local Government and Ministry of Transport (1962) *Town Centres: Approach to Renewal*, London: HMSO.

Ministry of Housing and Local Government (1970) *Development Plans: A Manual on Form and Content*, London: HMSO.

Moir, C. (1990) 'Competition in the UK grocery trades', in C. Moir and J.A. Dawson (eds) *Competition and Markets: Essays in Honour of Margaret Hall*, London: Macmillan.

Montgomery, J. (1990) 'Counter revolution: out of town shopping and the future of town centres', in J. Montgomery and A. Thornley (eds) *Radical Planning Initiatives: New Directions for Urban Planning in the 1990s*, Aldershot: Gower.

Morgan, M. (1992) 'Centres of attention', *Chartered Surveyor Weekly* 14 May: 44.

Morgan, P. and Walker, A. (1988) *Retail Development*, London: Estates Gazette.

Mortishead, C. (1992) 'A costly investment strategy', *Investors Chronicle* 17 July: 30.

Myers, B. (1992) 'City judgements', *Grocer* 19 September: 28–29.

Mynors, C. (1991) 'The Planning and Compensation Act 1991: (3) development plans, minerals and waste disposal', *The Planner* 13 September: 7–8.

Nabarro, R. (1989) 'Investment in commercial and industrial development: some recent trends', in D. Cross, and C. Whitehead (eds) *Development and Planning 1989*, Cambridge: Policy Journals.

Nabarro, R. (1990) 'The investment market in commercial and industrial development:

some recent trends', in P. Healey and R. Nabarro (eds) *Land and Property Development in a Changing Context*, Aldershot: Gower.

Nabarro, R. and Key, T. (1992) 'Current trends in commercial property investment and development: an overview', in P. Healey, S. Davoudi, M. O'Toole, S. Tavsanoglu, and D. Usher, (1992) *Rebuilding the City: Property-led Urban Regeneration*, London: E. & F.N. Spon.

Newman (1988) *Retail Directory 1988*, London: Newman.

Nielsen (1992) *The Retail Pocket Book 1992*, Oxford: NTC Publications.

Northen, R.I. and Haskoll, M. (1977) *Shopping Centres: A Developer's Guide to Planning and Design*, Reading: Centre for Advanced Land Use Studies.

O'Brien, L.G. and Harris, F. (1991) *Retailing: Shopping, Society, Space*, London: David Fulton.

Oxford Retail Group (1989) *Planning for Major Retail Development*, Oxford: Oxford Institute of Retail Management.

Oxford Retail Group (1990) *Retailing Issues for Development Plans*, Oxford: Oxford Institute of Retail Management.

Peart, J.D. (1989) 'Planning agreements: a method of achieving planning gain', in R. Grover (ed.) *Land and Property Development: New Directions*, London: E. & F.N. Spon.

Penny, N.J. and Broom, D. (1988) 'The Tesco approach to store location', in N. Wrigley (ed.) *Store Choice, Store Location and Market Analysis*, London: Routledge.

Petherick, A. (1992) *Living Over the Shop: A Handbook for Practitioners*, York: University of York.

Phillips, M. (1992) 'The evolution of markets and shops in Britain', in J. Benson and G. Shaw (eds) *The Evolution of Retail Systems, c.1800–1914*, Leicester: Leicester University Press.

Planning (1993) 'Gain package ruled lawful', 1006: 10.

Potter, R. (1982) *The Urban Retailing System: Location, Cognition and Behaviour*, Aldershot: Gower.

Purvis, M. (1992) 'Co-operative retailing in Britain', in J. Benson and G. Shaw (eds) *The Evolution of Retail Systems, c.1800–1914*, Leicester: Leicester University Press.

Raggett, B.P. (1984) 'Principles of partnership schemes: theory and practice', *Land Development Studies* 1: 83–99.

Rees, J. (1989) 'Social polarisation in shopping patterns: an example from Swansea', *Planning Practice and Research* 3, 1: 5–12.

Retail Business (1993a) 'DIY and hardware shops', *Retail Business Quarterly Trade Reviews* 25: 21–33.

Retail Business (1993b) 'Company profiles: Texas Homecare', *Retail Business Quarterly Trade Reviews* 25: 50–55.

Reynolds, J. (1992) 'Generic models of European shopping centre development', *European Journal of Marketing*, 26, 8/9: 48–60.

Reynolds, J. (1993) 'The proliferation of the planned centre', in R.D.F. Bromley and C.J. Thomas (eds), *Retail Change: Contemporary Issues*, London: UCL Press.

Richards, J. and MacNeary, A. (1991) 'A City view of retailing: challenge and opportunity in the nineties', in A. Treadgold (ed.) *The City View of Retailing*, London: Longman.

Royal Town Planning Institute (1988) *Planning for Shopping into the 21st Century*, London: Royal Town Planning Institute.

Sainsbury (1990) *Local Attitudes to Central Advice: A Survey of the Response of Planning Authorities to Government Planning Guidance*, London: J. Sainsbury plc.

Sainsbury (1992) *Annual Report and Accounts*, London: J. Sainsbury plc.

Saunders, K. (1990) 'Turnover rents: the retailer's view', *Shopping Centre Horizons* 19: 8–10.

Savitt, R. (1985) 'Issues of tenant policy control: the American perspective', in J.A. Dawson and J.D. Lord (eds) *Shopping Centre Development: Policies and Prospects*, Beckenham: Croom Helm.

Sawicki, D.S. (1989) 'The festival marketplace as public policy: guidelines for future policy decisions', *American Planning Association Journal* 55: 347–361.

Schiller, R. (1986) 'Retail decentralisation: the coming of the third wave', *The Planner* 72, 7: 13–15.

Schiller, R. (1987) 'Out of town exodus', in E. McFadyen (ed.) *The Changing Face of British Retailing*, London: Newman Books.

Schiller, R. (1991) 'Britain's biggest institutions', *Property Research Summaries: October 1991*, London: Hillier Parker Research.

Schiller, R. and Boucke, O. (1989) 'Are shop numbers rising or falling?', *Retail and Distribution Management* 17, 2: 16–19.

Scott, N.K. (1980) 'Rebuilding town centres', *Estates Gazette* 254: 181–185.

Scott, N.K. (1989) *Shopping Centre Design*, London: Van Nostrand Reinhold.

Scottish Development Department (1978) *National Planning Guidelines: The Location of Major Shopping Development*, Edinburgh: Scottish Development Department.

Scottish Development Department (1986) *National Planning Guidelines: The Location of Major Retail Developments*, Edinburgh: Scottish Development Department.

Shaw, G. (1985) 'Shopping centre developments in Toronto', in J.A. Dawson and J.D. Lord (eds) *Shopping Centre Development: Policies and Prospects*, London: Croom Helm.

Shaw, G. (1992) 'The evolution and impact of large-scale retailing in Britain', in J. Benson and G. Shaw (eds) *The Evolution of Retail Systems, c.1800–1914*, Leicester: Leicester University Press.

Shaw, G. and Wild, M.T. (1979) 'Retail patterns in the Victorian city', *Transactions of the Institute of British Geographers* 4: 278–291.

Shaw, S.A., Nisbet, D.J. and Dawson, J.A. (1989) 'Economies of scale in UK supermarkets: some preliminary findings', *International Journal of Retailing* 4, 5: 12–26.

Shepherd, P.M. and Thorpe, D., (1977) *Urban Redevelopment and Changes in Retail Structure 1961–1971*, Manchester: Manchester Business School, Retail Outlets Research Unit, Research Report No. 27.

Sheppard, E. and Barnes, T. (1990) *The Capitalist Space Economy: Geographical Analysis after Ricardo, Marx and Sraffa*, London: Unwin Hyman.

Shopping Centre (1992) 'Church stumbles as Crown progresses', August: 2.

Sim, L.L. and Way, C.R. (1989) 'Tenant placement in a Singapore shopping centre', *International Journal of Retailing* 4, 3: 4–16.

Simmons, J. (1964) *The Changing Pattern of Retail Location*, Chicago: University of Chicago, Department of Geography, Research Paper 92.

Skeel, S. (1991) 'Food wars', *Management Today* July: 40–44.

Sljivic, N. (1990) 'The German retail property market', *International Journal of Retail and Distribution Management* 18, 1: 8–10.

Smiddy, P. (1991) 'Significant issues in UK food retailing', in A. Treadgold (ed.) *The City View of Retailing*, London: Longman.

Sparks, L. (1983) 'Employment characteristics of superstore retailing', *Service Industries Journal* 3: 63–78.

Sparks, L. (1987) 'Retailing in Enterprise Zones: the example of Swansea', *Regional Studies* 21: 37–42.

Sparks, L. (1990) 'Spatial-structural relationships in retail corporate growth: A case-study of Kwik Save Group PLC', *Service Industries Journal* 10: 25–84.

Sparks, L. and Aitken, P. (1986) 'Retail planning policies in Scottish structure plans', *Land Development Studies* 3: 59–75.

Spriddell, P. (1980) 'Retailing – town centres in the 1980s', in *Town Centres of the Future: Report of an URPI Conference*, Reading: Unit for Retail Planning Information.

Stanley, G. (1992) 'Making the first move: British Land takes on the superstores', *Chartered Surveyor Weekly* 27 August: 14–15.

Stansbury, M. (1993) 'Town centre management – the story so far', in C.M. Guy (ed.) *Town Centre Investment and Management*, University of Wales College of Cardiff, Papers in Planning Research no. 143, Cardiff.

Stocks, N. (1989) 'The Greater Manchester shopping inquiry. A case study of strategic retail planning', *Land Development Studies* 6: 57–83.

Sunday Times (1992) 'Disaster in Docklands', 31 May: 3.2.

Tate, G. (1991) 'Meadowhall Shopping Centre, Sheffield', *Shopping Centre Horizons* 21: 21–27.

Teale, M. (1989) 'Retail shopping: the need for more space', in D. Cross and C. Whitehead (eds), *Development and Planning 1989*, Cambridge: Policy Journals.

Telling, A.E. (1990) *Planning Law and Procedure* (eighth edition), London: Butterworth.

Tesco (1991) *Annual Report and Accounts*, Cheshunt: Tesco plc.

TEST (1988) *Quality Street: How Traditional Urban Centres Benefit from Traffic-calming*, London: Transport and Environment Studies.

TEST (1989) *Trouble in Store? Retail Locational Policy in Britain and Germany*, London: Transport and Environment Studies.

Thomas, C.J. and Bromley, R.D.F. (1987) 'The growth and functioning of an unplanned retail park: the Swansea Enterprise Zone', *Regional Studies* 21: 287–300.

Thomas, K. (1990) *Planning for Shops*, London: Estates Gazette.

Thompson, N.H.C. and Wythe, J. (1988) 'Development funding for retail development', in A. West (ed.) *Handbook of Retailing*, Aldershot: Gower.

Thornley, A. (1991) *Urban Planning under Thatcherism: The Challenge of the Market*, London: Routledge.

Thorpe, D. (1990) 'Economic theory, retail output and capacity in British retailing', in C. Moir and J.A. Dawson (eds) *Competition and Markets: Essays in Honour of Margaret Hall*, London: Macmillan.

Thorpe, D. (1991) 'The development of British superstore retailing – further comments on Davies and Sparks', *Transactions of the Institute of British Geographers* 16: 354–367.

Thurrock Lakeside Shopping Centre (nd) *Your Personal Guide to Lakeside*.

Treadgold, A.D. and Reynolds, J. (1989) *Retail Saturation: Examining the Evidence*, London: Longman.

Unit for Retail Planning Information (1976) *Hypermarkets and Superstores: Report of a House of Commons Seminar*, Reading: Unit for Retail Planning Information.

Unit for Retail Planning Information (1977) *District Shopping Centres: Report of an URPI Workshop*, Reading: Unit for Retail Planning Information.

Unit for Retail Planning Information (1987) *Register of Managed Shopping Centres*, Reading: Unit for Retail Planning Information.

Unit for Retail Planning Information (1990) 'Planning inquiries for proposed regional shopping schemes 1987–1990', *URPI Information Brief* 90/5, Reading: Unit for Retail Planning Information.

Unit for Retail Planning Information (1991) 'Regional shopping schemes in the pipeline', *UpData* February, Reading: Unit for Retail Planning Information.

Unit for Retail Planning Information (1992a) 'New direction for major planning applications', *UpData* March, Reading: Unit for Retail Planning Information.

Unit for Retail Planning Information (1992b) *1992 Register of UK Hypermarkets and Superstores*, Reading: Unit for Retail Planning Information.

Valuation Office (1990) *Property Market Report: Spring 1990 Supplement*, London: Valuation Office.

Wakeford, R. (1990) *American Development Control: Parallels and Paradoxes from an English Perspective*, London: HMSO.

Walker, R. (ed.) (1990) *Living Over the Shop*, London: National Housing and Town Planning Council.

Wells, I. (1991) *Town Centre Management: a Future for the High Street?*, University of Reading, Geographical Papers no. 109.

Westlake, T. (1993) 'The disadvantaged consumer: problems and policies', in R.D.F. Bromley and C.J. Thomas (eds), *Retail Change: Contemporary Issues*, London: UCL Press.

Whitehand, J.W.R. (1987) *The Changing Face of Cities: A Study of Development Cycles and Urban Form*, Oxford: Basil Blackwell.

Wicks, R. (1990) 'Retail parks – time for reassessment', *Investors Chronicle* 6 July: 78.

Wild, M.T. and Shaw, G. (1979) 'Trends in urban retailing: the British experience during the nineteenth century', *Tijdschrift voor Economische en Sociale Geografie* 70: 35–44.

Wilson, A.G. (1988) 'Store and shopping centre location and size: A review of British research and practice', in N. Wrigley (ed.), *Store Choice, Store Location and Market Analysis*, London: Routledge.

World Commission on Economic Development (1987) *Our Common Future (The Brundtland Report)*, Oxford: Oxford University Press.

Worpole, K. (1992) *Towns for People: Transforming Urban Life*, Buckingham: Open University Press.

Wrigley, N. (1987) 'The concentration of capital in UK grocery retailing', *Environment and Planning A* 19: 1283–1288.

Wrigley, N. (1988) *Store Choice, Store Location and Market Analysis*, London: Routledge.

Wrigley, N. (1991) 'Is the "golden age" of British grocery retailing at a watershed?', *Environment and Planning A* 23: 1537–1544.

Wrigley, N. (1992) 'Sunk capital, the property crisis, and the restructuring of British food retailing', *Environment and Planning A* 24: 1521–1527.

Wrigley, N. (1993) 'The internationalisation of British grocery retailing', in R.D.F. Bromley and C.J. Thomas (eds), *Retail Change: Contemporary Issues*, London: UCL Press.

Index